P9-DFN-337

The GOD Factor

The
GOD
Factor

Inside

the Spiritual Lives

of

Public People

CATHLEEN FALSANI

SARAH CRICHTON BOOKS
Farrar, Straus and Giroux / New York

Sarah Crichton Books
Farrar, Straus and Giroux
19 Union Square West, New York 10003

Copyright © 2006 by Cathleen Falsani
All rights reserved
Distributed in Canada by Douglas & McIntyre Ltd.
Printed in the United States of America
First edition, 2006

Some of these interviews originally appeared in a slightly different form in the Chicago Sun-Times.
Some direct quotations have been edited for clarity.

Grateful acknowledgment is made for permission to reprint the following previously published material:
"Not While I'm Around," from Sweeney Todd. Music and lyrics by Stephen Sondheim. Copyright
© 1979 Ritling Music, Inc. (ASCAP). All rights administered by WB Music Corp. (ASCAP).
Lyrics from "Gloria" by Bono. Reproduced courtesy of Universal Music Publishing BV.
Quotes from Sherman Alexie used by permission of Sherman Alexie. Copyright © 2005.
All rights reserved.
John Patrick Shanley's biography from Doubt, copyright © 2005 by John Patrick Shanley. Doubt
published by Theater Communications Group. Used by permission of Theater Communications Group.

Library of Congress Cataloging-in-Publication Data
Falsani, Cathleen, 1970–
    The God factor : inside the spiritual lives of public people / by
    Cathleen Falsani. — 1st ed.
        p.   cm.
    "Sarah Crichton books".
    ISBN-13: 978-0-374-16381-5 (hardcover : alk. paper)
    ISBN-10: 0-374-16381-2 (hardcover : alk. paper)
    1. Spirituality. 2. Faith. I. Title.
BL624.F35 2006
200.92'2—dc22   2005027229

Designed by Abby Kagan

www.fsgbooks.com

1 3 5 7 9 10 8 6 4 2

For my faithful mother,
who insists on praying without ceasing

For my darling husband,
who reminds me that I'll never know if I don't ask

And for my beloved daddy,
who makes the idea of a Heavenly Father so very appealing

All truth is God's truth.

—ARTHUR FRANK HOLMES

CONTENTS

The GOD Factor

INTRODUCTION

C all them glimpses of grace, moments of clarity, or epiphanies. However you choose to describe them, we've all had them—split seconds when something suddenly makes sense, when the pieces of the puzzle fit together.

If you are particularly lucky—blessed, some would say—you can assemble those bits of transcendence into a clear vision of how things really are and how life, every now and again, comes full circle.

The circle started for me in the living room of my friend Rob Lunetta's house in 1982, and it comes back around here, in this book.

I can remember it vividly, a twelve-year-old me standing there with my buddy Rob, fiddling with the stereo, as he put on an album someone recently had given him. "I think you'll like it. They're an Irish rock band, but they're Christians," he said, as the first track started up. Drums faded in, a bass guitar thumped, and a man's rogue tenor voice the likes of which I'd never heard before started howling, "Gloria, glo-reeeee-aaah TWO, THREE, FOUR!" as a guitar began to keen.

"I try to sing this song, I try to stand up but I can't find my feet, I try, I try to speak up but only in you I am complete. *Gloria in te domine, Gloria exultate*, Gloria, Gloria, O Lord, loosen my lips!" the guy yawped, guitars wailing.

My soul did a backflip.

"I try to sing this song, I try to get in but I can't find the door. The door is open, you're standing there, you let me in—GLORIA!"

The words were familiar—a psalm, a chant from the liturgy, an image of Christ standing at the door (of our hearts) and knocking. I recognized them all from church. But somehow they'd never had that kind of effect on me. As the next tracks played, one after the other filled with biblical imagery and declarations of spiritual yearning, I was absolutely transfixed by the extraordinary mix of faith with rock 'n' roll—a forbidden fruit at my house, where we were supposed to be in the world but not of it. Who were these guys? How were they doing this? And who else was managing to do it, too?

Hearing U2's album *October* for the first time set me on a course that continues today: To discover God in the places some people say God isn't supposed to be. To look for the truly sacred in the supposedly profane. To find the kind of unmatched inspiration and spiritual elation elsewhere in culture that I had found that day in Rob's living room.

I'd always been fascinated by religion—my parents tell stories of me at age five or six sitting on the floor of our family room poring over a coffee-table book of world religions, with its pictures of whirling dervishes, Muslim women in hijab, Hindu girls with hennaed hands, gilded icons of Russian Orthodoxy, and giant Japanese Buddhas. Religion was a huge part of my life growing up, first in Roman Catholicism and then in the strange new land of evangelical Protestantism. I was—and am—a believer. But after my musical baptism, I became consumed by the idea that spirituality could be expressed just as articulately, perhaps even more so, outside a house of worship as in it, and that faith could be lived in radically different ways.

Twenty-odd years later, I'm still looking, fascinated as ever. It's what motivated my decision to study journalism as well as theology with the intention of becoming a reporter who covers the diverse world of religion and spirituality in culture broadly. It's also what inspired a series of long-form spiritual profiles of public people I began writing in the pages of the *Chicago*

Sun-Times, where I am the religion reporter and columnist, in the spring of 2004. I called the project "The God Factor," and through it I hoped to draw a more detailed picture of the spiritual lives of people who shape our culture and consciousness. So I sat down with Senator Barack Obama, Hugh Hefner, Annie Lennox, Melissa Etheridge, and others to find out what they believed (or didn't) and how it affected the way they lived their lives.

In our mainstream media, little of what we learn about the beliefs of public figures goes beyond labels—this actor's a Catholic, that one's a Buddhist. But labels don't mean a damn thing. They offer little information about how a public person's private beliefs might affect his or her life and, in turn, shape the world in which the rest of us live. The timing seemed right to move well beyond superficiality. After all, some of the most astute theological and social observers have been wondering whether we might be in the midst of the Third Great Awakening, and, if so, whether its real prophets might be found marching across a silver screen or dancing behind a microphone instead of pounding on an actual pulpit.

The response to the *Sun-Times* series was overwhelming. People wanted to know what these icons of culture believed, how their faith—or lack thereof made its way into their work, their art, their politics. Some readers were purely curious, some were searching for a spiritual place to call their own and looking for guidance from people they admired. Still others seemed to be using the profiles to hold up a mirror to their own faith, to see how what they believed, how they lived their faith, appeared by comparison. Whatever the source of their interest, I clearly had hit a nerve. So I decided to move beyond a newspaper column and broaden my inquiry into a book, where I could expand its cultural scope to include actors, writers, athletes, scientists, politicians, musicians, entrepreneurs, and gadflies of all faiths and none. I did so because it seemed essential now, in these tense and trying times, that a choir of diverse voices be heard in the public square. More candid talk about spirituality, beliefs, faith, and morality can only increase knowledge, and knowledge empowers, casting out fear.

I wanted to peel back the labels and see what was underneath, certain I would discover interesting results. These were remarkably interesting, incredibly accomplished people I was meeting. But what I wasn't expecting was this: the openness and honesty with which my questions were met moved me deeply. More often than not I found the depth—and breadth—of their commitments to be both surprising and inspiring. I didn't go looking for answers to my own spiritual questions, at least not intentionally. I'm not a seeker in the traditional sense. I am a Christian. I'm not particularly good at it, but that's where my faith firmly lies. Still, I believe strongly in the idea that all truth is God's truth, and so I expected to learn something from each person I interviewed that would enliven and enrich my own faith. And I was not disappointed.

These kind people allowed me into their lives. The insights they shared with me were sometimes painfully candid, always rich, and often controversial. Without fail, the conversations I had with these boldface names in venues far afield—from a church in Nebraska to the Playboy Mansion, from the dugout at Wrigley Field to the White House—revealed intimate glimpses into the private lives of people who have made our modern reality what it is. For better and for worse.

The profiles that follow here in *The God Factor* paint a spiritual portrait of popular culture that will explain—through the compelling voices of strangers with familiar faces—how society is changing.

And how faith, essentially, is not.

BONO

Rock Star

I'm not a very good advertisement for God.

A.K.A. *Paul David Hewson*

BIRTH DATE: *May 10, 1960*

RAISED: *Christian, Church of Ireland (Anglican)*

NOW: *"A believer" of the Christian persuasion*

ATTENDS: *Nowhere regularly*

WORDS TO LIVE BY: *"The idea that the same love and logic would choose to describe itself as a baby born in shit and straw and poverty is genius. And it brings me to my knees, literally."*

If God is a gracious God—and I believe God is—Bono has no recollection of the first time we met.

It was September 2002, and well after midnight in the VIP section of a nightclub in Dublin called Lillie's Bordello. It was my birthday, and I had been, ever so slightly, er, *overserved*. And while I certainly cannot speak for the legendary Irish rock star, activist, and lead singer of U2, if I had to guess, I'd say he was a bit stiff himself. While my memory of the events is unquestionably hazy, and I'm not sure what, exactly, we talked about, I do remember my parting words, as my inner sycophant got the better of me:

"Everything you do is art."

Mirthfully peering at me over the rims of his tinted glasses before ducking into the chauffeur-driven car waiting to spirit him through the dark streets of Dublin toward home, Bono chuckled and said, "Cheers!"

Jesus help us. How embarrassing. I die a little every time I think of it.

The second time we met was about two months later at a church in Lincoln, Nebraska. Hopefully that's the encounter he remembers.

We both were attending the morning service at St. Paul United Methodist Church, which was serving as the launch for the Heart of America tour, a weeklong bus trip through the Midwest to raise awareness about the AIDS emergency in sub-Saharan Africa. The tour was arranged by the not-for-profit organization Debt AIDS Trade Africa, better known as DATA, of which Bono is cofounder. I would be tagging along and filing daily stories for the *Chicago Sun-Times* as the rock star and his band of humanitarians made stops at churches, colleges, and theaters in six states from Nebraska to Tennessee.

Before the DATA tour, I'd written occasionally about the need for the American church writ large to come to the aid of the more than 25 million Africans infected with HIV, so I had a personal interest in the issue. And because I knew Bono is a Christian, I also thought it might make an interesting religion story if he would talk a bit about how faith motivates his humanitarian efforts. I wasn't sure if he would open up. He hadn't exactly been wearing his Christianity on his sleeve since the mid-1980s, when he was burned by less-than-kind media coverage accusing "Saint Bono" of being holier than thou. And when the media weren't attacking him for his faith, fellow Christians were criticizing him for not being, in their view, appropriately pious, and questioning the authenticity of his spiritual devotion. It seemed that, either way, he couldn't win. So he more or less avoided discussing his faith publicly, except, of course, in U2's music, where he continued to bare his soul.

As The Rock Star (as Bono refers to himself sarcastically) made his way toward the stage at St. Paul's, in front of an Easter morning–sized crowd, he looked a little unnerved. His first order of business was to make fun of himself.

"Rock star in the pulpit shot—nope," he quipped, moving away from the imposing wooden lectern to the other end of the raised platform at the front of the sanctuary. Bono felt out of place and told the congregation as much. "I'm not often comfortable in church," he said. "It feels pious and so unlike the Christ that I read about in the Scriptures."

When the tiny microphone on his lapel failed, The Rock Star reluctantly moved back to the pulpit, where he slung his arm over the side and managed to look thoroughly at ease. "I've always wanted to get into one of these," he said wryly, before launching into an impassioned speech about the African AIDS pandemic, citing health statistics and Bible verses with equal aplomb.

Each and every day, 6,300 men, women, and children die of AIDS in sub-Saharan Africa because they cannot afford the dollar a day it would cost to buy lifesaving antiretroviral drugs readily available everywhere in the developed world, he told the congregation. Only 500,000 of the 4.7 million HIV-positive Africans in *immediate* need of the antiretrovirals that work so well their results are called the Lazarus effect have access to them. "Jesus only speaks of judgment once," in the Bible, Bono said, before quoting, from memory, a passage in the Gospel of St. Matthew where Jesus instructs his followers to care for the sick, the hungry, and the poor because when "you do it to the least of these, you do it to me."

The next day, when we had a chance to speak privately for the first time as his tour bus motored east toward Iowa, I still didn't know how forthcoming Bono would be about his spiritual life, so I was pleasantly surprised when our conversation quickly moved from Africa to faith.

"The idea that there's a force of love and logic behind the universe is overwhelming to start with, if you believe it," he told me in his raspy brogue, sipping black coffee out of a Styrofoam cup. "But the idea that the same love and logic would choose to describe itself as a baby born in shit and straw and poverty is genius. And it brings me to my knees, literally. To me, as a poet, I'm just in awe of that. It makes some sort of poetic sense. It's the thing that makes me a believer, although it didn't dawn on me for many years. I don't set myself up to be any kind of Christian. I can't live up to that. It's something I aspire to, but I don't feel comfortable with that badge. It's a badge I want to wear. But I'm not a very good advertisement for God."

In the days that followed on the Heart of America tour, and on a number of occasions in the years since, Bono and I would have the chance to talk more about his faith and mine, our responsibility to help the least of those among us, and the challenges of living up to our spiritual convictions. Bono is keenly aware of his shortcomings—religious and otherwise—and is hell-bent on trying to be a responsible steward of the blessings he's been given in what he refers to as his "extraordinary life." Celebrity is currency, he says, and he feels an urgent moral obligation to spend his wisely. "This is a defining moment for us. For the church. For our values. For the culture we live in."

Through our conversations over the years, I have come to know Bono as an irreverent, complicated man of faith who is not afraid to challenge notions of what is sacred and what is profane as he struggles to be the person he believes God wants him to be.

"I think you can relate to this," he says one day by phone from his vacation home in the south of France, where he is enjoying a rare couple of weeks off with his family—his wife, Ali, whom he wed in 1982, their teenage daughters, Jordan and Eve, and their two young sons, Elijah and John. U2 has just completed the European leg of a tour in support of their latest album, 2004's *How to Dismantle an Atomic Bomb*.

"In my religious life, I feel like I am a boy in a hall of mirrors, where each turn I take I see a more grotesque picture. It's supposed to be you in those mirrors, but it's not. They're bent and out of shape. You walk into the next hall of amusements and it's a haunted house. It's just a game. There are just a lot of noisy voices—big, bellicose voices sounding off. And all the while you're looking for a voice of reason, something that reminds you of your father in heaven, or, indeed, what you hope your father on earth would be," he says. "My religious life is like an obstacle course where I'm trying to dodge what you might think are weird and wonderful people, but who are sometimes dangerous. Dangerous in the sense that spiritual abuse is rather like any kind of physical or sexual abuse. It brings you to a place where you can't face the subject ever again. It's rare for the sexually abused to ever enjoy sex. So, too, people who are spiritually abused can rarely approach the subject of religion with fresh faith. They wince and they twitch. My religious life has been trying to get through the minefield without coming out of it at the other end in a wheelchair. And I have. Well, okay, I walk with a limp," he says, laughing. "But that's kind of rock 'n' roll, know what I mean? The wobbly knees thing works well in leather pants."

I get it. We've talked about how dreadfully judgmental and unkind Christians can be toward one another, as if they're trying to keep the more unsavory elements out of their private club.

In 2003, I wrote a cover story for *Christianity Today* magazine about Bono and his crusade to persuade American evangelicals to respond to the AIDS emergency in Africa, a tragic phenomenon he calls "the defining moral issue of our time." In it he takes fellow Christians to task for their initial reticence to get involved, pleading with the church to lead the crusade to alleviate the suffering of impoverished Africans. People of faith represent perhaps the greatest hope to turn the tide of apparent apathy toward a continent reeling from the one-two punch of a pandemic and extreme poverty, he says, if they can get past their prejudices.

"Somewhere in the back of the religious mind was this idea—they reaped what they sowed—missing the entire New Testament, the new covenant, and the idea of grace," Bono says. "I think our whole idea of who we are is at stake. I think Judeo-Christian culture is at stake. If the church doesn't respond to this, the church will be made irrelevant. In the way you heard stories about people watching Jews being put on the trains, we will be that generation that watched our African brothers and sisters being put on trains. It's absolutely clear what's on God's mind. You just have to read Scripture. Two thousand, one hundred and three verses of Scripture about the poor. I mean, *really*. People have been perverting the Gospels and the Holy Scripture since they were first written. Mostly the church. And it's clear. You don't have to guess. This AIDS emergency actually is just such a valuable example of everything that's wrong and perverted about Christianity today.

"There should be civil disobedience on this," he tells me, indignant, as we drive down Fifth Avenue in New York City not long before Christmas 2002. "You read about the apostles being persecuted because they were out there taking on the powers that be. Jesus said, 'I came to bring the sword.' Today it's a load of sissies running around with their 'bless me' clubs. And there's a war going on between good and evil. Millions of children and millions of lives are being lost to greed, to bureaucracy, and to a church that's been asleep. And it sends me out of my mind with anger. I want to implore the church to reconsider grace, to put an end to this hierarchy of sin. All have fallen short. Let's stop throwing stones at people who've made mistakes in their lives and start throwing drugs," he says. "God is on his knees to the church on this one. God Almighty is on his knees to us, begging us to turn around the supertanker of indifference on the subject of AIDS."

Sadly, in an editorial that accompanied the *Christianity Today* article, the magazine's editors upbraided Bono—stopping just short of calling his faith into question—for deigning to criticize the church when he's not a regular churchgoer himself. It was painful to read.

Undaunted, Bono, who along with his wife initially became involved with humanitarian work in Africa in the mid-eighties, around the time of the

Ethiopian famine, continued his efforts as well as his critique of the church universal, of which he considers himself a member. A year after the Heart of America tour, he tells me he is pleased with the way the American church heeded his call to action. "I really am surprised and even a little disappointed that I can't continue to beat up the church, because they really have responded," Bono says. "I'm actually amazed. The sleeping giant kind of woke up and is playing a huge role in getting the job done. I'm amazed and moved by it." But he wasn't done trying to nudge the church to go further. "What if now the churches really become sanctuaries? How 'bout they open their doors and start becoming centers for HIV testing? And how 'bout if they start using their pulpits to deal with the issue of stigma in Africa, where people are afraid to admit they've had sex and they may be HIV-positive? There's an opportunity for the church to really, truly become a sanctuary, to be the place people go to feel safe and a place where people go to be honest with themselves and with God."

Religion can be rough going for someone like Bono. He doesn't fit the mold. Never has. And that makes people nervous.

He doesn't attend any particular church regularly, preferring, instead, to go "wherever the Spirit leads," whether it's the back of a Catholic cathedral or the front row of a Baptist revival. He prays frequently, likes to say grace before meals, and tries to have what he calls a "Sabbath hour" as often as he can. He has a favorite translation of the Bible—Eugene Peterson's contemporary English paraphrase, *The Message*—and a few years back wrote an autobiographical introduction for a special edition of the Psalms, saying his favorites were the ones where King David expressed his sense of abandonment by God. Bono regularly hangs out with supermodels, rock stars, and Hollywood's A-listers, but it's not unheard of to find him breaking bread with the megachurch pastor Bill Hybels, the Christian author Philip Yancey, or the singer Michael W. Smith—roughly his star-power equivalent in the "Christian" music world.

Bono, whose given name is Paul David Hewson, was reared in a mixed-marriage household on Dublin's working-class north side. His father, Bob, a postal clerk who died in 2001 after a long battle with cancer, was Roman Catholic. His mother, Iris, who died of a brain aneurysm at the funeral of her own father when Bono was fourteen, was Protestant. In 1970s Ireland, with the sectarian Troubles raging just over the border in Northern Ireland, the

Hewsons were something of an anomaly. (A few years ago, a relative of Bono's who was doing some family research discovered that his mother's family, whose surname was Rankin, may actually have been Jewish. Ireland has a tiny Jewish population—about seventeen hundred in the north and south combined. Iris Rankin grew up around the corner from Dublin's Clanbrassil Street, at one time the cultural and commercial center of the city's small Jewish community. "It's interesting," Bono says of this recent development in his unique spiritual history. "My mother was dark haired and had the nose. Rankin. It's a Scottish Jewish name.")

When his mother was alive, Bono, whose peculiar nickname (given to him by boyhood friends) was taken from the name of a hearing aid brand, and his older brother, Norman, attended Sunday services with her at a Church of Ireland (the equivalent to the Episcopal Church in the United States) parish, while their father headed off to Mass at a Catholic church down the hill.

"They couldn't be nicer people," Bono says of the Church of Ireland. "It's a religion of niceness. Manners are everything, and more and more important to me. I think Church of Ireland people have gotten by the sectarianism of Ireland by keeping their heads low, by working very hard, and, it would appear, by never throwing anything out. They're very active participants in jumble sales, which I love. The Church of Ireland is kind of a car boot religion, garden fetes. But watch out—death by cupcake," he says.

"The best story I could tell you of growing up 'C of I,' as they are known, was when a friend of my mother lost his wife. He was distraught, as you would be, and went to the local clergyman for comfort. During his tearful breakdown he asked the pastor, 'Do you really believe in an afterlife?' To which the pastor replied with really kind eyes that he really wasn't sure. Therein lies one of the most attractive qualities of Protestantism in the south of Ireland. And also the most bewildering. They're so beholden to the Enlightenment, to the mores of modernity, and so in genuflection to academia, that the Church is suspicious of faith in any experiential sense, and has become more of a theater of morality. No absolutism, which was sort of attractive, because there's no bullshit there, and more intellectual than emotional, I suppose. A little dry.

"My mother's clergyman was a fellow by the name of the Reverend Sidney Laing, who really was very cool. Groovy, even. He had two beautiful daughters and a wife who were well loved by everyone in the parish. He was a great man in his service to the community and his openness on matters of faith. Not a dogmatist. I felt in that church in Finglas, Dublin, the love of God, but I wasn't sure what it was," he says.

Bono continued his spiritual education by paying close attention to the neighborhood eccentric. "I had a friend who lived up the road whose father was straight out of a Flannery O'Connor novel. It was like the prophet Jeremiah lived on our street. Rather interestingly, he suspected the end of the world was coming very soon, so he used to collect things. Friday evenings, he'd read the small-ads column in the local newspaper and purchase the most extraordinary items at bargain price. He bought a herd of sheep once. Piled up around their house would be about twenty-five motorcycles, a half-dozen cars, and a couple of vans. He then collected on another piece of property large containers of tires, batteries, bric-a-brac—anything you might need at the end of the world, I suppose. Everyone, of course, found this eccentric behavior very amusing. I certainly did. And yet, he really impressed me," he says. "I always remember the color of the language he used when preached at us, and the conviction of the words he used. I think it prepared me for the shock of televangelism in the United States. At a young age I could get through the rhetoric and the madness of these salespeople for God and actually look at their wares a little more dispassionately than most people around me, who just thought, Let's get out of here quick. I can't underestimate the impact he had on me."

A couple of years before his mother's death, Bono was introduced to Protestantism's more evangelical branch at a Bible camp. "A friend took me and didn't *tell* me it was a Bible camp. I'd never been anywhere for a holiday other than a converted train carriage in the middle of the dunes of north County Dublin with my grandfather. So when I arrived I couldn't believe it. They had football teams with names like the Ephesians and the Colossians!" he says, laughing so hard he momentarily loses the ability to speak.

Which team was he on? "I thought they were both *Martians*," he says, still laughing. "And yet I learnt valuable stuff. I was given a *Good News Bible*, which is a paraphrased version with illustrations that looked like Keith Haring paintings. Oddly enough, when I went to see a Keith Haring exhibit in Toronto years later, I saw amongst his treasured things a *Good News Bible*. So from an early age I developed an interest in the Holy Scriptures. For a kid who grew up in a house where the one thing you *didn't* talk about was religion, unless it was how Ian Paisley and the Provisional IRA should both be stopped by St. Peter at the pearly gates for their peddling of hatred, this was unusual behavior.

"Over the years I met some preachers who did connect with me, for sure, and whose words return to me. I remember hearing about this fellow called Billy Graham. Church people would push him on you like your friends at school would push Elvis Presley records. Actually, they looked kind of similar—both stars from the South who spoke with a twang and had giant crowds come to see them."

Graham is a hero to Bono. A few years ago, The Rock Star had a chance to meet privately with the man known as "America's pastor," at the ailing preacher's mountaintop home in North Carolina. "I got a call from someone in his office who said Billy wanted to give me a blessing," Bono recalls fondly. "In fact, he was prepared to give the whole band a blessing. I told them, I said, 'This is a big deal. This is BILLY GRAHAM!' And they all said, 'That's great, but we're in the middle of a tour.' So I rented a plane and flew there right away in case he might forget. I was picked up by his son Franklin and driven a couple of hours up to their house. I met himself and his wife, Ruth. I think I've mentioned to you before that the blessings of an older man mean a great deal to me. Particularly this man. I gave him a book of Seamus Heaney poetry, and I wrote a poem for him in it." Bono can't recall much of the poem he penned for Graham, but he remembers the final line: "The journey from father to friend is all paternal love's end."

While he spent most of his formative years in the Church of Ireland, Bono is quick to acknowledge the equally significant impact his father's Catholicism—and growing up in an overwhelmingly Catholic country— had in shaping his faith. "I read Thomas Aquinas, Thomas Merton. In fact, all of the Thomases played an important role in my life—Doubting Thomas included," he teases. One of Bono's prized possessions is a set of black rosary beads Pope John Paul II gave him in 1999 during a visit to Castel Gandolfo, the pope's summer retreat outside Rome. At the time Bono was deeply involved in the Drop the Debt campaign, urging the world's leading nations to forgive the crippling debts owed them by some of the poorest countries in the world, an effort the late pontiff also championed. Bono often wears the rosary around his neck or carries it in his pocket.

"The Catholicism of the friends I grew up with on the street was much more mysterious" than the Church of Ireland's brand of spirituality, he says. "Catholicism had all the glam rock aspects—the smoke, much better clothes, much better stage gear. And mystery—the not knowing. I remember when the priests faced the other way on the altar. I remember the priests facing towards us. And I remember it not making a blind bit of difference because you couldn't understand them anyway. People had these heated debates over which was better. But I had a lot of respect for the meditative quality of Catholicism. When I was younger I thought the more baroque, unknowable God of Catholicism was slightly more frightening. The mumble and the chanting. As a young boy, I would look a little nervously over my shoulder. I grew up equally comfortable and uncomfortable in both" Protestant and Catholic churches, he says.

As a teenager, Bono attended Mount Temple, Ireland's first nondenominational coeducational high school where Catholic and Protestant students learned side by side. It was at Mount Temple that he met Alison Stewart, the girl who would eventually become his wife, as well as David Evans (a.k.a. The Edge), Larry Mullen Jr., and Adam Clayton, with whom, at the ripe old age of sixteen, he would form the band U2. It was around the same time, in the late 1970s, that Bono, Edge, and Mullen became involved with a nondenominational evangelical Christian group in Dublin called Shalom. The group's members met frequently for Bible study, prayer, and charismatic worship, and pooled their financial resources in an attempt to model themselves after first-century Christians, who lived collectively.

Over time, the Shalom group evolved into something more structured, more akin to the institutional religion Bono often finds so discomforting. Some of Shalom's members began questioning whether being in a rock 'n' roll band was compatible with an authentic Christian life. Eventually, Mullen, Bono, and Edge left Shalom behind, choosing to exercise their faith in a radically different way.

For many fans of a certain generation and spiritual predilection, combing through the lyrics of U2 songs (nearly all of them penned by Bono) in search of biblical images or references to Jesus Christ and his teachings is almost a sport—a cross between exegesis and capture the flag. There is plenty of material to work with. U2's fourteen albums are full of unquestionably spiritual content—whether songs about praising God or songs questioning God's existence. For nearly twenty-five years, Bono's fans have been attempting to gauge his spiritual well-being by what he sings, what he says in interviews, on talk shows, and at awards programs, and what he does or doesn't do in public. He knows his personal faith is of great interest to others, but he's certain their fascination is misplaced.

He's a rock star, he says. No more. No less. Bono has tried to avoid becoming some kind of idealized poster child for Jesus. Still, "I don't want you to think I've shunned the life of discipline, because I have not," he tells me. "It's just that I'm a really crap disciple. I am the runt of the litter. That's why I have a hard time talking about it. Maybe if I were better at it, though, I'd be more like one of those monsters I described earlier—the Ayatollah Bono." He laughs.

I suggest that one of the reasons people are so drawn to him and U2's music is grace. He's written many songs about grace, some mentioning it by name, others not. It's a subject we've talked about before, and a condition we agree we cannot live without.

The best explanation of grace I've ever heard goes something like this: Justice is getting what you deserve. Mercy is *not* getting what you deserve. And grace is getting what you absolutely don't deserve.

"I think I understood grace instinctively before I did intellectually," Bono says. "You first glimpse it in your mother. A mother's unconditional love—*agape* [the Greek word for unconditional love]—I think that leads to grace. Now, you can imagine that a person like myself would put a stretch on *agape*," he jokes. "But grace, I see it more in women than I see it in men. I didn't realize it was the oxygen of religious life on earth. Because without it, religion will surely suffocate you. It creates an impossible standard."

This reminds him of a story about Jesus in the Gospel of St. Matthew, which he paraphrases with typical irreverent panache. "Jesus has all these religious people around him—the Pharisees, the Sadducees; you know, the Jedi—and he says, 'You've heard it said that any man who commits murder shall be guilty before the court.' And they all nod and say, 'Yes, of course.' And he says, 'I say unto you, anyone who says unto his brother, *Raca*,' which means 'idiot,' 'shall also be guilty.' Now this is a *very* high standard. You can imagine this raises the game somewhat, even in the comfort of these paratroopers here. But these are the kinds of folks who get up very early and have a cold shower and beat themselves with a big stick, so they say, 'Okay, okay, we can hack this.' And then Jesus says, noticing them getting used to his raising the standard, 'You've heard it said that any man who commits adultery shall be guilty before the court.' And they all go, 'Yep, that's right. We know that one. Ha ha. Nothing new here.' And *then* he says, 'But I say unto you, any man who looks at another woman with lust in his eyes shall be guilty before the court.' Now, I'm imagining that no one in the room at this point can breathe. I'm imagining a shortness of blood supply. And Cathleen, that's where I learnt about grace," Bono says.

"That's it! Christ's attempt to bring you out of your religiosity to an impossible standard you cannot reach without grace," he says. "Grace is the reason I discovered my gift. It's the reason I have children. It's the reason I found my voice in different areas.

"Grace is the reason I'm here."

DECEMBER 2002, MARCH 2003, DECEMBER 2003, AUGUST 2005

HUGH HEFNER

Publisher

I'm a pretty moral guy.

✳

BIRTH DATE: *April 9, 1926*

RAISED: *Methodist*

NOW: *Enthusiastic humanist*

ATTENDS: *Doesn't*

WORDS TO LIVE BY: *"I urge one and all to live this life as if there is no reward in the afterlife and to do it in a moral way that makes it better for you and for those around you, and that leaves this world a little better place than when you found it."*

When I decided to make my living as a religion writer, I never expected the job to entail giving my name and credentials to a "talking rock" outside the imposing gates of California's Playboy Mansion on my way to have a conversation with Hugh Hefner about God.

What am I getting myself into? I thought, maneuvering my rental car past the rock, which kindly opened the gates for me, and up the winding wooded driveway where cutesy painted "Playmates at Play" signs mark the way toward the infamous mock-Tudor mansion. I crane my neck, looking both ways, fully expecting to see flocks of naked, pneumatic blondes skipping across the manicured lawns.

But there are no naked girls in sight—only a handful of fully clothed male gardeners and a small flock of flamingos—and what I find inside the Playboy Mansion during the visit with the man everyone calls Hef thoroughly surprises me. Almost as much, he will tell me eventually, as I surprise him.

"I have strong feelings about the way organized religion—with the codification of all the rules related to sexuality—became law and played havoc with people's lives. And I think that—dare I say it?—is very un-Christian," Hef says at the beginning of our conversation. We are sitting next to each other on a comfy couch in the mansion's library, not far from where an original Matisse, with a burn mark where a tipsy John Lennon once left a lit cigarette, hangs. Behind the couch is a life-size bust of a topless woman. (Someone later tells me it is Hef's former girlfriend Barbi Benton—the bust, not the Matisse.) "I think that there are great unanswered questions that I don't have the answers for, and I think it is presumptuous for some people not only to suggest that they do have the answers but to codify them and establish them as a set of rules, some of which are wonderful and some of which are hurtful, in the name of the Almighty."

That Hef would chafe at the confines of organized religion is hardly a shock. Much of what he says initially about religion and religious people appears to be well-rehearsed material, thoughtful sound bites that he's delivered during innumerable interviews throughout his fifty-plus-year career as publisher of *Playboy* magazine. "Religion was a very important part of my upbringing. I saw in it a quality, in terms of ideals and morality, that I embraced. I also saw part of it, the part related to human sexuality and other things, that I thought was hypocritical and hurtful. And I think that is the origin of who I am. The heart of who I am is a result of trying to make some sense of all of that.

"Sex is there for procreation and a good deal more," Hef continues. "I was raised in a setting in which it was for procreation *only* and the rest was sin, and that included not only a whole lot of behavior but also a whole lot of people. That's abominable."

Hef, who is dressed in his usual uniform—red-and-black-satin smoking jacket, pajamas, and slippers—is charming, disarmingly so for a man in his late seventies. He is also incredibly literate, introspective, and kind in a grandfatherly way. But there is a certain tension at the beginning of our conversation, as if he's worried that I'm going to judge him or, worse, try to convert him, as another interviewer apparently had a few weeks before me.

"I was saved a long time ago," Hef says, not quite sarcastically. "I think I am a spiritual person, but I don't mean that I believe in the supernatural. I believe in the creation, and therefore I believe there has to be a creator of some kind, and that is my God. I do not believe in the biblical God, not in the sense that he doesn't exist, just in the sense that I know rationally that man created the Bible and that we invented our perception of what we do not know.

"I would believe in a god who created this world and also some more rational insights to make it better, and would indeed give us an afterlife. An afterlife would be a really good deal. Yeah, I would vote in favor of that," he says, chuckling. "But in the meantime, I urge one and all to live this life as if there is no reward in the afterlife and to do it in a moral way that makes it better for you and for those around you, and that leaves this world a little better place than when you found it."

Is that how he defines morality, then? Living in a way that makes life better for those around you and trying to make the world a better place? He looks a little concerned about the question, like I'm going to stand up, point my finger at him, and yell "shame on you!" or something.

"Yes," he says tensely.

Don't hurt anyone. Try to do the right thing. Make the world a better place. The Hefner moral code.

Hef believes he has lived up to the code, although he's keenly aware there are people—many of them deeply religious—who would insist he has done exactly the opposite by building an empire based on unfettered sexuality and, some say, the objectification of women. To them, the image of the man is simple: Hugh Hefner, sinner extraordinaire.

"*Sin* is a religious term for immoral behavior, but it's a *religious* term," Hef says, adding that his definition of sin is "things that are hurtful to people."

Has he sinned?

"Oh, sure," Hef says, "but I haven't pursued very much immoral behavior. I'm a pretty moral guy. Now, it's morality as I perceive it. Morality is what is perceived as good for people. I try to do what's right, to do what I believe to be truly humanistic and rational and loving."

So, how did he learn his definition of morality?

"First and foremost from my parents and secondly, in a very real way, from the movies. I think the movies were my mentors, my other parents. It's where I escaped into dreams and fantasies, and it also provided me with a set of values that were immigrant dreams—what we call the American dream, dreams of democracy. I was a big fan of Frank Capra before I knew who Frank Capra was. I was born in 1926, so I grew up with the films of the 1930s.

Very romantic, during the Great Depression. And those dreams came from Jewish immigrants, by and large, and that is what we think of as the American dream. It has become a universal dream, a dream of democracy, of personal and political freedom for everybody, a right to live your life on your own terms as long as it doesn't hurt anybody."

What films have you learned the most from spiritually? I ask, and appear to have stumped him.

"One of the difficulties in the context of what you're asking is that spirituality has different meanings for different people and suggests for most people a supernatural phenomenon," he says, tentatively. "And you know . . . most of the movies that have had the most impact on me in terms of what I would call spiritual were romantic films, but they are . . . you know . . . I don't know if I can use the word *spiritual* in its proper sense—"

"Let me tell you mine," I interrupt. "It's *Harold and Maude*."

"Oh," Hef says, his face folding into a big grin and the tension seeming to evaporate between us. "Oh, I *love Harold and Maude*. Well, now you're broadening the definition of *spiritual* in a really wonderful way. *Harold and Maude* is one of my favorite films, and Bud Cort [Harold] is a friend and [is] here for parties all the time. And of course, Ruth Gordon [Maude] is wonderful. We show classic films here every Friday night," he says, motioning toward the screening room (complete with a full-size pipe organ) adjacent to his library. "It's called Casablanca Night. Last Friday we ran a film written by Ruth Gordon's husband. *Born Yesterday*. Judy Holliday's first film. And that's a very spiritual film, too.

"It's about a woman who is a kept mistress of a corrupt guy, played by Broderick Crawford, who is trying to make a deal in Washington. And in her rather Pygmalion relationship with the teacher, William Holden, she sees the world in a whole new way and she is reborn in the real sense. It's a very spiritual film," he says.

Another movie he finds spiritually inspiring is the 1942 film *The Male Animal*, starring Henry Fonda and Olivia de Havilland. Fonda plays the mild-mannered midwestern university professor Tommy Turner, whose job is threatened after he reads a controversial essay to his class that is perceived to be pro-communist.

"It has to do with conviction of belief beyond what is popular, and it had a tremendously moving impact on me," Hef says. "When I talk about spiritual, that's what I'm talking about."

Me, too, I tell him.

"How nice to have someone like you dealing with the subject of religion," he says, looking relieved. "How did you ever get this gig? I didn't expect *you*."

Despite what he calls a "typical midwestern Puritan" upbringing—and Hefner, a tenth-generation direct descendant of the *Mayflower* passenger William Bradford, uses the term *Puritan* quite specifically—the *Playboy* baron's own spirituality is decidedly unconventional.

Call it The Playboy Theology. Hef doesn't believe in a "biblical God," but he is fairly adamant about the existence of a "Creator." He hasn't been to a church service that wasn't a wedding, funeral, or baptism since he was a student at the University of Illinois in the late 1940s, but he says he worships on a regular basis while walking the grounds of his own backyard. And he follows a system of morals, but not those gleaned from the Methodism of his childhood—at least not the ones that pertain to sexuality.

Hef grew up in Chicago, the elder of two sons born to Grace and Glenn Hefner. As a child he spent little time with his father, an accountant. "It was the Depression, and he was away before I got up and often not back before I went to sleep, so we only saw him on weekends," he says. "Our family was Prohibitionist, Puritan in a very real sense. Never smoked, swore, drank, danced—all the good stuff. Never hugged. Oh, no. There was absolutely no hugging or kissing in my family.

"There was a point in time when my mother, later in life, apologized to me for not being able to show affection. That was, of course, the way I'd been raised. I said to her, 'Mom, you couldn't have done it any better. And because of the things you weren't able to do, it set me on a course that changed my life and the world.'

"When I talk about the hurt and the hypocrisy in some of our values— our sexual values—it comes from the fact that I didn't get hugged a lot as a kid, and I understand that."

While his mother was steadfastly Puritanical, Hefner says she wasn't particularly dogmatic. "We had to go to church every Sunday, but she let us try other churches. We went to a Congregational church for a while, which is similar to Methodist. I went a couple of times to a Christian Science church because I had a crush on a girl in high school who was a Christian Scientist. I went to Catholic church on a number of occasions with my first wife because she was Catholic."

He married his first wife, Millie Williams, in 1949 at a parish on Chicago's blue-collar Northwest Side. He can't recall the name of the parish, but he does remember—vividly—his brush with Catholicism. "Millie got very upset when she went to the doctor for birth control information and the doctor turned out to be Catholic and started singing 'Rhythm is my business.' She was so affronted," Hefner says. That was the end of Hef's connection, tenuous as it was, to the Catholic Church—or to any organized religion.

The couple, who divorced after ten years of marriage, raised their children, David and Christie (who is now CEO of Playboy Enterprises), without any formal religious tradition. His younger children, teenage sons Marston and Cooper, who live with their mother, Hefner's second wife, Kimberly Conrad, on an estate adjacent to the Playboy Mansion, are also being reared religion free, he says. (Hefner and Conrad, *Playboy*'s 1989 Playmate of the Year, married in 1989 and have been separated amicably since 1998.)

Back in the 1960s, when Hefner and Playboy Enterprises were involved with the civil rights movement and *Playboy* was in its heyday, Hef spent time with various clergymen, including the Reverend Jesse Jackson, with whom he could knock around his ideas about theology and morality. In fact, Hef says, for a time *Playboy* magazine offered a special discount subscription rate for ministers. During this era, the *Playboy* founder also met the Episcopal priest and author Malcolm Boyd. The two men have remained close friends for more than forty years.

"Hef is a seeker," says Boyd, an openly gay octogenarian who lived briefly at the Playboy Mansion in Chicago in the mid-1960s and is artist in residence at Los Angeles's Cathedral Center of St. Paul. "He's on an adventure in life, and it's at a very deep level a spiritual adventure. He's looking for meaning, for context, for answers. He tries to size people up in a kind of spiritual way.

"Hef is almost a fierce individualist, and I think a great many people have never really understood him," Boyd says. "He doesn't have a conformist image that people are invited to buy into. He's himself."

When Hef prays, which he admits is not with any regularity, he says his conversation with the Creator usually goes something like this: "Thank you, Lord."

"I'm blessed. If life is a card game, I got the winning hand, and most people have only a small idea of how really good it is," he says, grinning. "Usually, you know, our religious values suggest you have to pay the fiddler, that if you get a lot of good breaks, there has to be something wrong with it, and usually there is. Not to suggest that my life hasn't been full of trials and tribulations. Of course, it has. It wouldn't be a life without it. But I know how lucky I am."

As we're talking, a peacock rests on the low branch of a tree in the backyard of the Playboy Mansion, which he shares with his girlfriends Holly Madison, Bridget Marquardt, and Kendra Wilkinson. All three women are in their twenties. Located in Los Angeles's Holmby Hills, the 5.7-acre grounds of the mansion are elaborately landscaped. There are fifty coastal redwoods, a meandering pool with waterfalls, and, of course, the notorious "grotto," a cave-like alcove off the main swimming pool that houses a series of hot tubs, all of different depths and temperatures. (Of the myriad intimate encounters that have reportedly occurred in the grotto over the years, the saying goes, "What happens in the grotto, stays in the grotto.")

There's also a zoo. Squirrel monkeys, parrots, toucans, and other exotic creatures live only a few dozen yards from Hef's back door. "The animals we have here are a direct connection to my childhood and my love of animals and my belief that we should be somehow living in harmony with nature, as the animals do. The Tarzan myths fascinated me as a kid. It was man and his mate in harmony with nature, and the enemy was the white hunter—civilization.

"Some of my most spiritual moments, if I can call them that, come from walking through the forest, come from walking the backyard; feeling connected to the wonder of what this is all about," he says, his eyes wandering out a picture window to the mansion's rolling, bucolic grounds.

"I think it brings your emotions to the surface, to a level where you are just totally overwhelmed. Sometimes you know why and sometimes you don't. It touches you in places that are hidden, that are from very early childhood, that are hurts, yearnings, and those are wonderful, magical, spiritual moments. And they can come sometimes from left field." One of the regular stops on his backyard strolls is a Tabebuia, or trumpet tree, he planted near the tennis courts in honor of his mother, who died in 1997 at the age of 101. "A good walk in the woods is very revitalizing," he says. "If you think you've got problems or something hurtful has happened, take a walk in the woods and think about how lucky you are just to be alive."

So, why are we here? What's the meaning of life, the highest moral value?

"Love," he says, without hesitation. "Love. Why do we keep fucking it up? Love. It is the Golden Rule."

Love is all we need?

"Well, John Lennon thought so, but we need a little reason to go along with it," Hef says as he sees me out of the library before disappearing upstairs to his bedroom. "This has been a truly spiritual afternoon for me. Not in my wildest dreams could I have imagined this."

Me neither, Hef. Me neither.

AUGUST 2004

SANDRA BERNHARD

Actor, Writer, Performer

Our spiritual purpose is to tell people where it's at.

✳

BIRTH DATE: *June 6, 1955*
RAISED: *Jewish*
NOW: *Jewish*
ATTENDS: *Weekly Shabbat services at The Kabbalah Centre in New York and Los Angeles or a local synagogue every Saturday when she's traveling*
WORDS TO LIVE BY: *"There is no reason to be out of control. There is no reason to be freaked out. There are tangible meditations and ways of changing that consciousness."*

To the best of my memory, I first learned the word *Kabbalah* in a newspaper article about Sandra Bernhard in the mid-1990s. The story caught my eye because Bernhard, the iconoclastic performer, had been a favorite of my group of college friends. One of them, a fellow called Petie, was more or less obsessed with her and her seminal comedy album, *Without You I'm Nothing*, reciting her monologues by heart.

"We'd just had dinner at the Stardust Hotel, one of the eight international restaurants—I believe it was Aku Aku, the *Polyneeeesian*," is a line I remember Petie repeating over and over again, even when we'd ask him to stop. "My mother grabbed a handful of after-dinner mints, and she started choking on them. So me and my brother walked really far ahead in the casino. And my dad finally got her a glass of water, and she washed it all down. She went, 'Oh my God, there must have been dust on those mints!'" Petie would recite, cackling, "DUST. ON. THOSE. MINTS!"

So when I saw the article about Bernhard—the actor-writer-singer-comedienne perhaps best known for her psychotically funny role in Martin Scorsese's 1983 film *The King of Comedy* and more conventionally comic stints on TV shows such as *Roseanne* and *Will & Grace*—and her new devotion to a little-known corner of Judaism, I was intrigued. It seemed so . . . unlikely.

Kabbalah is difficult to define. Mystical traditions are like that—it's intrinsically difficult to get your arms around them. But broadly speaking, Kabbalah, which means "to receive" in Hebrew, is an esoteric assemblage of Jewish doctrine that attempts to explain the nature of God, his creation, the role of human beings in the world, and the fate of their souls. It's an ancient tradition—some say it's been around as long as the Torah, the Jewish law compiled largely in the first five books of the Hebrew Bible. One of the central themes of Kabbalah is that the Torah itself is divine, and by studying its texts, one can unlock the hidden mysteries of creation, of light and energy, good and evil. Its principal text is the Zohar, a dense commentary on the Torah written in Aramaic and popularized in the thirteenth century by a Spanish Jew named Moses de León, who claimed to have discovered the text allegedly written by the famed second-century rabbi Shimon bar Yohai.

Kabbalists have a number of meditative, devotional, mystical, and even magical practices, and traditionally they believe that the secret knowledge of how the universe works—the laws of light—has been handed down from one especially enlightened rabbi to another. For much of its history, Kabbalists would pass on their mystic teachings only to Jewish men over the age of forty. Most modern Jews in Conservative and Reform branches have considered Kabbalah to be an obscure part of Judaism, though the mystical tradition has long been an important part of extreme Orthodox practice, particularly in the Lubavitch movement.

In recent years, as Kabbalah's quirkier contemporary incarnations started to receive more attention from the media, Bernhard's name would invariably be invoked as the catalyst for their current popularity among the rich and famous. It has been widely reported that Bernhard introduced Madonna and a number of other Jewish and non-Jewish Hollywood types to the study of Kabbalah. (Once good friends, she and Madonna are no longer close.) And since Madonna's name became associated with Kabbalah, Kabbalah has evolved into a full-blown fad, with stars such as Demi Moore, Ashton Kutcher, Paris Hilton, and Britney Spears all said to be devotees.

That Bernhard is somehow the Godmother of Kabbalah is a notion she scoffs at with characteristic caustic candor.

"The practice of Kabbalah is two thousand years old and *I'm* getting credit for bringing it out? That in itself is the most absurd thing in the world," she says, sipping her drink while hidden in a corner booth during the lunch rush at the über-hip eatery Pastis in New York City's Meatpacking District. "I don't even fucking care. I just hope some people who *say* they're into Kabbalah have *actually* changed. I'm not really sure that some of these people have changed enough that I want credit for it." She is a serious spiritual student, and while it may be a fad for others, Bernhard isn't toying with Kabbalah. She is deeply committed to the study and practice of a spiritual tradition she says changed her life more than a decade ago.

Bernhard began studying Kabbalah in 1995, when her personal trainer took her to Los Angeles's Kabbalah Centre on her fortieth birthday. "My trainer at the gym was Brazilian and not Jewish. He'd been studying at The Kabbalah Centre for a while and was always telling me about it while we were training. It was very interesting to me," she recalls.

As her fortieth birthday approached, Bernhard decided she wanted to make "some big changes" in her life. Kabbalah was her conduit for doing that. She explains, "I'm definitely more aware of my impatience and my level of anger and bitchiness. I've kind of been able to rein in a lot of that. In my relationship with the person I'm involved with, we can have conversations and she can point out things to me that five or ten years ago I would not have wanted to hear from someone else. I would have gotten a lot more defensive. But that is not what Kabbalah is really about, from what I've read. Kabbalah is really about cleaving to God."

Bernhard and her daughter, Cicely, born in 1998, try to keep kosher at the home they share with Bernhard's girlfriend, and they attend weekly Shabbat services at The Kabbalah Centre when they are in New York, their primary residence, or Los Angeles, where Bernhard lived for years. But Bernhard always seeks out a local synagogue to attend Saturday services no matter where in the world she finds herself. "I want to hear the Torah reading, because that's the energy of the week. It cleans the palate for the coming week and gives you a spiritual grounding and explanation for the things that have happened. The Torah portion represents the energy of that week, and if you understand what you're getting yourself into, you're a little less likely to blame external things."

She's worshiped in synagogues all over the world. "I've been to some *shuls* that are a hoot. From Morocco to Ireland to Paris and even across the States. I went to a great *shul*—I think it was in North Carolina—a *Chabad* where one of the rabbis was black. His wife was wearing her *sheitl* and the whole thing. I have to say I was pretty fascinated by that." She'd like to go back and make a documentary of the synagogues she's visited around the world but isn't sure how she'd get around one major roadblock: Many synagogues don't allow cameras inside, especially on the Sabbath.

Travel inspires Bernhard. She loves experiencing different cultures, and she celebrated her fiftieth birthday in Marrakech, Morocco, with a bunch of friends. Her daughter's middle name—Yassin—is Moroccan. It means "girl with a beautiful face" or "messenger of good news."

"Part of the reason I ended up having a kid," she says, "is because I was on a spiritual path. I don't think I would have been open enough to the experience of having a kid before. I was used to being on my own and just dealing with my own life all the time. But I wanted to make room for something else. I felt that I wanted to make a change." Bernhard does not get all goo-goo-eyed or ethereal when she talks about motherhood. "I'm a little less into the wonderment of it all, ya know? I still feel like I'm her *mutha*, know what I mean?" she says, emphatically. "Cicely is someone who is extremely kind and aware of people. Just a good soul. And she just came into the world that way. I feel that's just the soul that I drew down. I mean, she's a kid. She can be difficult. You don't want a placid kid, you want somebody who can be feisty as well. But her basic makeup is very calm. She's a good kid, and she understands spirituality and love."

Bernhard never lets Cicely out of the house without her *roite bendel*, the red string bracelet that many Kabbalists believe wards off evil energy. Bernhard wears one as well. "It can't hurt to have something that's keeping away bad vibes," she says almost apologetically, turning her arm to show me the red string wrapped around her slender left wrist. "I used to always rush Cicely to The Kabbalah Centre to have one of the teachers tie hers on, but now I do it myself. I know the prayers, and I feel like I have my daughter's best interests at heart more than some teacher at the centre does."

While she loves traveling, performing, and writing—she's published three books and seven albums since the late eighties—it's in her quotidian existence that Bernhard feels the most spiritually attuned. She's raising Cicely in a more Kabbalistic, Orthodox home than the one she grew up in, and she begins her day with a series of small rituals. "I do all my meditations in the morning. I wouldn't leave the house before I do them," she says. "The first thing I do when I get up in the morning is say a prayer of thanks that my soul has returned to my body, because during the night your soul elevates and recharges. It's a little bit like being out of your body, which is why sleep is such a kind of fragile place to be. So when you wake up in the morning, you give thanks that your soul has come back into your body. And then you do a prayer washing your hands because, obviously, all the negative energy comes out of your fingertips. You wash your hands and do a prayer to wash away the negativity. Those are the first two things I do when I wake up in the morning. They're kind of traditional Orthodox Jewish prayers.

"Then in my day-to-day life it's about how I'm feeling that day and whether I can stay in that positive frame of mind all day and not be felled like a tree in the forest by one or two things that shake me up, whether it's work or relationship or my daughter or something that I feel is off. You can't always be in that state of mind. You just can't. It's very hard. So that's part of the work, you know? On a physical level, I work out a lot because it helps me feel grounded. I like to shop, I like to clean the apartment, I like to do laundry, I like to make my phone calls. Routine is very important to me, which is why I like all the rituals of these meditations and prayers. It's about order. Order in the home. Order in the universe."

Bernhard's first guide through the mystic waters of Kabbalah was Rabbi Eitan Yardeni, a boyish-looking Israeli, then in his early thirties, who is one of the master teachers at The Kabbalah Centre, a not-for-profit group founded by Rabbi Philip Berg and his wife, Karen, in 1984. The Bergs' brand of Kabbalah is perhaps the best-known modern manifestation of the ancient Jewish mystical tradition. It has also become the most maligned.

Yardeni gained notoriety in recent years as Madonna's Kabbalah teacher. "Everybody knows who Eitan is now, but ten years ago it was a little different," Bernhard says, sounding a little bitter. "He really impressed me. He was good, powerful, and I liked everything he had to say, so I started studying with him. They were very small classes, and to me the study seemed a lot less watered down than it is now. I didn't know much about Kabbalah then, but now that I've read other books from other teachers and I have a little more insight, looking back, I realize when I first started studying at the centre it was closer to the real stuff. The centre has become like the fast food of Kabbalah.

"They want to bring people in, and I'm sure that ten, twenty years ago they had the right consciousness and they wanted to effect a change in the world and in people, but I feel they've gotten terribly sidetracked by a lot of things that are pitfalls, according to them, pitfalls they themselves have been become trapped by. Fame. Money. Private jets. Excitement. Glamour. All of those things are fine. I like all of those things, you know what I mean? But I don't believe you can be a teacher of spirituality and profess all this stuff and then be hanging out with people like *that*," she says.

Bernhard is talking about the Bergs—Philip (known popularly as "The Rav"), his wife, and their two sons, Michael and Yehuda. The Bergs have been criticized for commercializing Kabbalah, neutering its teachings to appeal to a broad audience, and reducing it to little more than New Agey self-help pap. They have also come under attack for living the high life in multimillion-dollar homes in California, financed, it would appear, by the sale of myriad Kabbalah Centre products, ranging from Kabbalah water (at nearly $4 a bottle; they claim it has curative powers) to candles, books, assorted tchotchkes, the ubiquitous $26 "red string" bracelets, and a range of classes that run about $250 per course.

"All these little gimmicks that they have seem to be all that's talked about, as opposed to getting up and being disciplined with your life and tapping into the resources and the study of Kabbalah and quietly going about your way," Bernhard rails. "Just to be into it because it's 'cool'—aagh! When I hear about Posh Spice and David Beckham getting a Hebrew tattoo, I'm like, *What the fuck?* First of all, as a Jew you're not *supposed* to get a tattoo at all, let alone a tattoo of Hebrew letters! What is that? It's pure bunk. I'm not judging people, but you're just not supposed to do that. It's an oxymoron. Thank you."

While the increasingly celebrity-centric, big-business aspects of The Kabbalah Centre have soured Bernhard, she hasn't cut ties with it. Yet. "I still go. I go to Shabbat, and I go to some of the holidays in L.A. and here in New York. But I go to other synagogues when I'm traveling. I'm interested in reading what other people have to say. I'd like to find another teacher, somebody that I feel has the right intentions. I haven't found anybody yet, but I'm sure I will," she says, adding that she's not shy about sharing her enthusiasm for Kabbalah, if not for The Kabbalah Centre itself. "If I feel like somebody's really off their path or off their track and they're miserable, it's not gonna hurt to turn them on to some of the principles of Kabbalah. But I'm certainly not going to drag somebody kicking and screaming. Along the way I certainly have brought a lot of people in, and a lot of people certainly have benefited from it. But after a certain point, everybody's got to take responsibility for themselves. Yeah, I talk to people about it and give them—as much as I can—little insights and glimmers of what I've learned from it. I did a lot more at the beginning, because it was new for me and I also felt like the centre was not as jaded and contrived as it is now. It was easier for me to get behind it.

"I'm the same way about a new product. If I find something I like, I'm like, Oh my God! I found this product and you *have* to try it! It still works for me, but I don't necessarily feel that great about bringing anyone to the centre anymore because there are too many mitigating factors there about what they want," she says, a little wistfully. Bernhard wants to be clear about something: despite feeling somewhat estranged now, she is grateful for what the Bergs' Kabbalah Centre has given her. "I feel fortunate that I actually got to go to the centre and study at a time when I feel it still had the best intentions. That's what I got to connect with, which is why it still has meaning for me. Even if I end up somewhere else and I end up studying with someone else, I'm thankful for that introduction. I haven't outgrown the practice. They've just gone down a superfunky path. I don't know what else to say except it's just friggin' weird!"

The youngest of four children (she has three older brothers), Bernhard was born in the working-class town of Flint, Michigan. Her parents—her mother an abstract artist and her father a proctologist—moved the family to Scottsdale, Arizona, when Bernhard was ten years old. She was reared Jewish, and while she describes herself spiritually as "very loose and very fluid," she has never strayed from her religious roots. No dabbling in Buddhism, Sufism, or Baha'i for this *meydele*. "I always loved being Jewish," she says. "I love the tradition of it, I love the family, I love the holidays. And I liked something deeper in those times. I liked something that grounded me and made me feel a certain emotion every year at the same time. Once I started studying Kabbalah, I understood that each holiday represented the energy of that time of the year. That's what I was relating to on a soul level, but as a child I didn't really fully understand that what I was doing had spiritual connotations at all.

"I went to Hebrew school, I was bat mitzvahed and confirmed. But we didn't have a super-Jewish household. We didn't have mezuzahs up in the house, we didn't keep kosher, we ate shrimp. My dad is not really involved at all. We went to the High Holy Days, but it was pretty loose. Conservative. Easy-breezy. But I think that was very reflective of the times, postwar, post-Holocaust. American Jews just wanted to kind of blend in. Now I feel there's kind of a return to something that has deeper meaning."

When I ask her what her first idea of God was, she talks about the baggage she believes she arrived with in this life. (She believes in reincarnation.) "I came into this world with a lot of fear, a lot of anxiety. It had to have come from another life. Why all of a sudden does a kid have anxieties? It doesn't make any sense. If your parents are a mess and there's disruption in the house, then, yeah, that's certainly part of it. But I think you come in with a certain blueprint, and I was very fearful and very scared all the time. I wanted protection and needed a lot of protection from my parents. And I wanted God to protect me."

From what, I wonder aloud.

"Bad things happening, to me, to my parents, to people I loved. But I've gotten much more relaxed and certain and confident about things in my life and have had to let go of a lot of that. Because of my spiritual study I've learned you just have to, otherwise you're miserable all the time and freaked out and it's just a bummer. I really found it through Kabbalah. I've learned that there is no reason to be out of control. There is no reason to be freaked out. There are tangible meditations and ways of changing that consciousness."

Bernhard wants to learn more about the history of Kabbalah, which traces its modern roots to medieval Europe and its ancient roots back at least another millennium, according to adherents. She'd like to explore other teachers, perhaps even study with traditional kabbalists, maybe a rabbi from the Lubavitch movement. In recent years, some Orthodox kabbalists have become more open to taking women on as students—something unthinkable a few generations ago. "It's a whole esoteric study that seems very hard to grasp. I'm interested in knowing that on an intellectual level, and I feel like The Kabbalah Centre is not interested in that," she says. She wants to go deeper in her faith and keep it steeped in something genuine. "I just don't think I know enough about it sometimes to fully believe and fully understand these practices I'm involved with," she admits. "The centre has taken this kind of rebel stance in Kabbalah, which I find difficult. I feel like, yeah, make it available to everybody, but *what is it?* What is your dissemination and interpretation of it? Just because you don't feel like following the doctrine or the rules of it, is your interpretation really right, or are you just making shit up? I want to know."

She doesn't believe Kabbalah is just for Jews, but she does have some misgivings about the way some non-Jews approach the mystical tradition. "At a certain point, it's still a Jewish practice," she says, forcefully. "You still go to Shabbat, you still read the Torah, they want you to keep kosher for spiritual reasons. If I was a non-Jew studying Kabbalah and I wanted to really go all the way, I'd like to think that at some point I'd want to become Jewish. I mean, it's a lot of work for a non-Jew. We're the chosen people, and we were chosen to do the extra work. I don't know why non-Jews would want to have to deal with all that if they didn't have to. You guys can get up and go to church for an hour on Sunday and call it a week. You can eat shrimp! You can eat lobster! You could have a nice B.L.T. What the hell do you want all this shit for?"

It's comments like that—part humor, part hard truth—that might make the fainthearted wince. But brutal honesty is a hallmark of Bernhard's spiritual practice as much as it is an integral part of her personality and her public persona.

"I feel that my spirituality in great part comes from a place of honesty. To my understanding, part of our spiritual purpose is to tell people where it's at and for everybody to make everybody else better through criticism. Not destructive criticism, but observation and being able to say to somebody, 'You're a mess. You're doing this wrong. You're irresponsible. You're a bummer. You're self-indulgent,'" she says. "Spirituality is also applying those same rules to myself—to introspection—constantly checking myself and my limitations."

AUGUST 2005

STUDS TERKEL

Author

I like being agnostic.

✳

A.K.A.: *Louis Terkel*

BIRTH DATE: *May 16, 1912*

RAISED: *Jewish (nonreligious)*

NOW: *Agnostic*

ATTENDS: *Nowhere regularly*

WORDS TO LIVE BY: *"I believe in God in you and God in me. I suppose you could say I'm a transcendentalist of sorts. I think we're capable of extraordinary things, human beings. I call that 'God-like.'"*

Respect your elders. Honor them.

Why? Because they've been around longer than the rest of us.

Because maybe they've learned something, found some wisdom, uncovered a truth or two that haven't yet blown our way.

It's a lesson I was taught early in life, one that has managed to stick. And it's what brought me, quite unusually, to one of Chicago's tony private clubs on a particularly crisp autumn afternoon, surrounded by important patrons of the arts and tables of ladies who lunch.

My dining companion, Studs Terkel, is the oldest person I know. He picked our lunch joint, as he'd call it. I didn't argue.

In his early nineties, Studs can't hear "worth a damn" and walks a little slower than he used to, but he is still sharp and one of the keenest observers of life I've ever had the pleasure of encountering.

We had arranged to meet to talk about what the world would be like if the next pope were a black African. It was one of the more intriguing angles of the near hysterical prognosticating in the last months before his death about who Pope John Paul II's successor would be. (Most of the forecasting was, of course, dead wrong.)

I thought Studs might have something interesting to say about race and the church, as he's observed it from a distance for the last nine decades. I wanted to ask his impressions of past popes—he's lived through nine of them.

Even though he's agnostic by choice and Jewish by heritage, Studs is an enthusiastic historian, and I figured he'd paid attention over the years.

He had. And while we discussed the possibility of a black pope, Studs had a lot more he wanted to say about religion in general and God in particular.

He talked. I listened.

"As the old saying goes, some of my best friends are religious," Studs said, sipping a glass of merlot after deciding it was too early for a martini. "You see, I respect religion very much. But to what ends? What purpose?

"I think about the role of religion in its worst way, of course—what fundamentalism has done. But I think religion is wonderful for the people it serves and helps. A lot of people think it's beautiful."

One of those people was John Donahue, the executive director of the Chicago Coalition for the Homeless, who had died several days earlier of lung cancer. Studs counted Donahue, a former Roman Catholic priest, one of his great friends.

It is in the work that Donahue, and so many other "religious" friends, have done over the years that Studs finds the value of religion. In them, he says, he sees God.

"John is not dead, ya see," he told me. "I don't believe it. Because among the dispossessed of this city—the homeless—where there is community working together, there is hope. And John is there. And so, in spirit and in actual *being*, he's here.

"That's pretty religious stuff! I'm saying life has little meaning if you haven't lived it."

As for the Almighty, Studs equivocates, as if that bit of wisdom has yet to come clearly into focus for him.

"Me, I have my own way. Do I believe in God? Sure. I can't define him. I believe in God in you and God in me. I suppose you could say I'm a transcendentalist of sorts. I think we're capable of extraordinary things, human beings. I call that 'God-like.'"

Maybe he's not really an agnostic, I ventured.

"But I like being agnostic," he said, laughing. "I like questioning. You know what an agnostic really is? A cowardly atheist."

He looked up from his sirloin and mushroom sauce, smiling mischievously.

"Are you trying to convert me?"

No, Studs. Not my shtick.

"I'm just kidding," he tells me, obviously pleased to have gigged me a bit.

"Even though I'm an agnostic, and I kid around with that, I respect those who believe in the hereafter. Not only respect, I envy them! If they feel that they will meet some dear ones later and it gives them solace, are you kidding? Of course it's okay.

"I'm a fan of religion," Studs said, by way of summarizing. "I don't think it'll suffer the fate of the Cubs, but I'm a fan."

While he'd sooner call himself a Republican than a religious man, matters of faith clearly have been on his mind in recent years. In 2001 Studs, who lost his wife of more than sixty years in 1999—he keeps fresh yellow daisies (Ida's favorite) next to her ashes on a windowsill in his home and admits he still talks to her from time to time—published a book called *Will the Circle Be Unbroken?: Reflections on Death, Rebirth, and Hunger for a Faith*. When he dies, Studs wants to have his ashes mixed with Ida's and spread across Bughouse Square.

The title of the book is an homage to one of his favorite hymns, which asks, "Will the circle be unbroken by and by, Lord, by and by? There's a better home a-waitin' in the sky, Lord, in the sky."

Not long before our lunch, he had published yet another new book, *Hope Dies Last: Keeping the Faith in Troubled Times*. It's a study of that intangible, spiritual notion: hope.

"Death has little meaning if you haven't lived," Studs continued as our conversation meandered through politics, race, religion, the arts, literature, and the media.

Eventually, though, as his long tales always do, Studs returned to the original question: What would the world be like if the pope were a black man?

While he is intrigued by the idea of the most recognizable face of Christianity in the world being a black one, Studs, a champion of racial causes, said it mattered little to him what color the next pope would be.

"What's his perspective? Will it be reminiscent of Pope John XXIII? Open? Open to the world? Open to changes? Open to what Christ is really about? Or will it be closed? Shut down?"

Then he told me a story, one of his favorites, he said, that an old friend once told him.

"A. J. Muste says there were two guys in this town, and it's a small town. One guy is the rich guy, and he says, 'What counts is what I do for me and my family. What counts is here, right here now. No other place matters to me, no other people matter to me.' They nicknamed him Here.

"And then there was a schoolteacher, an impoverished schoolteacher who was telling the kids, 'There's a world outside that's related to us, too. Out there. We must be involved out there as well as here because we're all related.' And they nicknamed him There.

"So Here, the rich man, dies. Who shows up at his funeral? His relatives fighting over the will. Nephews and nieces, a few cousins, and a few gossips . . . When the man they called There died, everybody appeared! And the eulogy was the shortest eulogy on record. It said, 'We loved him here because he was always there.'"

Studs threw his hands up in triumph when he finished the story and said, loud enough for everyone in the dining room to hear, "To me, that's what life is all about."

I'm glad I asked.

NOVEMBER 2004

BARACK OBAMA

U.S. Senator

I have an ongoing conversation with God.

✳

BIRTH DATE: *August 4, 1961*
RAISED: *Christian (nonspecific)*
NOW: *Christian, United Church of Christ*
ATTENDS: *Trinity United Church of Christ, on Chicago's South Side*
WORDS TO LIVE BY: *"I think there is an enormous danger on the part of public figures to rationalize or justify their actions by claiming God's mandate."*

Casually straightening his tie with one hand as he holds the door for a stranger with the other, the young politician strides into the café on Chicago's South Michigan Avenue, greeting the counter guy by name and flashing a big grin at the rest of the room. He grabs a bottled protein shake from the cooler in the back and settles at a table near the soft-drink dispenser, doffing his suit jacket along the way.

Barack Obama is alone on this Saturday afternoon in the city, his press secretary nowhere in sight. He's not carrying anything with him. Not even notes.

Yet he appears perfectly confident as he answers questions about his spiritual life, a subject that would make many politicians—on or off the campaign trail—more skittish than a long-tailed cat in a room full of rocking chairs.

It's a few weeks after Obama has won the Democratic primary in Illinois for the open United States Senate seat he will eventually win in a landslide against the Republican candidate, Alan Keyes. And while it's months before his debut at the Democratic National Convention, where Obama will become a household name in the rest of the nation, here at home, people for months have been whispering that he's sure to be the first black president of the United States. It's just a matter of time, they say. He shrugs coolly at such suggestions, striking a balance between self-deprecation and the calm assuredness of someone who is wise enough to realize his own place in history.

So if a public conversation about his faith unnerves him, the lanky senator-to-be with the boyish good looks is not letting on. He fields without hesitation the first question: *What does he believe?* "I am a Christian," Obama says, as one of the nearby customers interrupts to congratulate him on winning the primary. Obama shakes the man's hand and says, "Thank you very much. I appreciate that," before turning his attention directly back to the question. "So, I have a deep faith. I'm rooted in the Christian tradition. I believe that there are many paths to the same place, and that is a belief that there is a higher power, a belief that we are connected as a people, that there are values that transcend race or culture, that move us forward, and that there's an obligation for all of us individually as well as collectively to take responsibility to make those values lived. I probably spent the first forty years of my life figuring out what I did believe, and it's not that I have it all completely worked out, but I'm spending a lot of time now trying to apply what I believe and trying to live up to those values."

He is saying, essentially, that all people of faith—Christians, Jews, Muslims, animists, everyone—know the same God. It is, perhaps, an unlikely theological position for someone who places his faith squarely at the feet of Jesus to take. But that depends on how you hear a verse from the Gospel of St. John, where Jesus says, "I am the way, the truth and the life. No one comes to the Father but by me," Obama says.

His theological point of view was shaped by his uniquely multicultural upbringing. Obama was born in 1961 in Hawaii to a white mother who came from Protestant midwestern stock and a black African father who hailed from the Luo tribe of Kenya. The future senator describes his father, after whom he is named, as "agnostic." His paternal grandfather was a Muslim. His mother, he says, was a Christian. "My mother, who I think had as much influence on my values as anybody, was not someone who wore her religion on her sleeve," he says. "We'd go to church for Easter, but she wasn't a 'church lady.'"

What she really was, as he put it in his 1995 memoir, *Dreams from My Father: A Story of Race and Inheritance,* was "a lonely witness for secular humanism." He says now, "My mother's confidence in needlepoint virtues depended on a faith I didn't possess, a faith that she would refuse to describe as religious; that, in fact, her experience told her was sacrilegious: a faith that rational, thoughtful people could shape their own destiny."

When he was six years old, after his parents divorced, Obama moved with his mother and her new husband—a non-practicing Muslim—to Indonesia, where he attended a Roman Catholic school and lived until he was ten. "I went to a Catholic school in a Muslim country, so I was studying the Bible and catechisms by day, and, at night, I'd hear the [Muslim] prayer call," Obama recalls. "My mother was a deeply spiritual person and would spend a lot of time talking about values and give me books about the world's religions and talk to me about them. Her view always was that underlying these religions was a common set of beliefs about how you treat other people and how you aspire to act, not just for yourself but also for the greater good."

Obama earned a degree in political science from Columbia University in 1983 and in 1991 graduated magna cum laude with a law degree from Harvard University. Since 1993, he has been a lecturer at the University of Chicago Law School. Those intellectual experiences, as much as his multireligious childhood, affect how he expresses his faith. "Alongside my own deep personal faith, I am a follower, as well, of our civic religion," he says. "I am a big believer in the separation of church and state. I am a big believer in our constitutional structure. I mean, I'm a law professor at the University of Chicago teaching constitutional law. I am a great admirer of our founding charter and its resolve to prevent theocracies from forming and its resolve to prevent disruptive strains of fundamentalism from taking root in this country. I think there is an enormous danger on the part of public figures to rationalize or justify their actions by claiming God's mandate. I don't think it's healthy for public figures to wear religion on their sleeve as a means to insulate themselves from criticism, or avoid dialogue with people who disagree with them."

Even so, Obama is not shy about saying he has a "personal relationship with Jesus Christ." As a sign of that relationship, he says, he walked down the aisle of Chicago's Trinity United Church of Christ in response to the Reverend Jeremiah Wright's altar call one Sunday morning in 1988.

The politician could have ended his spiritual tale right there, at the point where some people might assume his life changed, when he got "saved," transformed, washed in the blood. But Obama wants to clarify what truly happened. "It wasn't an epiphany," he says of that public profession of faith. "It was much more of a gradual process for me. I know there are some people who fall out. Which is wonderful. God bless them. For me, I think it was just a moment to certify or publicly affirm a growing faith in me.

"I retain from my childhood and my experiences growing up a suspicion of dogma, and I'm not somebody who is always comfortable with language that implies I've got a monopoly on the truth, or that my faith is automatically transferable to others," he continues. "I'm a big believer in tolerance. I think that religion at its best comes with a big dose of doubt. I'm suspicious, too, of too much certainty in the pursuit of understanding. I think that, particularly as somebody who's now in the public realm and is a student of what brings people together and what drives them apart, there's an enormous amount of damage done around the world in the name of religion and certainty."

When he is in Chicago, he attends the 11:00 a.m. Sunday service at Trinity in the working-class Brainerd neighborhood every week—or at least as many weeks as he is able. But how exactly did he become a churchgoer? It began in 1985, when he arrived in Chicago as a $13,000-a-year community organizer, working with a number of African-American churches in the struggling Roseland, West Pullman, and Altgeld Gardens neighborhoods, which were dealing with the devastation caused by shuttered steel plants.

"I started working with both the ministers and the laypeople in these churches on issues like creating job-training programs, or after-school programs for youth, or making sure that city services were fairly allocated to underserved communities," Obama explains. "And it was in those places where I think what had been more of an intellectual view of religion deepened because I was spending an enormous amount of time with church ladies, sort of surrogate mothers and fathers. Everybody I was working with was fifty or fifty-five or sixty, and here I was, a twenty-three-year-old kid, kicking around. I became much more familiar with the ongoing tradition of the historic black church and its importance in the community. And the power of that culture to give people strength in very difficult circumstances, and the power of that church to give people courage against great odds. And it moved me deeply."

Obama reads the Bible, though not as regularly as he'd like given the ever-increasing demands on his time that political life has brought. But he does find time to pray. "It's not formal, me getting on my knees," he says. "I think I have an ongoing conversation with God. Throughout the day I'm constantly asking myself questions about what I'm doing, why I am doing it. One of the interesting things about being in public life is that there are constantly these pressures being placed on you from different sides. To be effective, you have to be able to listen to a variety of points of view, to synthesize the viewpoints. You also have to know when to be a strong advocate and to push back against certain people or views that you think aren't right or that don't serve your constituents. And so the biggest challenge, I think, is always maintaining your moral compass. Those are the conversations I'm having with God internally. I'm measuring my actions against that inner voice that, for me at least, is audible, is active. It tells me where I think I'm on track and where I'm off track.

"This election comes with a lot of celebrity. I always think of politics as having two sides: There's a vanity aspect to politics, and a substantive aspect to politics. Now, you need some sizzle with the steak to be effective, but I think it's very easy to get swept up in the vanity side of it, the desire to be liked and recognized and important. It's important for me to take stock throughout the day, to say, Now, am I doing this because I think it's advantageous to me politically or because I think it's the right thing to do? Am I doing this to get in the papers, or am I doing this because it's necessary to accomplish my motives?"

He uses prayer as a litmus test for altruism? "Yeah, something like that," he says, smiling sheepishly. "The most powerful political moments for me come when I feel like my actions are aligned with a certain truth. I can feel it. When I'm talking to a group and I'm saying something truthful, I can feel a power that comes out of those statements that is different than when I'm just being glib or clever."

Is that power the Holy Spirit? "I think it's the power of the recognition of God, or the recognition of a larger truth that is being shared between me and the audience. That's something you learn watching ministers—what they call the Holy Spirit. They want the Holy Spirit to come down while they're preaching, right? Not to try to intellectualize it, but what I see there are moments that happen within a sermon where the minister gets out of his ego and is speaking from a different source. And it's powerful. There are also times when you can see the ego getting in the way, where the minister is performing and clearly straining for applause or an amen. And those are distinct moments. But I think those former moments are sacred."

Obama has many friends in the clergy who help keep his moral compass set, such as the Reverend Michael Pfleger, a white Roman Catholic priest and pastor of St. Sabina Church, a mostly black activist congregation in the rough Auburn-Gresham community on Chicago's South Side. "I always have felt in him this consciousness that, at the end of the day, with all of us, you've got to face God," says Pfleger, who has known Obama for almost twenty years. "Faith is key to his life, no question about it. It is central to who he is, and not just in his work in the political field but as a man, as a black man, as a husband, as a father. I don't think he could easily divorce his faith from who he is."

Another person Obama seeks out for spiritual counsel is Illinois State Senator James Meeks, who is also the pastor of Chicago's Salem Baptist Church and heir apparent to the helm of the Reverend Jesse Jackson's Rainbow/PUSH Coalition. The day after Obama won the primary in March 2004, he stopped by Salem for Wednesday-night Bible study. "I know that he's a person of prayer," Meeks says. "The night after the election, he was the hottest thing going from Galesburg to Rockford. He did all the TV shows, and all the morning news, but his last stop at night was for church. He came by to say thank you, and he came by for prayer."

Obama recognizes that it's not easy for most politicians to talk about faith, at least not in any real, genuine way.

"The nature of politics is that you want to have everybody like you and project the best possible traits onto you," he says. "Oftentimes, that's by being as vague as possible, or appealing to the lowest common denominators. The more specific and detailed you are on issues as personal and fundamental as your faith, the more potentially dangerous it is. The difficult thing about any religion, including Christianity, is that at some level there is a call to evangelize and proselytize. There's the belief, certainly in some quarters, that if people haven't embraced Jesus Christ as their personal savior, they're going to hell."

Obama doesn't believe he, or anyone else, will go to hell. But he's not sure if he'll be going to heaven either.

"I find it hard to believe that my God would consign four-fifths of the world to hell. I can't imagine that my God would allow some little Hindu kid in India who never interacts with the Christian faith to somehow burn for all eternity. That's just not part of my religious makeup," he says. "What I believe in is that if I live my life as well as I can, that I will be rewarded. I don't presume to have knowledge of what happens after I die. But I feel very strongly that whether the reward is in the here and now or in the hereafter, aligning myself to my faith and values is a good thing.

"When I tuck my daughters in at night and I feel like I've been a good father to them, and I see in them that I am transferring values that I got from my mother and that they're kind people and that they're honest people and that they're curious people, that's a little piece of heaven."

APRIL 2004

ANNE RICE

Author

I was given the gift of faith again.

✳

A.K.A. *Howard Allen O'Brien Rice*
BIRTH DATE: *October 4, 1941*
RAISED: *Roman Catholic*
NOW: *Roman Catholic*
ATTENDS: *Mary, Star of the Sea, Catholic Church in La Jolla, California*
WORDS TO LIVE BY: *"If you focus on loving and focus on faith and God as well, you won't have a whole lot of time for hating people."*

Johnny Depp would make a perfect Jesus. At least that's what Anne Rice thinks. And she's given it a lot of thought.

"Definitely Johnny Depp," she says decisively, casting, in her imagination, the hypothetical leading man of the television series she hopes to develop for HBO based on her latest novel, *Christ the Lord: Out of Egypt*, which chronicles Jesus' life. "I haven't told Johnny Depp yet, but wouldn't he be perfect?"

Hmm . . . Strong. Beautiful. Edgy. Soulful eyes. A graceful person but not effeminate. Roguish yet strangely wise. Yes, Depp as Jesus—I can see it.

Rice envisions a show that would do for Jesus' everyday life what *Deadwood,* which she insists is the best show on television—perhaps ever— has done for the Wild West. "It would be everything that's going on in Jesus' village—all the arguments, disputes, whatever—and we'd take maybe five years to get to Jerusalem," she says. "In my book, Jesus is only seven years old, so we would start there and have a boy play him, and then we'd move on up." To Johnny Depp.

I would watch that, I tell her. "I would, too," she says, eyes dancing with enthusiasm. "That's all I want to do. Somebody's gonna do it. If I don't do it, somebody else will, because I can't want to do something this badly and have wanted to do it for so long without somebody else thinking of it. That's what I keep telling my agents—go out there and get it set up, please!"

Jesus is on Anne Rice's mind these days not just as a novel or a television series but as Lord and savior, the embodiment of a faith she abandoned as a college girl and has since returned to, transformed.

"For me, spiritual concerns are totally pervasive. There is nothing separate from it. It's complete and sort of urgent," she says, sipping coffee from a tiny porcelain cup and saucer at a tea table perfectly set with starched floral linens and lacy napkins, overlooking the lush backyard of her home in La Jolla, California. Reared Roman Catholic in a largely Irish American community in New Orleans, Rice returned to the church in 1998 after having abandoned it for the better part of forty years.

"I really did want to go back to Communion, back to the banquet table," she says, her voice gentle and measured. "I did believe that the body and blood of Christ were there and I believed in the incarnation and I wanted to be received back. It didn't seem to me that all the other problems I had with the church mattered. The important thing was to go and be reconciled, to rejoin, to reapproach. And I felt like I was given the gift of faith again and I was able to go back to the table."

She walked away from it when she was an eighteen-year-old student at Texas Women's College. "It was a crisis of faith. I just stopped believing," she says. "The idea of God was just so completely intertwined with the idea of the Catholic Church that when I lost faith in my church and the world in which I had grown up, I think my loss of faith was complete. It was a very rigid, authoritarian system that I had grown up under. It wasn't until years later that I could separate out what was custom and tradition from what was true church teaching and theology. What I wanted desperately at the time was freedom, freedom to read anything that I wanted to read. At that time there was still an index of forbidden books, and you weren't supposed to read all kinds of authors if you were a strict Catholic. I think, really, I had been just too rigid and too completely inflexible as a Catholic. I sort of snapped and really suffered a severe loss of faith in God."

When she disinterred her Catholic roots, Rice was living in New Orleans (she moved to California in 2005) and had begun visiting the church of her childhood, even supporting it financially. She started attending Mass again and slowly reacquainted herself with the church. A friend who is a professor of religious studies went with her and coached her through the parts of the Mass she didn't remember. "It's been quite an education. I didn't really know much about the church. I couldn't even have told you the pope's name for the first six months. I just went back to church. For the first time ever I saw an English Mass. When I left, it was in Latin," she says, chuckling.

"I wanted to come back for a long time, and I really just finally got up one afternoon and went to confession and went back," she says. Confession? Really? "Oh, yes," she says, surprised at my surprise. "You have to go back to confession to go back to church." Yes, but a lot of people might skip that part, what with owning up to nearly forty years of sin in one sitting. "Oh, no," she says. "I went back to confession and was reconciled and then got married in the church."

Anne had been legally married for thirty-seven years to the poet and artist Stan Rice, a man she describes as "my Bible Belt atheist" because of his zeal for resisting all things remotely theistic, when she returned to Catholicism and asked him if he would agree to get married again in a church. "He said sure, he didn't mind," she recounts. "We were married December 12, 1998, in St. Mary's Church. I invited my Irish Catholic cousins—there really are a thousand of them, but only about twenty or twenty-five were there—and then we all went over and had a little reception. Two days later I almost died. I went into a diabetic coma. My heart stopped beating, and I was unconscious for two days. One of the last things I remember is our wedding reception and going to Mass and Communion that afternoon. After that, it's pretty much a blur."

That diabetes-induced coma wasn't her first, or her last, brush with peril. Rice has led a dramatic life, weathering a number of health-related issues— including a burst appendix a year after the coma. "The doctor told me to say my goodbyes," she says. "But I was saved again." Even during the thirty-eight years that she was a "fashionable atheist," she feels she was being shielded from harm for a higher calling.

"I think I certainly was protected. There were many times when I could have been hurt. I lived so carelessly. I mean, I was married the whole time and was faithful to my husband and was only with him, but I also went through a long period of very, very heavy drinking. I took a lot of risks. But I was protected. I was given another chance over and over again," she says. In hindsight, even though she didn't believe, does she think Jesus might have been walking with her during those years in the wilderness? "Yes. I guess he was," she says pensively. "Yes . . . I think so.

"I have a great sense of mission. I really want to make a big difference, and I want to keep writing, I want to keep going, and I feel I have before me a lot of tasks that I want to do. I've always been obsessed with what we really want. Even when I wrote *Interview with the Vampire*, I thought what we really wanted to know is what's going on in a vampire's mind. We really want to go home with him, not with the victim. That's what I want to do, and I feel the same way now, that what we really want is not what we're being offered in the entertainment industry. It's something different. You can be offered mystery and romance in very legitimate ways, in profound ways, and have it without the cheap car chases and garish violence that they keep throwing in our faces. Who wants it? I've been sort of exploring that all my life, trying to get to what I think is really important. I would like to write books within the Judeo-Christian framework that are every bit as exciting as anything I've ever written in the past that was thought to be exciting," she says.

Rice is a fan of Mel Gibson's film *The Passion of the Christ* and says claims by critics that it is the "most violent film ever made" are ridiculous. "I couldn't believe it. I thought, You haven't seen *The Last of the Mohicans*? You didn't get dragged to a Freddy Krueger movie by your eleven-year-old son like I did? I was hiding under the seats while he's sitting there eating popcorn as Freddy murders people," she says, laughing. "The most violent movie ever made? Come on. Do kids really wake up in the middle of the night screaming that they're afraid of Roman soldiers?"

Anne and Stan Rice had two children together—the novelist Christopher Rice and a daughter, Michelle, who died of leukemia in 1972. Stan died in December 2002 of brain cancer. In the summer of 2002, a few months before Stan passed away, Rice decided to write a book about the life of Christ, but she had to complete *Blood Canticle*, the last book in her Vampire Chronicles, first. She says that novel, in which her beloved vampire, Lestat, takes an interesting moral turn, is, in a manner, really about her decision to turn her literary and spiritual attention toward Jesus. *Blood Canticle* "starts off with the hero [Lestat] saying, 'I want to be a saint. I want to save souls by the millions,'" she says.

"Once it was finished, that was it, and I went right into the life of Christ. By that time, I already knew I couldn't possibly do the life of Christ without years of intense studying, that it was something that required enormous research in archaeology, in history, and in Bible study. I had a very clear focus on what I wanted to do, and very quickly I realized the type of book I wanted to do was about the Jesus of the Gospels."

She didn't want to reinvent Jesus as something that he wasn't. Her Jesus would have to be historically and theologically accurate. "Anybody could write a book about him being a liberal, homosexual, married guy with three lovers," she says. So she studied and studied and consulted with experts, theologians and clergy, and studied some more—for three years. "It was the most thrilling experience," she says, "because everything in my devotional life and everything in my creative life, my professional life, and my personal life was all one. I never foresaw what it would be like to be that unified, that completely at peace with oneself, and yet fired up and eager and determined to do something and as divinely discontent as ever, but everything was together."

While she wrote *Christ the Lord*, she says she could feel Jesus' presence. "Just talking to him all the time, walking around the house, praying, talking to him, going to Mass," she says. One of the reasons she bought this sprawling, airy home in California was its proximity to a parish she likes. "You can walk to church from here," she says. Rice attends Mass as often as her health allows. "I don't go out a lot. It sounds ridiculous to say it, but one of the reasons I have a big house is because I don't go out a lot. So I have all of my books here, my whole world is here." Her home is bright, decorated with a kind of English country sensibility, and filled with her late husband's vibrantly colored paintings. One room on the main floor holds a portion of her enormous doll collection, and the basement level houses many of the thousands of books she uses for research.

What Rice discovered during her years of study in preparation for *Christ the Lord* surprised her. "I had no idea that I was entering a field where people cannot agree on anything, where the arguments and the controversies were so heated and passionate," she says, referring to centuries of scholarship about the life of Christ. She ended up dismissing a preponderance of modern criticism of the Gospels and the so-called search for the historical Jesus—"It's a joke and everyone knows that," she says—finding more traditional scholarship and the Gospels themselves the most compelling in explaining who Jesus was, what he did, and what it means. "So many of the assumptions made by scholars in the early twentieth century have really proved to be flimsy assumptions. They just really don't prove out," she says.

While the Jesus of *Christ the Lord* is a fictionalized Jesus, living in a fictionalized Nazareth, she believes the novel reflects the truth of who Jesus really was. "He was a literate, trilingual carpenter from the village of Nazareth, who worked, probably every day, in the city and went to Jerusalem three or four times a year," she says. "He spoke Greek, certainly, and he probably spoke Aramaic—that was the language he spoke every day and spoke at the time that he was teaching. But he also spoke and understood Greek, and he understood and read Hebrew. He was an observant Jew. And of course, all of that is based on the Gospels. There's nothing radical about that. I believe that he was definitely all of those things and that he preached a new religion that was a repudiation of the temple system, and that he was condemned for it, crucified, and then he rose from the dead and ascended into heaven. And that's who he was: the Son of God.

"The challenge for me is to take the Jesus of the Gospels and make him as believable as I made vampires and witches to people," she says. "If you have adults calling you and *seriously* asking you, 'Are the vampires real?' you can get in the mind of a character—Jesus Christ—born of a virgin in Nazareth, visited by shepherds and wise men."

People might think that when Rice found religion she felt the need to lose her vampires, to turn away from the "dark side." They'd be mistaken, she says. "All of those books were just milestones on a quest. And it's a wonderful experience as a published author to have all that behind you, to have that record of your quests and how you felt at all the different points along the road. But there's no repudiation on my part of something that was at odds with Christianity. It's part of the progression, the moving on toward the same salvation that Louis was looking for in *Interview with the Vampire*, that same looking for meaning, looking for the context that will rescue everything, that will somehow redeem all the suffering. I feel that I have found it."

MAY 2005

MANCOW MULLER

Radio Personality

Yes, I'm a believer.

✳

A.K.A.: *Mathew Erich Muller*

BIRTH DATE: *June 21, 1966*

RAISED: *Roman Catholic, then Protestant*

NOW: *"Journeyman Christian"*

ATTENDS: *St. Mary of the Angels Roman Catholic Church in Chicago*

WORDS TO LIVE BY: *"The message is love, and it's a very simple message. And I think that we have really messed it up and messed it up good."*

Believe it or not, ladies and gentlemen, Mancow Muller loves Jesus. Yes, indeed, the shock-jock ringmaster of *Mancow's Morning Madhouse*, the goateed provocateur on the FCC's hit list, the guy with a sidekick named Turd and a pseudo-memoir that describes, among other things, his enthusiastic embrace of a smorgasbord of carnal pleasures in Amsterdam's Red Light district, is a Christian.

"Am I saved? Yes. Yes," says the man who was christened Mathew Erich Muller but who's better known to legions of listeners across the nation as, simply, Mancow. "I went and got baptized and all that stuff. How old would I have been? Probably thirteen or fourteen. And I was very, very much into it." He still is. "If you go through and read the red parts of the Bible [quoting Jesus' own words], that's what I believe," Mancow says. "I'm a real guy, I live in a real world, and yes, I'm a believer."

Mancow knows what a lot of people will think when they hear him talk about this Christian faith—that he's full of, well, a word that he can't say on the air without getting fined again. But he swears he's telling the truth. "Having to prove you're Christian, though, is like having to prove you're not a pedophile or something. But why should I have to prove it? I can't prove it," he says. "People are always going to be suspicious, but so what? . . . I can't control what people think."

Born and reared in a small town outside of Kansas City, Missouri, Mancow grew up Roman Catholic until he was in grade school, when his parents decided to leave that religious tradition and began attending Baptist and various Protestant churches. "We did go to a lot of different churches just to experience different things," he says. "My dad and I went to different churches together. We went to a church called the Berean Church, where they were speaking in tongues. That just terrified me, scared me to death. I went to Catholic school for a year. I got kicked out for kicking a nun. Our Lady of Lourdes in Raytown, Missouri. Third grade. They asked me not to come back."

Through portions of middle school and high school, Mancow attended a couple of private Christian academies. It was during those years that he became a born-again Christian and considered, rather seriously for a time, becoming a minister. "I felt that I had gotten the calling to do that. However, I lost the call," he says. "My fear about becoming a preacher was that I thought I'd be very good at it. That was my fear. And I would have been doing it for the wrong reasons."

Which were?

"I would have probably liked the showbiz aspect of it too much," he says, deadly serious. "I had done some preaching and some talking, and I could see what these guys were doing wrong. And if the goal was saving people and getting people in the church, I could have done that, and it would have been a good show. I saw these guys in the bad suits, and I thought, I can do better than this. In fact, I could be great at this."

See, he says. Wrong reason. And then there were The Questions, theological conundrums he says he couldn't solve, even with the help of his pastors. "I had some questions that they couldn't answer, and that also caused me to stray some," Mancow says. "I had a real problem with the attitude that those who were not saved were going to suffer eternity in hell. And that's what the church believes, certainly the Baptist and other Christian churches.

And there's no way around that. I said, 'What about somebody in India or in the jungle of Africa who has never heard the Word?' Their answer was, 'That's why we've got to get the Word out.' You mean, people are going to suffer for eternity if they don't get born again? So. That was one of my questions. That's probably a question a lot of people get hung up on. And there were others."

So instead of seminary or Bible school and a sacred calling to the ministry, Mancow headed off to Central Missouri State University, a career in broadcasting, and an entirely different kind of pulpit. Erich Muller became Mancow Muller and began earning a national reputation in his twenties with his brand of provocative radio shtick. Some would say too provocative. By mid-2004 the Federal Communications Commission had cited his home radio station, WKQX-FM in Chicago, six times for indecent content on *Mancow's Morning Madhouse*, with accompanying fines of $42,000.

Most people confuse Mancow the shock jock with Mancow the man, he complains, his wife, Sandy, nodding in agreement from a chair not too far away in the chicly decorated living room of their condominium in a tony Chicago neighborhood. Mancow protests that's like assuming the actress Linda Blair is possessed or that the actor Anthony Hopkins is a cannibal because they played those roles on film. Radio is, after all, a form of theater. "This is a radio *show*. My real name is not Mancow. The show is called *Mancow's Morning Madhouse*, and it has a carnival barker–type appeal, where you have the pretty girl out front to titillate people into coming into the tent, but the thing is, once they're in the tent, there are some heavy ideas being expressed. There is a lot of fear and confusion in the world right now. It's kind of like Tony Montana at the end of *Scarface* when he's going 'Come on, Come on!' To have a radio show and take as many phone calls as I do—and I've been doing it since the late eighties—I have never felt such fear and hatred and confusion about everything that's going on in the world right now." He makes a point to tell me that he prays before he goes on the air.

"It's weird, the stuff he believes and then how he is on the air," Midge Ripoli a.k.a. DJ Luv Cheez, one of Muller's morning-show crew, says during a break in the Q101 radio station studios in Chicago from where the nationally syndicated morning show is broadcast. "It's like two people."

The porn star Ron Jeremy has been a frequent guest on the *Madhouse* over the years, and Mancow's Web site features more than a few photos of scantily clad girls. Mancow recently showed up—fully dressed and joking with the proprietor—on an episode of HBO's series *Cathouse*, a documentary-style program about Nevada's Moonlight Bunny Ranch brothel. (The shock jock swears he did not partake of any of the ranch's services. He's got witnesses.) In contrast to some of his racier friends, Mancow was close to Malachi Martin, a friend of Pope John XXIII and former Jesuit priest who wrote thrillers about the Catholic Church. He considered Martin a confidant until his death in 1999.

Mancow is fascinated by faith, religion, and the spirit world, topics that come up regularly in the frenetic morning banter of his *Madhouse*. In the early 1990s, when he was working for a radio station in San Francisco, he claims he traded a pair of Prince concert tickets for the chance to touch the Dead Sea Scrolls with his bare hands. He would like to write a couple of books on religious subjects—one about the legendary Spear of Longinus, the weapon supposedly used to pierce Jesus' side as he hung on the cross; the other book about St. Paul, who Mancow believes may have been the Antichrist. (It's a *long* story.)

When Mel Gibson held a private screening of his film *The Passion of the Christ* for a group of pastors at Willow Creek Community Church in a Chicago suburb a few months before the controversial film opened in theaters, Mancow was among the guests. "I couldn't watch a lot of it. But again, the fact that it gets people talking . . . yeah, I liked it," he says. "One of the things I loved about *The Passion of the Christ* is that Jesus wasn't some guy with a halo around him. We created that, I think, phony-baloney image of him. In the movie he's a real guy."

Despite his private piety, Mancow's public persona rubs certain religious people the wrong way. The shock jock once attended a Christmas party at the Gold Coast home of Cardinal Francis George, Chicago's Roman Catholic cardinal-archbishop. Mancow was the guest of an invited guest. "I had a long conversation with the cardinal," he says. Pictures were taken. Then, according to Mancow, someone from the archdiocese, apparently displeased that there was photographic evidence of the shock jock in the archbishop's house, sent out a photo taken with the cardinal with Mancow's image excised by scissors. "It broke my heart," he says. (After I asked church officials about the incident in the spring of 2004, a representative from the archdiocese phoned Mancow to apologize and sent him fresh photos—with his likeness included.)

"I've probably done a poor job of something because I've allowed myself to be categorized as something I'm not," Mancow laments. "But there's nothing I can do about that."

His professional success has at times been accompanied by excess. He chronicled some of his debaucherous adventures in his 2003 book, *Dad, Dames, Demons, and a Dwarf: My Trip Down Freedom Road*. It's not for the faint of heart—a lot of drugs, doubts, and whoring about. He now admits parts of the pseudo-memoir are pure fiction. "Some of it is just fantasy. Some of it is, I thought at the time, just fun. And some of the stories are true. It is a bit of a time capsule, and I did go through a time of questioning. The moral of the story is I had everything that could be offered to me—all the sex, drugs, and rock 'n' roll I could handle, and it was served up to me on a platter. I was like a kid in a candy store. I did indulge. And I got sick," he says.

Mancow insists he's a different man today. "You're talking about a twenty-five-, twenty-six-year-old guy. Even Amish kids are given a couple of years when they can go and fool around. Sins of the flesh. Interesting, interesting," he says, his voice trailing off for a moment. "Sex was definitely my weakness. I think it's every man's weakness. I talked to Michael Douglas once on my show. He said he was a sex addict. I just don't believe it. I think every man is a sex addict. Do you want to have this conversation with me?" he says, looking concerned. "Am I embarrassing you?" I tell him no.

"For me, it was a dead end. Look, I'm happily married. When you find the right woman, you don't need to go searching. I'd say I'm five years on the other side of it. But I spent years being miserable. Of course, what person is going to read this and believe that?"

In 2003, Mancow married Sandy Ferrando, a former staffer from his radio show. The wedding was celebrated at Chicago's St. Mary of the Angels Roman Catholic Church, a parish staffed by priests from the Opus Dei prelature. Neither Mancow nor his wife, who used to sing in St. Mary's choir, is a member of Opus Dei, but they are regular churchgoers. Before they were married, Mancow also used to attend a small Baptist church up the street from his condo, Chicago's Greater Little Rock Baptist. "I would hear the music, and I just went into it, and I loved it," Mancow says. "You could really feel the Spirit. And I loved it." But then the church members started welcoming him publicly from the pulpit. They meant well, he says, but it made him uncomfortable.

"Look, I do believe that you have to go to church. I don't believe these people who say, 'Well, you can feel God in your living room.' I think that's true, and I think I feel closer to God on a canoe trip with my brothers than I do in any church. But I do think it's important to go and hear the Word . . . And I certainly think when we have kids, it's something I won't want to miss."

On the way to an evening Palm Sunday Mass at St. Mary of the Angels, the Mullers are talking about the pre-Cana classes they attended before their Valentine's Day wedding a few years earlier. "I found it interesting, when we had our meeting with the priest before we got married, that he told you we had to have relations often, that it was part of the relationship," Mancow says, smirking mischievously.

"They asked him if he could perform his husbandly duties," Sandy says to me.

"They want more Catholics," Mancow retorts, as Sandy adds, "Yeah, the whole point of getting married is to have children." (The Mullers welcomed twin girls—Ava and Isabella—in August 2005.) Mancow parks their car in the church lot, gets out to open the door for Sandy, and says to me, "What's that line from Monty Python? 'Every sperm is sacred'?" Sandy shoots him a disapproving look; he smiles, clearly pleased with himself; and they walk into the sanctuary to find a seat in a back pew, picking up palm fronds along the way. After Mass, the Reverend John Debicki, associate pastor at St. Mary's and the priest who presided at their wedding, mentions to me that he's never heard Mancow's radio show. "I've never gotten to listen to it. The thing is, it's the wrong time for me. I've got Mass in the morning," Debicki says.

"Good. Don't encourage him to listen to it," Mancow interrupts, playfully. "It is true that my show isn't aimed at Catholic priests."

Debicki has heard from plenty of people who have listened to Mancow's show and don't approve. "I've heard many things about it," the priest says, smiling. "I'm not worried about that. One of the things is that I know him. I know him as a *person*."

A few days later, Mancow is thinking, as he seems to do often, about his reputation and how he believes he is misunderstood, the victim of unfair presumptions. "First of all, I don't think I've ever done anything obscene on the show. I don't think I've ever done anything that was—what's the word they use—indecent. There are things in every show that I regret. If we put a mic for five hours in front of Father Debicki, he would probably offend half the population, too. I never set out to be a shock jock, and I never set out to be offensive. These are honest opinions, and people are offended."

When it comes to spiritual counsel, Mancow often turns to John Calkins, a Christian Scientist trained in spiritual healing who lives in Italy. The two men met in 1990, when Muller rented a home from Calkins in California. "Like everything else he does, he's intense and comes at things from a different direction," Calkins says of Mancow. "If he has a problem and calls for counsel and I pray with him, he accepts it, and within a half hour, things are different. His faith is genuine, definitely. And it's fairly simple. I think he genuinely believes that love is the solution, and that's the message: to love your neighbor as yourself and to get on with it. There's some of the punishing God that he's working on getting rid of, and I think that's good, and I think that's right. He's the most fearless person I know, and if Jesus is right that perfect love casts out fear, and if Mancow is the most fearless, he also is the most loving."

The Mullers read the Bible regularly, and they pray. "I believe in prayer, although it didn't work for my father," Mancow says. His father, John Muller, died of cancer in 1995. "Unanswered prayers are sometimes the best. There's a reason in all of it. But yeah, I do pray every night." What do he and Sandy pray for? "We pray for each other. We pray for our marriage," he says. Sandy is attempting to read the entire Bible in one year and reads Scripture each night before going to bed. Mancow, a voracious reader in general, regularly turns to the Bible, saying, "The more I study, the more I believe."

One spring morning, between discussions of *The Apprentice* and *The Da Vinci Code*, Mancow tells his listeners about something he has gleaned from his biblical studies: Jesus would enjoy a dirty joke. "Look, he was a carpenter," Mancow explains later. "He hung out with fishermen. You ever hung out with sailors? Do they have dirty mouths? He wasn't sitting around with the Pharisees, pontificating. He was hanging out, in the dirt, with the regular people."

APRIL 2004

BILLY CORGAN

Rock Star

I'm comfortable with God in any form.

✳

BIRTH DATE: *March 17, 1967*

RAISED: *Roman Catholic*

NOW: *No label applies*

ATTENDS: *Mass occasionally at a Chicago-area parish*

WORDS TO LIVE BY: *"God is asking you to step up and say, 'Okay, I'm worthy. What do I need to do? Point me in the right direction, no matter how crazy it seems.'"*

You could see it in her eyes, a kind of wounded yearning. She was probably in her late teens, a little chubby, pale skin, dyed black hair, pierced eyebrow, pierced lip, lots of black kohl eyeliner, and a retro-punk outfit in, of course, all black. It seemed as if her outward appearance was meant to be a protective shell for the frightened girl inside. She feigned an effective ennui, but when I put *Blinking with Fists*, a book of poetry by the rocker Billy Corgan, down on the counter in front of her, her face lit up. "I LOVE Billy Corgan. I LOVE him. Smashing Pumpkins are like my absolute favorite!" she said, gently sliding the slim collection of poetry into a plastic bag. "Did you know he's touring? His new album comes out next week! I can't WAIT! He's so great! I just LOVE him!"

"The Goths love me," Corgan, the former lead singer of the bands Smashing Pumpkins and Zwan, tells me a few days later as we chat in the corner booth at a diner in downtown Chicago. He's having a strip steak, medium

rare. And herbal tea. The next day, he will leave on a tour to support his first solo album, *The Future Embrace*, and he's trying to keep his energy up, in a healthy way. I've just told him about the salesgirl at Borders. "All I'm trying to do is *olé* them back to themselves, like a bullfighter. I'm not trying to draw people to me for me. I'm trying to draw them to me to give them back to them. Do you know what I mean? This is a new thing, it's not that profitable. Because you stand the chance that when they go back to them, they think, I don't need you anymore. But that's okay. I trust that."

The Goth kids—and increasingly people in general these days—are searching for something, he says, and it's not him. But he can try to point them in the right direction, toward the thing he was searching for as a Goth teenager and as a depressed, self-absorbed young adult during most of his Smashing Pumpkins years. (The hugely popular Pumpkins formed in 1988 and broke up in 2000.) "They're looking for God, they're looking for God," he tells me with fierce gravity. "I can sit here and speak from personal knowledge and say I was in the number one band in the world and it didn't get me what I was looking for. It was great being in the number one band in the world, but it sucked because it had no foundational meaning beyond what I thought it did. Now I actually realize that we did a lot of good even despite ourselves, and that was what is beautiful about it. Because our hearts were in the right place, enough of that came through even if we didn't have the right context to put it in. Most of it doesn't have any context, and the negative context is constantly being reinforced.

"Watch the news. Who gets on the news? The person who says the offensive thing, the person who gets the good sound bite. You watch the debates. Who gets the most publicity at the debate? The person who was most clever, not the person who made the best points. It was who dodged the bullet. These things are constantly being reinforced. Everybody is walking around all thirsty. Why doesn't my government reflect who I am? Why do I feel dispossessed? They're looking for God, but you can't tell somebody who is individuating that what they're looking for is God. There is a reason that, in essence, God on one level has been pushed out of the mainstream, because it's just not cool, it gets in the way. No, fuck that. I see God everywhere I go.

"Here's what people don't understand: They can find God through themselves. They don't need an old man on a hill. That's *their* problem. Look at how incredible your life is. Look at the fact that you are just a biomechanical thing that works. I go like this and my hand moves. We take so much for granted. Look at it this way, let's say you don't believe in God at all, zero. The fact that you were created by two human beings, that you came out, that you walked, talked, moved, that alone should give you some belief, some faith in something."

"All Things Change," the lead track on *The Future Embrace*, seems to sum up what Corgan is trying to explain. The song's lyrics say in part: *"All is faith, unwound . . . we can change the world."*

A decade or two ago, Corgan probably wouldn't have been saying such things. Born on St. Patrick's Day 1967 in suburban Chicago, Billy had a rough early life, one he has chronicled extensively in an Internet blog. His parents were young and unstable when he was born—they got married when his mother, Martha, became pregnant with him. He says he never felt wanted, and by all indications, he had good reason to feel that way. His parents divorced when he was young, and he was shuttled between the homes of relatives before moving in with his younger brother, stepmother, and father. According to Corgan, his home was physically abusive. His stepmother beat him regularly, waking him in the middle of the night to scream and hit him, he says. His father, a musician, did drugs and ignored him. His mother was unable or unwilling to care for him herself. He felt like an outcast and was teased by other children about the large strawberry birthmark that covers much of his left hand and wrist. When his father and stepmother divorced, Billy stayed with his stepmother. It was not a happy childhood by any stretch of the imagination. And the scars still show.

"My niece is very spiritual," he says. Corgan often makes his point by telling stories. "The way she looks at me is crazy—she's three years old, and I feel like I'm being scanned by an X-ray. She's got that look in her eyes. What would her construct of God be?" He shrugs. "She's very connected, though. She's as connected as she needs to be. But if I see her in ten years from now and that glow has gone out of the eyes, I'll know that that's something that needs to be reclaimed. But I know she has it. I think I was the same way. I got the shit kicked out of me, and I had to find my way out of that hole, I had to figure that out. And everything from having a disabled brother and watching him be sort of shunned and teased because he had this crazy chromosomal disability, to my birthmark and being picked on because people thought I was deformed. And Dad on drugs or whatever the fuck went on.

At the time, those things were extremely, extremely painful. But now they're positive in light of something good that came out of them. That's why they put cow shit in the field."

You seem like you're in a pretty good place, I tell him.

"For now," he says, smiling.

Corgan was raised Roman Catholic, at least for a time. "I regularly went to church between the ages of five and eight with my stepmother," he says. "It was sort of required. You went to church; it's just what you did. And then one day we were walking home when I was around eight years old and I turned and said to her, 'I don't want to go anymore.' She said okay. And I didn't step foot in a church for twenty years after that, unless you count one visit to a Christian Science church, which was surreal. But that is a whole other story."

On the day he stepped back into the church, he wasn't planning on doing it. "I think I was having a sort of personal crisis moment, and I was walking down the street and I saw a church and I was like, I need to go to church. I need a quiet, safe place to pray, which was not a common thought for me to have. Praying was not part of the picture, ever."

But it is now. "I pray every day," he says. "It takes a lot of different forms. Sometimes they're like lightning bolts to the head, shut-the-fuck-up-and-listen stuff. But I basically try to pray when I get up and I try to pray before I go to bed, even if it's just for a minute. I feel like I should pray more. I wish I prayed more. My life benefits greatly when I do pray. I think there's a sort of stubborn ego thing that I haven't worked out yet." How long has he been praying regularly? "About four years, give or take a prayer." He doesn't attend church regularly, but every once in a while he does. It's always a Catholic church. "I understand the lay of the land there," he says. "One of my friends wanted me to go with her to a Korean temple, a Buddhist temple or something. She was describing it to me and it seemed beautiful, but I would be more of a tourist there, you know? I'm comfortable with God in any form, so I don't really care. But I think from that point of view, if I'm thinking about church I want to go to what I know. It's like *Gilligan's Island*. I know how they all end, do you know what I mean?

"The parables of Jesus and Mother Mary are really powerful. They have a particular resonance for Western culture, and I think there is a reason for that. I can't say I know all the reasons, but I have a sense that there *is* a reason. There is something about the mother-father paradigm and the cross.

There is something about the egoism of this particular part of the world that has everything to do with the cross and how that all manifests itself out. I think there is a reason they're not obsessed with the cross that much on the Eastern side of the planet, because they have more of a group consciousness. And when you have a solo consciousness, like a lot of Westerners do, it is really about being on the cross. You're the one putting yourself up there. And I think the whole point is to try to figure out how to get off the fucking cross. I believe we are sort of genetically programmed to resonate with certain things. That's just what I believe. I don't know why. I haven't figured it out yet."

Corgan seems comfortable not knowing everything. He says "I don't know why" frequently and without apology. "It's like how I don't have to know how the telephone works. But I know that it works when I pick it up. I respond very well to Christian iconography, but I'm not sure why. It's not because I'm so in love with the Catholic Church, it's nothing like that. I generally avoid talking about this stuff because people automatically assume that. And because people have such negative views about the Catholic Church they start to turn that against you. The church is not making a lot of friends lately. I just look at the Catholic Church like another major label. Just another major record label."

If his music is a reflection of his spirituality—and he insists that it is because everything in his life is—it appears there has been a significant shift in his soul in recent years. His new music sounds more hopeful, sonically and lyrically. "Everything I do is offset by how I perceive it in spiritual terms. Everything. Fucking, lying, eating—everything. Everything," he says forcefully. Gangly tall and wan, with a cleanly shaven head, Corgan is intense, in a tightly coiled kind of way. But he has a sweetness about him, a tenderness in his eyes that is almost tangible.

I ask him if I'm right about this apparent spiritual shift in his music. "Yes and no," he answers. "I think the most overt shift is that it's public. In 1985 I wanted to communicate the same things I want to communicate now, but it was easier to couch them in a language of hiding behind a persona that people would either believe or disbelieve. Being negative, nihilistic, or whatever, and then sort of sneaking in hope. I have been criticized a lot through the years for taking that position, but my thing has always been that, look, you can't walk down into the ghetto and go, 'Hi, I'm from Minnesota!' You have to be able to speak somebody's language in their context. I don't mean just *talk* that way, I'm saying speak from the context by which they view the world. We got the shit kicked out of us. We had parents doing drugs and all sorts of this other crazy shit that was unique to our generation. We still had the fifties violence but with parents who were divorcing. We had the worst of both worlds. So I communicated that language very succinctly and in a way that resonated with people. Now, being older, [I feel] that language no longer needs to be simple. I'm willing to step out and say, This is what I believe in. Now I have a deeper context to draw upon, but the message hasn't changed at all. How I'm doing it has. I'm not punching listeners in the head anymore. I don't feel I need to—at least not right now."

He traces the beginning of his spiritual evolution to the alt-music tour Lollapalooza in 1994, where he encountered someone who would leave a lasting impression on him in an unexpected way. "God has a way of sort of putting people in your life and giving you little nudges when you need them," Corgan says. "I walked around for like a year telling everyone I was a Buddhist because I was reading books like *The Tao of Pooh*. And suddenly I was a Buddhist. I'm serious—I'm not even joking. And I was having this miserable period in my life. I was taking a lot of pills, and I was grumpy and miserable like you can be when you're taking a lot of pills." And then he met a Tibetan Buddhist monk that Adam Yauch of the Beastie Boys had brought on tour with the bands to raise awareness about efforts to free Tibet from Chinese control. Corgan recalls, "We played basketball with the monks and hung out with the monks, and this one monk took a liking to me. He would kind of pull me aside and say, 'What's wrong with you?' And I'd say, 'Oh, damn this and miserable that.' He'd just start laughing. He'd laugh 'Ha ha ha ha ha! Oh, that's just so silly.' I would try to engage him on an intellectual level, arguing, 'Well, you don't understand.' But he didn't want to hear it. He wasn't interested. And it wasn't even reactionary. He would just laugh. That man's laughter stuck with me. He was a holy man and he thought my life was funny, but for the right reasons.

"So it started there, and then just little things happened along the way. I met different people, and weird and different little things would come from out of nowhere and sort of knock me upside the head to say, 'You're not quite on the right journey here,'" he says before starting the story of an intuitive—some people would call her psychic—woman who did something that transformed the way Corgan thinks about faith. This woman, the friend of a friend, has a business providing herbal remedies for ailments by intuitively sensing what the person needs to take. Sometimes she doesn't even know why she gives the person the herb or root that she does. She just listens to her spirit guides and does what they tell her to do.

One day, as Corgan tells it, she boards a plane and has the shock of her life. "A few people have told me that when somebody is going to die, their spirit starts to leave and you can tell they're going to die. So she gets on the plane, and the whole plane is dead. So she starts to get off the plane because she's thinking, I'm not going to die," he says, leaning in, riveted by his own tale. "She's walking off the plane, and her spirit guide tells her, 'Get back on the plane.' Now this woman has built her whole life on listening to that voice. So she gets back on the plane and she is freaking out because she is convinced she is going to die. But she has trusted this voice all along, this voice has never steered her wrong. The plane takes off. She's praying her ass off. The engine dies. Emergency landing. Nobody dies. Okay? Now, that's faith."

It's like the Catholic mystic St. John of the Cross and his *Dark Night of the Soul*, a lengthy poem Corgan has recently read. "His point is there is a reason this is hard. Unless you're willing to go into the valley in the middle of the night and take that walk, God is basically saying, 'Fuck you, where's your commitment? Show me commitment,'" he says with characteristic bluntness. "God is asking you to step up and say, 'Okay, I'm worthy. What do I need to do? Point me in the right direction, no matter how crazy it seems.'

"Speaking personally, I get a lot of *stuff*—whether it's from me or from somewhere else doesn't matter—but I get a lot of *stuff* and think, Gee, that doesn't seem like a really good idea, but I guess, okay, that's what I've gotta do," he says. By "stuff" Corgan means messages, ideas, directions, hunches— those intuitive urges that are difficult to describe properly. When he listens to that *stuff*, those spiritual directives, does it work out well? I ask him. "Never how I think it's going to work out," he says. "That's the point. It's always different."

I wonder if what he's describing—the voice, the guide—is the still, small voice of the spirit of God that the Bible talks about. "It could be the big voice of my own insanity," he counters. "My point is, it doesn't matter. It doesn't matter. I believe in God, so to me it's all the same. It's not a very popular idea, but if you believe in God and you believe God made you, then God made you for a reason. At the end of the day it has to do with how you serve others. But you can't serve others if you don't know who you are."

Corgan has a story about serving others that seems particularly moving for him to recount. I'd say it brought him close to tears to tell it, but on his Internet blog he swears he's cried only six or seven times in the last thirty years, so maybe it was just me. "I had this one teacher I was fond of, she was a lot older. Very nice, though very formal. I was a teenager, and I was getting the shit kicked out of me, bad, bad. I don't know what condition I was coming to school in, but I must have looked pretty awful," he recalls. One day the teacher took him aside and asked him what was going on. He wouldn't tell her about the abuse at home. "And she said—I'll never forget this—she said, 'All right. That's fine, I don't need an answer. But I want you to know if the shit hits the fan, you can come live with me.' It's twenty-one years later, and I'm still thinking about that. I can't even remember her name. But that's it. That's what I'm saying. It doesn't matter. God, no God, white-bearded man in a chair—who cares? It's like the faith and the idea that somewhere there is a chain that works, just go with it, how bad can it be?

"Like I said, if all my life is about is selling some plastic—fuck off. I'll find something better to do than sell pieces of plastic," he says. "But every time I start thinking this is a waste of time, that I'm talking to a wall, I get an e-mail or I meet somebody on the street who totally gets it. And I go, *Okay*."

The sad-eyed Goth girl at Borders gets it. And so, it seems, do millions of other fans of Corgan. So maybe he should keep listening to that still, small voice, even when it sounds pretty damn crazy.

JUNE 2005

DUSTY BAKER

Professional Baseball Manager

You can be a Christian and be hard-nosed.

A.K.A.: *Johnnie B. Baker Jr.*
BIRTH DATE: *June 15, 1949*
RAISED: *Southern Baptist and Methodist*
NOW: *Baptist*
ATTENDS: *Hermon Baptist Church in Chicago*
WORDS TO LIVE BY: *"Just because you're spiritual doesn't mean you're perfect, because you're not."*

The toothpick. The dark sunglasses. The seemingly unflappable, ultra-cool exterior.

They're all accoutrements of Dusty Baker's personal battle between good and evil, an eclectic spirituality that the Chicago Cubs manager explains takes discipline, prayer, and periodic divine intervention to maintain.

"I have to work on it, I'm tellin' ya," Baker says, stretching back in his office chair in the Cubs clubhouse at Wrigley Field before a game against the Pittsburgh Pirates. "Because I can get—I've got a wild side to me that I don't like too much. It's fun, but, you know, like I said, I'm not exactly a saint. But I know what's right and what's wrong."

When he talks about his faith, and the spiritual journey that brought him to Chicago, Baker describes a kind of existential tug-of-war between the Good Dusty and the Bad Dusty. "I believe that if there's a north, there's a south. That if there's heaven, there's hell. That if there's God, there's a devil. I believe that I've been full of both of them at some point in time. At times, it's been fun being wrong, even though you know it's wrong," he says, his serious, dark eyes, the ones he usually obscures behind his trademark shades during the game, gleaming with intensity. "The good part is that you know you can be forgiven. You know where and how to repent for what you've done, thought, and said. I know I'm not perfect, and the Lord knows I'm not perfect. A lot of people, you tell them you're Christian, and they see you having too many drinks or doing this or that, and they say, 'Oh, yeah, he's a hypocrite.' But you're human. Just because you're spiritual doesn't mean you're perfect, because you're not. And you're not going to be."

Making the right choice takes practice, Baker says, and he works at it. Like his ubiquitous toothpicks. They're supposed to keep him from chewing tobacco.

Raised in a religious home in Northern California by his Southern Baptist father and his Methodist mother, Johnnie B. "Dusty" Baker Jr. has been entrenched in faith, church, Scripture, and the power of prayer since he was a small child. As an adult, he peppers deeply held Christian beliefs with Eastern philosophy and other religious traditions, New Age ideology, and what he says are firsthand experiences with the supernatural. It's a sort of all-truth-is-God's-truth approach to theology.

"Who's to say one's better than the other one? Know what I mean?" he says. "Jesus is the only way for me, but I understand how somebody else in another country or another whatever could feel differently about some things. We had to go to church every Sunday. It wasn't always pleasant, but the Bible says, 'Raise a child in the way he should go, and he will someday return,' or something like that. I'm paraphrasing."

For more than a decade, Baker has read from the biblical book of Proverbs each morning, picking the chapter that matches the day of the month. (There are thirty-one chapters.) It's a spiritual discipline that he says gives him a daily dose of wisdom and direction. "There are some things in the readings each day that I'm about to think or do, and it'll say don't do that or whatever. It helps," he says.

On a corner of his clubhouse desk, amid stacks of team paperwork and piles of light blue envelopes filled with game tickets, sits a copy of *The Purpose-Driven Life*, its dust jacket tucked into the middle of the book. Written by the California megachurch pastor Rick Warren, the book is a kind of spiritual home-improvement guide that takes readers through forty days of Bible study and questions designed to jump-start their faith. "I've read about three-quarters of it," Baker says, getting up from his chair to rifle through a nearby bookshelf that's topped with unopened bottles of wine that appear to have been gifts.

He's looking for another devotional book he's been reading recently called *Secrets of the Vine: Breaking Through to Abundance*. That one was written by Bruce Wilkinson, a Christian author who also wrote *The Prayer of Jabez*, a tiny book that expounds on an obscure verse of Hebrew Scripture about a man named Jabez who prays for God to bless him "and enlarge [his] territory." And, apparently, God does.

After a few minutes, Baker finds what he was looking for—another book by Wilkinson called *A Life God Rewards: Why Everything You Do Today Matters Forever*—a few crowded shelves below a biography of Sammy Sosa. "I read these just to stay grounded," Baker says, "because I can get . . . well . . . wild."

Bible-related literature isn't the only thing Baker reads, he's quick to add, lest he sound too pious, and points toward another stack of books and papers behind his desk. "I read Sun-tzu and *The Art of War*, trying to get some understanding, too. *A Book of Five Rings* [by a seventeenth-century Japanese samurai], and a book on Attila the Hun about leadership. I try to understand, like I said, that if there's a north, there's a south. If there's an east, there's a west. Know what I mean?"

Baker's sister and brother-in-law run a bilingual church in Sacramento, California, that Baker has spiritually and financially supported over the years. Baker and his wife, Melissa, donate money regularly to half a dozen congregations, he says. "I tithe, that's why I'm blessed," he says, referring to the biblical concept of giving 10 percent of one's income back to God. "Well, I don't tithe ten percent like you're supposed to, but I do pretty good. Sometimes I tithe to a couple of small churches. One time it was a church that didn't know it was me. I signed the check 'Johnnie' and sent them something every month. It was a Catholic church. My wife was raised Catholic. And one day a letter came from the church, it said, 'Good luck in the playoffs, Dusty,'" he says, laughing.

Baker's faith plays a significant role in how he manages his baseball team. "It's all about faith, which is what life's about, which is what my job's about here," he says. His players, with whom he has, by all accounts, forged close relationships, know he's "not afraid to spare the rod." When it comes time to "chastise" a player, Baker says he does it privately, out of respect and because his faith demands it.

"We don't have the chance to sit down and talk about Christian things, but the time that we do have, he always shows how he feels about God," says the Cubs pitcher Carlos Zambrano, a Pentecostal Christian from Venezuela known for displaying his own spirituality by praying on the field. "He believes a lot. He's very communicative. He likes to talk a lot with the players. He's a great man, and he believes in God. Any man who believes in God is a good man."

But Baker's deep faith and generally beneficent character don't mean he's a softy when it comes to keeping his players on course. "I've had to work on patience, believe it or not," he says. "I expect a lot. I try not to give out too much grief, but I don't take any at all. I really try to be as fair as possible—firm, but fair. Love with discipline. And that's what spirituality and Christianity [are] about, to me. Love, discipline, and patience. I believe God gives me the strength to do what I've got to do, instead of just giving me the strength to wait there for things to happen. I believe he gives me the strength and the mind and the feeling and the motivation to go get it. Know what I mean?"

"I'm not a turn-the-cheek type of Christian," he says, bobbling the toothpick balanced on his lip as he talks. "I believe in a more gladiator-warrior type. A lot of people think because you're a Christian, you're not going to be a hard-nosed player. That's not what the Lord wants, to me. You can be a Christian and be hard-nosed. Like Reggie White and a whole bunch of dudes that will kick your butt, and help you up."

There is one thing Baker does not seem to believe in: It's the so-called Church of Baseball. He shies from overspiritualizing the game. He says the hallowed ground of Wrigley Field is no more or less a sacred place for him than the streams he enjoys fishing. Not once does he mention praying to win a game. As for the infamous curse that allegedly has dogged the Chicago Cubs since some unfortunate usher at Wrigley Field turned William "Billy Goat" Sianis and his pet goat, Murphy, away from game four of the 1945 World Series, Baker equivocates. A little. "They talk about that around here, about the curse and stuff," he says quietly. "That's not from the good side, know what I mean? The dark side has some real power, especially in the world today. To me, it seems like it's getting stronger. Evil's more accepted and more prevalent. But the good shall prevail. No matter what happens—the curse or whatever—the good shall prevail. Maybe that's why I'm here."

Baker's experiences have made him an unflinching believer in the spirit realm, the world that exists beyond what he can see with his eyes. A Hawaiian kahuna once told him that he has spiritual gifts. "He told me I have special gifts and power that I had kind of felt but didn't want to believe, know what I'm sayin'? Cuz I see things," he says, leaning in as if he were telling a secret. "I can *see* things." Like, more than what's here? "Yeah. I *feel* things. I've got a pen and paper next to my bed, and every night, if I wake up with a thought, I'll write it down or something. There are just a number of things that have happened in my life that let me know what I believe is real. I've been delivered a bunch of times."

In the late eighties, Baker had a brush with evil. "I've seen a lot of stuff," he explains, "that's why I know what's bad and what's good. I witnessed an exorcism once. About fifteen years ago. I was frightened. That let me know that it's real, know what I mean?" he says, stuffing a pinch of tobacco under his lip. "But you tell people different spiritual things that happen, and they think you're some weirdo."

The fear of being labeled a weirdo, however, does not stop him from talking about his "grand council," a kind of baseball communion of the saints to whom he says he turns for advice. "I've got some people up there who help me make decisions during the game," he says, pointing toward the ceiling. "A grand council of guys I know are looking out for me, guys that help me. Bill Lucas, [Hank's brother] Tommy Aaron, Joe Black, Roy Campanella, Lyman Bostock—guys who were influential in my life that are gone," he says, listing famous African-American baseball players from the past. "I can just sort of tell sometimes. *I'm at a crossroads here. Now, help me. Tell me what to do.* And I know. Most of the time I get the answers immediately."

Baker believes in the power of prayer, he says, because he's seen it work miracles. He's got a lot of stories about answered prayers, but the one that seems to move him deeply (he starts to tear up) is about his youngest child and only son, Darren, who was born in 1999. "The joy and the miracle of having my son at a late age, after my wife had two miscarriages trying to have him—I didn't think and she didn't think we'd be able to have a son, a child, period," he says. "There's just a number of things that have happened in my life that let me know that what I believe in is real."

He believes God answered his prayers and intervened the time one of his relatives went missing. "One who tripped out, he's manic-depressive and stuff, and we couldn't find him," Baker says. "I was praying one day, looking all over town. Nobody's seen him in months. And I was just leaving town—me and my wife—and I said a prayer, and there he was, sitting at the bus stop as I was leaving town. That's one of thousands of examples."

In the middle of batting practice before his Cubs beat the Pirates 4–1, Baker ambles to the dugout to tell me another prayer story. This one's special, he says. It's about how he ended up coaching in the major leagues after an eighteen-year career as a player that ended in 1986.

"I had had enough baseball by 1987," he says, launching into a long tale about what happened the following year, in 1988, when he was first approached about becoming a coach. "The Giants were after me at the time. Al Rosen and Bob Kennedy had approached me about joining the Giants, and I said, 'Nah. I don't think so.' But they kept asking me and asking me. I was a stockbroker at the time. So I went to Lake Arrowhead to pray, me and my brother and our daughters, looking for a sign. Go to the mountain, you know? And I'm checking in at the Marriott, and right behind me in line is the owner of the Giants checking in at the same time. I called my dad and said, 'Is this a sign?' And he said, 'Son, you went up there looking for a sign, you prayed, and even before you got to the mountaintop, your answer is here.' So that's how my coaching career got started." Baker signed on as first base coach of the Giants in 1988 and in 1993 became manager. He joined the Cubs as manager in 2003. "I thought it was important to tell you that. It's pretty deep, real deep. And I had nothing to do with it besides trying to seek direction."

And then there's the story of Baker's bout with cancer. On a flight from San Francisco to Hawaii in 2001, a few months after Giants team doctors had diagnosed him with prostate cancer, and shortly before he had surgery to remove the malignancy, Baker read an article in an Aloha Airlines magazine that changed his physical and spiritual life. "They had a thing about a healing center in Hawaii, the Lawai International Healing Center on the island of Kauai," Baker says. "I visited before I went to the hospital. It's a spiritual place where there are shrines up on this hillside, and I just go there to think. I knew when I got there that everything was gonna be all right, once I had been there, once I had walked the mountain with my wife and son."

When he returned to California, Baker had a successful operation to remove his prostate, and he remains cancer-free. He's now an honorary member of the Lawai center's board of directors and spends time at the center each December.

"I believe I was saved at a very early stage of cancer for a reason and a purpose," he says, adding that it's probably not to be a major-league baseball manager. "I have a bigger purpose in life than what I'm just doing right now. What I'm supposed to do, I do not know, but I know it isn't this for the rest of my life."

JUNE 2004

IYANLA VANZANT

Author, Life Coach

People get nervous when they can't put you in a box.

*

BIRTH DATE: *September 13, 1953*
RAISED: *Christian, specifically Church of God in Christ*
NOW: *No religious label, but she's "a spiritual student"*
ATTENDS: *Her "home church" is Hillside Chapel in Atlanta, but she says she usually goes "where the spirit leads me."*
WORDS TO LIVE BY: *"Get there. Get to love and forgiveness. Forgive yourself, love yourself. Forgive others. Love them."*

She's the type of person strangers want to tell their secrets to because it feels like she already *knows*. That's how the bestselling author, Yoruba priestess, and self-described spiritual "life coach" Iyanla Vanzant was described to me months before we had a chance to meet.

"She just seems so *wise*," the woman said. "You just want to tell her *everything*."

Now, the woman doing the describing is a producer for *Starting Over*, the Emmy-winning daytime reality show that stars, among others, Vanzant. But when Vanzant strides onto the show's set—a multimillion-dollar home high in the Hollywood Hills, where a cast of six average women try to change their lives—it's immediately clear what the producer meant. Despite the fact that it's first thing on Monday morning and Vanzant is running late after battling grisly Los Angeles traffic, when she sits down to chat, she is intensely focused. Unflinchingly honest, and deeply kind.

Undoubtedly they are the same qualities that drew Oprah Winfrey to Vanzant in the early 1990s. The author of about a dozen books, at least half of which have spent time on the *New York Times* bestseller list, including titles such as *Tapping the Power Within: A Path to Self-Empowerment for Black Women*, Vanzant made frequent appearances on Winfrey's show for the better part of a decade before landing her own (short-lived) eponymous self-help show in 2001.

In person Vanzant is warm, soulful, knowing. I feel strangely compelled to tell her something personal, to tap into the well of whatever it is that seems to be bubbling just behind those wide, brown eyes, but I think better of it, for the sake of maintaining some sort of journalistic distance. An hour later, when we're done talking and she rushes to the set to begin taping that day's episode, I'll wish I had told her what was on my mind.

But on this day, the life coach isn't there to ask me questions. She's there to answer them. So I ask: How does she describe herself spiritually?

"A student, first of all, because in order to be a teacher, I have to be a student," Vanzant says. "I wouldn't apply a religious label to myself because God, the universal intelligence, is too vast to be contained in a label. I also have found that labels have a tendency to make people crazy, and we have enough insanity on the planet. For myself, personally, I do believe that Christ is the spiritual authority on the planet at this time. When I say Christ, I mean the highest, the most authentic self present in everybody, and I do believe that Jesus demonstrated that Christ*ness*. I don't think he was the only one who demonstrated it, but he certainly did demonstrate it because he taught The Principles. So did Buddha, and Krishna, and many other sages, prophets, and avatars. But I believe that Christ has the spiritual authority on the planet at this time.

"To me, spiritual authority means the energy that pervades people's hearts and minds. Christ taught love and forgiveness. And that is the authority, that is what people are being called to do right now: to forgive and love, love and forgive. That is the foundation of the Christ mind as demonstrated through the teachings of Jesus the Christ."

Vanzant's theology is not uncomplicated. It's got a lot of Christianity, mixed with healthy servings of traditional African spirituality, Eastern philosophy, and what she calls "The Principles." At its core is a solid ethic of love and forgiveness.

Fans of *Starting Over* fill the show's online bulletin boards with questions and speculations about Vanzant's religious predilections, trying to figure out just exactly what she is. Why does she talk about God so much? What's up with this Yoruba thing, anyway?

"People get nervous when they can't put you in a box," Vanzant says, flashing her huge grin. "'Is she New Age? Is she African? Is she Christian?' They really have a hard time figuring out who I am, and I don't feel the need to answer it." While she won't give any simple one-word answers to who she is spiritually, Vanzant, dressed in bright oranges and reds, bold African-influenced jewelry jangling as she talks with her hands, is forthcoming about her spiritual past, and the circuitous path that has led her to her unique present.

"I was raised in the Church of God in Christ, with a very mean, vengeful God, who would plucketh out thine eye and smoteth out thine being at the mere mention of wearing some red nail polish, you know? Just God didn't want you to do nothin'. You couldn't do anything. We went to church every Sunday. But in the corner, my grandmother, who is a Cherokee, taught me to pray on the full moon. *Shhh*, don't tell anybody. Don't cut your hair on the new moon. *Shhh*, Jesus is Lord!

"And then when I left my grandmother's care and went to live with my aunt and uncle and my cousin, who I was raised with like a sister, my aunt brought in the African aspect of my family," she says, explaining that her mother's ancestors are from the kingdom of Dahomey in West Africa.

"The African roots of my lineage were still very much alive. And so when I went to live with my aunt, I learned about ancestors, and I learned about nature, and I learned about water, which coupled with the moon. I always noticed the moon when it was full, and I've always honored nature. I know that when I'm really crazy, I need to walk barefoot on the earth. I know that. I know that trees are something other than fruit-bearing entities. I know that ocean water will cleanse you and river water will calm you, because that's how I was raised. What I could never figure out was how Jesus fit into all of that, because he would go to the water and *walk on it*.

"I had the indigenous nature, the indigenous cultures in me—both Native American and African—and those were wrapped up in the very strict, rigid, inflexible concept of the Church of God in Christ. So needless to say, I was very confused." Vanzant laughs.

How did she straighten it out? "I didn't figure it out. It kind of figured me out. I left the church at the first opportunity"—she interrupts herself with more laughter—"which was when I was about fifteen and nobody could really make me go. And I was just kind of wandering. But the good thing is, I had a foundation. The truth is, as the Scriptures say, if you raise a child the way they should be, they won't go far. And I never really went far from it."

Enter The Principles. "All of the sacred Scriptures—the Qur'an, the Bhagavad Gita, the Tao, the teachings of the *I Ching*, and the Holy Bible—teach principles," Vanzant says. "When you hear The Principles, see, people know. We know. At the very core and essence of our being is the calling of God. We know it. But we get so busy with bills and children and relationships and jobs and Kool-Aid, you know, that we don't pay attention to it. But if you listen to people, you can hear the common thread."

What *are* The Principles? "Faith. Trust. Honor. Respect. Awareness. Acknowledgment. Compassion," she says. "I did a lot of reading. I did a lot of comparison, and that's how I bumped into my gift. And my gift is to be able to look at it all and see the oneness. That's my gift."

In addition to writing books and appearing on television, in 1988 Vanzant founded Inner Visions Worldwide Spiritual Life Maintenance Center near her home in Maryland, an institute that promotes life coaching based on The Principles. A graduate of Medgar Evers College in New York, Vanzant also holds a law degree from Queens College Law School and was a public defender in Philadelphia for four years before she began writing books. In 2004, she was accepted into a graduate program at Union Theological Seminary in Virginia, where she hopes to hone some of that gift by formally studying world religions. But because of the demands of *Starting Over* and various other commitments, she's not sure when she will start the three years of study.

Born Rhonda Eva Harris in the back of a taxi in Brooklyn, Vanzant was raised largely by her grandmother Rissi Holloway after her mother, Sarah—"like Moses' wife," she says—died of cancer when Rhonda was just two years old. (She was given the African name Iyanla, which means "great mother," in a Yoruba religious ceremony at the age of thirteen. She legally changed her first name to Iyanla when she was thirty-five.)

Vanzant had a difficult youth. When she was nine, her uncle raped her. She had her first child at sixteen, and by the time she was twenty-one, she was the mother of three. There was an abusive marriage. Welfare. Constant struggles.

"When my life totally fell apart for like the third time—I must have been about twenty-five years old—I said, Okay, I've got to go someplace and find something, some help, because I'm just a mess here," Vanzant recalls. "I was scared of Jesus. I was scared of anything Christian because I would have gotten my eyes plucketh out and my life smoteth because I was a sinner and a heathen. And in the sixties, as a black woman, a white man on the cross didn't seem to hold much promise for me." She laughs. "I mean, look at what happened to him! And he was good! And I'm jacked up. I'm not hanging out with him! So for me, it was important to look back at African culture and the spiritual philosophy of African culture, which had visions and images of divinity that looked like me as a black woman and was all-encompassing."

It was during this time that Vanzant was initiated as a priestess in the Yoruba religion, an indigenous African spiritual tradition that she says is her "matriarchal lineage."

"When I was twenty-eight years old, it was brought to my awareness that part of my mission in life was to be this cultural custodian and to carry this tradition on and be initiated into the sacred rites of the Yoruba people," she says, and she explains to me the four basic tenets of Yoruba culture and philosophy. She pounds the coffee table for emphasis. "One: Have a relationship with God. Two: Have a relationship with the spirit of your own head, which in this society would be called your higher self, or your ego. Three: Have a relationship with your ancestors and your elders. And four: Have a relationship with your community and your clan."

These principles guide her life. "Today, I do everything knowing I am either going to bring honor to or shame upon my people," she says soberly. "When I think that someplace in my lineage—and I could tell that basically because of the hue that I am—that somebody lay in a bottom of a ship, chained, to get here, to pick cotton and be whipped, that they walked and ate slop so that I could go to college and have a TV in every room of my thirteen-room house, oh, I better be real clear about where I am and what I'm doing. Because only by the grace of God . . . if one of my ancestors had jumped ship and be lying in the bottom of the Atlantic Ocean, I wouldn't be here. There's a connection. So when I get to wherever I'm going when I leave this body, I don't want some big-breasted black woman with her hand on her hip, shaking her finger in my face. That is a frightening thought."

What is the greatest spiritual lesson anyone has taught her?

"Forgiveness," she says after pondering for a moment. "The greatest lesson of forgiveness for me was my uncle who raped me when I was nine." It's a lesson she says she didn't learn until many years after the sexual abuse took place when she forgave her uncle.

The difficult lesson began to take hold while she was watching a made-for-TV movie about a boy who was sexually abused by a priest. She can't remember the name of the film, but the details she is able to recall bring her to tears. "One thing I do remember is somebody in the picture said, 'That is not love. Whatever else it may be, it is not love,'" Vanzant recounts, her voice cracking. "And then I realized how I had wired up sex and love, abuse and love, dishonor and love, disrespect and love. And then I asked the question that will surely get you a spiritual buttwhipping: *Why?* Never ask that question. That's a bad question. You have to ask, 'What am I learning?'"

She did. And this is what she discovered: "No matter what happens to my body, it doesn't change who I really am. It doesn't change who I really am. I had been so angry about that for so many years. And then it was," she says, clapping her hands once as if to show how something had disappeared. "So as I began to forgive my uncle—first mouthing the words, and then reading about it and doing all kinds of forgiveness exercises—eventually one day it took place."

Act as if, as my twelve-step friends say? "Fake it 'til you make it," Vanzant says.

What does she struggle with spiritually? "I don't really struggle with anything, because I've really learned how to surrender. And for me the ultimate demonstration of surrender was Jesus on the cross," she says. "These people have dragged your butt up a road with a cross on your back, spit on you, put some nails on your head, nailed you to a cross, and you say, 'Forgive them, they know not what they do'? Oh, Lord!" she says, laughing and clapping. "I mean, look at the mundane stuff we go through. Getting fired from a job! And we go back and shoot people.

"This boy was hanging on a cross in the hot sun, bleeding! And he said, 'Forgive them.' Shoot. Could we learn from that? Could we *just learn from that?*" she says, with the passion of a street preacher.

Suddenly Vanzant is quiet. She stops and thinks for a few seconds. She has a confession: "I think my greatest perplexity or challenge right now is death," she says. "My perplexity about death is that I lost my daughter last December, and I don't know where she is." She's talking about her daughter Gemmia, who died in December 2003 from colon cancer at the age of thirty-one.

"Gemmia. It meant my precious jewel," she says, clearing her throat, teary. "Where is she? I've been asking that question since she died. Where is she? Where is she? I do believe there is life eternal and that she's someplace. I want to know where. What does she have on? What is she doing? Where is she?"

Even if she knew where Gemmia was, what difference would it make? "I'd find a way to get there. I'd find a way. Whether it's meditation or, I don't know. I'd FIND A WAY," she says. "I just want to know she's okay. I just want to know she's all right. I don't have to stay. I'll just go for tea. But I want to SEE her. I want to know she is all right, and I want her to tell me.

"I'm just asking. All you have to do is ask," she says, smiling. "If it is possible for her to connect and communicate, it will happen. It will happen. And I will know where she is and I will know she's okay. I mean, I've lost my mother, my father, my brother, my sister. And I never had this question. But with my child, I want to know. I want to know where she is. When the time is right, I'll know."

I can't imagine how that must feel, and the waiting must be terrible. I'm the most impatient person I know—it would just kill me, I tell her.

She smiles, grabs my hand, and says, "Well, you should sit in traffic at Hollywood and Highland. You'll get HEALED!" And she lets loose a body-shaking belly laugh. "Cuz there's nothing you can do when you've got people in front of you and the light's changing and they're cutting across and making U-turns. You'll get healed!" she says, clapping. "Go over there about noon. Your healing awaits you!"

AUGUST 2004

BARRY SCHECK

Attorney

This is a struggle—a spiritual struggle—for justice.

✳

BIRTH DATE: *September 19, 1949*

RAISED: *Jewish*

NOW: *Secular humanist*

ATTENDS: *Doesn't*

WORDS TO LIVE BY: *"We can all make mistakes, even when we're absolutely certain."*

I like to think of Barry Scheck as a kind of modern-day, sharpshootin' cowboy savior who rides into town just in time to fire off a round that breaks the rope around the neck of the innocent man about to hanged from the gallows for a crime he didn't commit. Except that he's a crusading Jewish attorney from New York City who uses DNA evidence and chutzpah instead of a horse and a six-shooter to get the job done.

In 1992 Scheck and his colleague, Peter Neufeld, founded The Innocence Project at Yeshiva University's Benjamin N. Cardozo School of Law, a not-for-profit legal clinic that uses DNA evidence to overturn the convictions of men and women who have been imprisoned for crimes they did not commit. In a very real sense they help set the captives free. It's heroic work, if you ask me; gut-wrenching, grueling work that carries with it an urgent spiritual import that is not lost on Scheck.

"Peter Neufeld and I undoubtedly know more of these exonerated individuals than anyone in this country—up close and personal," Scheck says over breakfast at a coffee shop in New York City's Union Square, not far from his Innocence Project office. "As we sit here today, there have been 155 postconviction DNA exonerations, and we were either assisting or working on, I think, 112 of those cases. I would say that among those exonerated individuals, I know very well close to a hundred of them. And not just them—there are other people who have been exonerated from death row with non-DNA evidence uncovered by journalists, by our dear friends at the Center on Wrongful Convictions at Northwestern University, and places all across the country. I've gotten to know many people whose cases I didn't work on but who, nonetheless, were in prison charged with crimes that they didn't commit, facing death. This is a struggle—a spiritual struggle—for justice. One that I know quite intimately."

Innovations in DNA technology and other scientific breakthroughs that have led to more careful examination of guilt and innocence have presented us as a society with "a learning moment," Scheck says. "It's a learning moment about the way our system works and how you can correct it to make sure it doesn't happen again. It should be a learning moment spiritually and morally for everyone involved and for the community at large. It teaches humility, and it should. We can all make mistakes, even when we're absolutely certain, in the most important of events."

While he is comfortable speaking in spiritual terms, at least when it comes to his legal work, Scheck, who, despite working on hundreds of cases over the years is probably best known for his role on the defense team at O. J. Simpson's murder trial, is not a religious believer in any traditional sense. "Secular humanist" is the label that fits him best, he says. But his own lack of faith hasn't stopped him from absorbing the impact of the faith of the men and women he so passionately defends.

"These exonerees go through a certain kind of spiritual journey. All of them," he says. "The first few years in jail, in prison for a crime you didn't commit, the anger is absolutely overwhelming. Overwhelming! And yet the people we meet, because they are, after all, survivors, because they reached out somehow, some way—to a journalist, to a lawyer, to somebody—to right this wrong, and survive, they found a way to transcend that anger. Because they knew the anger would kill them, the anger would destroy them, the anger would directly lead them to commit suicide or get involved in some sort of violent encounter in prison that would almost surely be a suicide. And each of these people in their own way found the strength to transcend the worst of injustices. I am always amazed by it. I always find it mind-blowing. They have achieved some kind of spiritual transcendence, and each of them is a tremendous spiritual teacher that way."

One exoneree Scheck mentions frequently is Delbert Tibbs. Arrested in 1974 and charged with murdering a white man—a recently discharged sailor—and raping the man's sixteen-year-old girlfriend on the side of a Florida highway, Tibbs, who is black, was convicted and sentenced to death. The alleged rape victim was the only witness to the crime and described her assailant as a dark-skinned black man, about five foot six, sporting a large Afro. Tibbs is light-skinned, six foot three, and wore a small Afro at the time. In 1976 Tibbs was released from death row when the Florida Supreme Court ordered a retrial, saying that the witness against him was unreliable and there was doubt he was the killer. In 1982, after years of legal wrangling, the state of Florida dropped the charges against him. The original prosecutor in his case would later say he had long had doubts about Tibbs's guilt.

"Delbert is a very graceful and profound person," Scheck says. "He says, 'If you free your heart of malice, then there's no reason to be afraid of anyone or anything.' He said he learned that from Gandhi. I think about that a lot. It's a telling point. You look at people like Nelson Mandela and Desmond Tutu, and you see that spirit. You look at the Truth and Reconciliation Commission in South Africa. Now, this is one of the most important spiritual events of our time. That a society could have achieved a largely bloodless revolution, overthrown apartheid, and then held these hearings where people who had committed the worst crimes and murders came forward, laid them out, asked forgiveness, and that most of the victims forgave—it is an extraordinary phenomenon."

Born and raised in New York City, Scheck attended Hebrew school but left religious Jewish life behind him after he was bar mitzvahed. His father, George Scheck, was a onetime professional tap dancer who went on to a successful career as an entertainment manager for clients such as Connie Francis, Bobby Darin, and the folk singer Odetta; Scheck describes his mother, Eleanor, as "very smart and very difficult." Neither was particularly religious. "I was the product of people who came out of the Depression and the Second World War, whose politics were left leaning," Scheck says. "The two main spiritual issues in our household, interestingly, were the Holocaust and how there could be a God if there was this Holocaust—this was a major question—and the civil rights movement. There was always a strong belief in civil liberties and a fear of persecution."

One significantly traumatic event in his childhood, Scheck admits, also left an indelible negative impression on him regarding religion and God. "Our house burned down. I was ten and my sister, Marilyn, was seven and she died in the fire. It had a terrible impact on my parents—my mother in particular. I remember when our house burned down, the first thing the rabbi wanted to know was if we were going to make a contribution to the temple in the name of my sister. That was not terribly helpful."

A different rabbi gave his mother some advice that, while not exactly a spiritual salvo, has stayed with Scheck all these years. "I view it as humanist advice," he says. "He said to her, 'People will tell you that you'll get over this, but you'll never get over it. If I cut off your arm, you're never going to get over that, but you may learn to live with it.' That's not 'God's gonna take care of this.' That's advice that *you* have to take care of it eventually, *you* have to learn to live with it, and I respected that."

Scheck doesn't believe in God, either as an entity or as some kind of supernatural force. "One thing I just can't do is intuit the existence of God, in the sense of the first creator, or an anthropomorphic figure that sits in the heavens and directs things, or one that sits back and watches us, or even as some transcendent consciousness that has suggested, posed, or created an order in the universe. I just don't intuit it. It has just never made any sense to me. The alternative, then, the only thing that ever really struck me in my core as a reasonable answer to the big ontological questions, is existentialism," he explains, pulling out a well-worn copy of *The Worlds of Existentialism*, a collection edited by Maurice Friedman. He opens to a chapter by Jean-Paul Sartre and begins to read.

"'If God does not exist there is at least one being in whom existence precedes essence, a being who exists before he can be defined by any concept, and that being is man,'" Scheck reads. "'Man is nothing else except what he makes of himself.'"

"Essentially, it seems to me that this is a profound statement of humanism," he says. "If you can't intuit God, and you really look at the physical universe as its constituent physical elements, and if you believe in science—and I'm a believer in science—you ultimately have to come back to some kind of humanitarian position where man, writ large, creates values for himself or herself. And that," he says, pausing for dramatic effect, "is what I believe."

Scheck also believes in justice, a notion that he holds so deeply sacred that he gets emotional speaking about it. "Justice is fair treatment of people. And justice is difficult, because following the law doesn't always give you justice. That is one of the very interesting spiritual foundations of the way I look at the world. The civil rights movement—civil disobedience—was a very important idea, directly from Gandhi to Martin Luther King to America to the most remarkable movements of our lifetime, which really represent the best about this country," Scheck says, his voice cracking with emotion as the Etta James song "At Last" wails from the restaurant's stereo system. "From the beginning I realized that justice did not necessarily follow the letter of the law, that we in society, in public institutions, can't lose sight of that. We have to constantly try to correct our social and legal institutions to reflect justice."

The first wrongful conviction case Scheck, who is a graduate of Yale University and earned his law degree from the University of California at Berkeley, became involved with was in the early 1980s. "Bobby McLaughlin," he says, smiling, as he begins to tell the tale. Robert McLaughlin was a nineteen-year-old whose only prior brush with the law had been a barroom brawl, when, in an apparent case of mistaken identity, he was convicted of second-degree murder and four counts of first-degree robbery for his supposed participation in the armed robbery on December 29, 1979, of fifteen people in the Marine Park section of Brooklyn. One person was shot and killed. McLaughlin was sentenced to fifteen years to life in prison. Scheck and a coalition of journalists, lawyers, and McLaughlin's stepfather worked tirelessly to get the case overturned. In 1986 they succeeded when the New York State Supreme Court in Brooklyn set aside McLaughlin's conviction. The state eventually paid him nearly $2 million in compensation for his six years of wrongful imprisonment.

"We got him out of prison," Scheck says proudly. "But like all these guys, Bobby ended up having problems after his incarceration. He's now overcome them. He lives in Minnesota. I just saw him the other day. He came here to lobby against the death penalty in New York, because if there had been one, he would have been executed, no question about it."

Scheck's mind wanders to another man he helped exonerate, Calvin Johnson, an African American from Georgia who served sixteen years in prison for rapes he did not commit. Johnson, a devoted Christian, has described his ordeal and how his faith saved him in the 2003 book *Exit to Freedom*. Scheck wrote an afterword for the book, in which he describes how he was moved by the power of Johnson's faith, even if he doesn't share it.

"I just admire the spiritual journey, but I don't have to believe in Jesus Christ or God to understand that as a spiritual force. I don't have to intuit God to understand this, the action. It's like what Delbert says, taking it a step further. If *I* lose malice in my heart, *I* don't have to be afraid of anything. I find that quite startling," Scheck says, tears welling in his eyes. "Some people, when they see these spiritual forces in the world, they say, 'The Mandelas, the Gandhis, the Martin Luther Kings, other great spiritual leaders—I guess God leads them in that direction.' I don't believe that any more than I do that the devil or some evil motivates people to commit evil acts per se. I think that it's just a product of man and the human spirit."

Guilt and innocence. Damnation and forgiveness. Good and evil. They are spiritual ideas, certainly, and play a key role in Scheck's lifework. Undoubtedly he's seen a lot of evil through the years, by virtue of what he does for a living. "Well, there absolutely can be evil acts," he says. "And there are evil or bad acts that can be committed by good people. We see that all the time. I see all these wrongful convictions, and I see all these people who have power, whether they are police or prosecutors, who really believe that they are good people, who have the authority and who begin to believe that if they decide somebody is guilty or has done something wrong, they are so righteous themselves and have done so much good in the world and avenged so much evil that their actions can't be questioned. And even more than that—that it's okay for them to bury exculpatory evidence, or to take shortcuts, to not follow fair process, to not even consider that they might be wrong because they are so good. Those people with that kind of self-righteousness very often commit acts of evil. And by evil I mean not just being wrong but doing things that are malicious. Gratuitously nasty.

"I look at evil *acts*, acts of malice, as opposed to a notion of evil as a force, as if there's something inside of people that inexorably leads them to take malicious, horrible, hurtful actions. There may very well be. I think that's an important distinction, because I see people all the time who, by any definition, describe themselves as good, and maybe in many other aspects of their lives you would not take issue with anything they do. They're good servants of the community, they're good to members of their family, they are, in many instances, very religious in the best of ways—kindness and charity and giving and good acts toward others—and almost *because* of their self-righteous belief that anything they do is good, they do evil," he says.

Surely there are plenty of undeniably guilty people serving time in prison for what they have done. I imagine he must have represented one or two of them in his day.

"I don't feel it to be immoral at all, in our adversarial system, to represent somebody vigorously who I may suspect is guilty," he says. "I understand that the job is to fairly—without cheating, without creating false evidence—represent the individual. Especially if the person is saying he's innocent. Even if I don't think so, I may be wrong."

With that, off he goes, armed with a briefcase of legal files, heading west on Sixteenth Street (not quite into the sunset) to try to right a few more wrongs and perhaps come to the rescue of yet another innocent man.

FEBRUARY 2005

DAVID LYNCH

Director

Bliss is our nature.

✳

BIRTH DATE: *January 20, 1946*
RAISED: *Presbyterian*
NOW: *Nothing in particular*
ATTENDS: *He's practiced twice-daily Transcendental Meditation for more than thirty years and is a* siddha, *or "yogic flier."*
WORDS TO LIVE BY: *"Change from within."*

The word critics use most often to describe the director David Lynch's films is *dark*.

Weird is a close second.

The cinematic otherworlds Lynch creates, whether they're the singularly eerie Lumberton and Twin Peaks, industrial Victorian England, or the shadowy underbelly of the Hollywood Hills, are surreal, sordid, nightmarish.

One might expect the soul behind such celluloid visions to be just as dark. But as Lynch explains what motivates him spiritually—in his life, in his art—he sprinkles the conversation with concepts such as "light," "peace," and "bliss."

Much has been written about the stark contrast between the director of films such as *Eraserhead*, *The Elephant Man*, *Blue Velvet*, and *Mulholland Drive*, who looks like a classic clean-cut everyman—think a fair-haired

Jimmy Stewart—and the bizarre, brutal characters he creates in his movies. But the greater contrast may lie much further beneath Lynch's surface.

"Negativity is like darkness—it goes away when you turn on this light of peace and unity," he says, between sips from his ever-present coffee mug and drags on his American Spirit cigarette. "Bliss is our nature. Bliss. We should be like little puppy dogs. So happy . . . And that includes unbounded, infinite intelligence, creativity, consciousness."

Be like puppy dogs? Where is this coming from?

"Pretty much everything I'm going to tell you I've learned from Maharishi Mahesh Yogi," Lynch says, staring off into the middle distance of the screening room in his sprawling home in the Hollywood Hills. "I've been practicing Transcendental Meditation, the Maharishi's Transcendental Meditation, for thirty-one years."

Maharishi Mahesh Yogi is an elderly Hindu monk from India best known for having been the Beatles' guru in the 1960s. About sixty years ago, Maharishi, as he is known, developed a simplified meditation technique based on the Indian Vedic spiritual tradition that is supposed to help its practitioner "transcend" to a higher state of consciousness and profound relaxation by silently repeating a one-syllable Sanskrit mantra for about twenty minutes a day.

Lynch, who describes Maharishi as "a holy man who teaches you how to become a holy person," says he was introduced to Transcendental Meditation by his sister in the 1970s, around the time he was making his first feature-length film, the black-and-white cult favorite *Eraserhead*.

Transcendental Meditation and the Maharishi's guidance have transformed his life, Lynch says. A framed picture of the smiling guru sits next to the phone and several bottles of Ayurvedic herbs on the desk in Lynch's industrial art studio, where abstract artwork (one piece includes what appears to be a baby doll's arm protruding from the canvas) hangs on the walls. Before he began meditating twice daily, "I had anger, I had fears, I had anxieties," Lynch says. "I still have them. I'm not enlightened. But life is much, much, much, much better. Life is so beautiful.

"Maharishi says there is an expression, 'The world is as you are.' They use the example that if you have dark blue, dirty sunglasses on, that's the way the world is to you. If you have rose-colored glasses, that's the way the world is to you. Change from within."

Born in Missoula, Montana, the son of a research scientist and a language tutor, Lynch was raised as a Presbyterian. He says that his earliest memory of God was "a feeling of happiness" and that he still believes in God, in a slightly less abstract form.

"The kingdom of heaven, God the almighty merciful father, is that totality," he says, when asked to define who or what God is. "It's that level. It's the almighty merciful father, and the divine mother, the kingdom of heaven, the absolute, divine being, bliss consciousness, creative intelligence. These are all names, but it is that.

"It is unchanging, eternal. It *is*. There *is* nothing. It's that level that never had a beginning, it *is*, and it will be forevermore," he says. "If you were to say, 'That's God,' I think you wouldn't be wrong."

Transcendental meditators insist theirs is simply a spiritual practice or discipline, and not a religion unto itself. There are transcendental meditators of every religion and of no religion. In bucolic Fairfield, Iowa, the Transcendental Meditation capital of the United States and home to Maharishi University of Management, the mayor, a meditator, is a practicing Roman Catholic.

"It's not mind control," Lynch says of Transcendental Meditation. "Anybody in any religion who practices Transcendental Meditation generally says that it gives them deeper appreciation of their religion, greater insight into their religion. The bigger picture starts unfolding, and things that used to bug you stop bugging you so much.

"It's not that you go dead or numb. It's just that there's too much happiness and consciousness and wakefulness and understanding growing for you to be, you know, suffering so much, or caught up in some narrow little thing. It just starts getting better, and better, and better, and better."

A twice-divorced father of two sons and a daughter (all of whom are transcendental meditators), Lynch says while he adheres to no particular religion himself, he respects all religions. "I think that the great religions are like rivers. Each one is beautiful, and they all flow into one ocean," he says. "And they lead somewhere. It's like a mystery, I love mysteries. And once in a while you're going along, feeling the mystery, and you become a seeker. It just happens. I don't know quite how it happens, but you want to know. You want to experience, and you learn about things.

"That's what happened with Transcendental Meditation. I heard about it and I said, 'I've gotta have it.' And I'm glad I took that."

Lynch's résumé is long and varied. Film director. Screenwriter. Painter. Furniture designer (he often designs pieces for his sets). Composer. Actor. Photographer ("I shoot nudes and factories," he says). And, most recently, flier.

Yogic flier, that is.

Advanced transcendental meditators, known by the Sanskrit term *siddhas*, practice what they describe as a dynamic form of meditation, in which they are physically lifted off the ground in a state of profound bliss.

In reality, so-called yogic flying looks a lot more like hopping on one's knees than like levitating. In the Golden Domes of Pure Knowledge in Fairfield, Iowa, more than a thousand *siddhas* spend hours a day "flying" on foam rubber cushions, spontaneously hopping in the lotus position, eyes closed, giggling blissfully.

"I'm not a great flier," admits Lynch, who has been a *siddha* for about three years and usually practices alone. "But the experience, when it kicks in, is so phenomenal, it's not funny. It's intense bliss. And I've seen the unbounded ocean pour into me, and it's so beautiful.

"It is what they call 'bubbling bliss,' and it is so intense and so fantastic. Bliss is physical, emotional, mental, and spiritual happiness. It's so beautiful it'll make you laugh like a little kid. It's like we're lightbulbs, it just fills you up with light. And then an offshoot of that, as we see in the lightbulb, the light goes beyond the bulb. So it affects the environment, and this is the principle that will bring perpetual peace on earth."

Lynch is talking about the physics theory of constructive interference and how it can be applied to the power of meditation. The best way to explain the theory is by looking at how stereo speakers work. If there is a single speaker on each side of a room, the sound produced is in stereo. But if the two speakers are pushed together, the sound is amplified exponentially. The same, according to Maharishi (who trained as a physicist before becoming a monk), is true of transcendental meditators. When he meditates alone, there is a certain peaceful impact on the meditator himself and on the environment around him. But when meditators practice together in the same room, that impact is magnified exponentially.

Many of Maharishi's devotees, including Lynch, believe that Transcendental Meditation not only produces positive effects—lowering blood pressure, reducing stress, increasing focus—in its practitioners but also does the same for society, reducing crime rates and even ending war. The greater the number of people meditating together, the greater the effect. A few years ago, after the events of September 11, Maharishi devised a plan to establish "peace palaces" around the world with thousands of people-meditating-full-time-for-peace. It's a cause to which Lynch says he is personally devoted.

"Large groups of yogic fliers together produce an exponential effect of bliss, coherence, peace," he says matter-of-factly. "The square root of one percent of the world's population, in a group, going day in and day out, will bring about peace.

"And that's what I've been trying to do in talking to people about this, and trying to raise the money to make it on a permanent basis, and I haven't had a whole lot of luck, but I'm still trying," he says.

Recently, the filmmaker established the David Lynch Foundation for Consciousness-Based Education and World Peace to ensure that any child who wants to learn Transcendental Meditation can do so. The foundation will cover the costs of meditation instruction (about $2,500 per person) and will provide some scholarships for students who want to attend colleges where Transcendental Meditation is taught, such as the Maharishi's university in Iowa.

"We're just this little ball of people floating near the edge of what we call the Milky Way Galaxy," Lynch says, "and there ought to be enough power to light this little ball up with peace."

Lighting up yet another cigarette—a no-no for most hyperhealth-conscious transcendental meditators, many of whom are strict teetotaling, caffeine-free vegetarians—Lynch explains that meditation has allowed him to tap into a deep well of creativity.

"It's the field of pure creativity," he says, his voice rising. "For artists, it seems to me, the greatest thing is to be able to dive in and go to the source of creativity. Ideas come from there. All these anxieties and fears and things that just kill us, all of those start going away. It becomes a fluid, pure, open channel of ideas. It is *really good*."

Many of Lynch's films—*Mulholland Drive*, for example—have surreally complicated plots and can be difficult to explain to the uninitiated. Is it easier, perhaps, to describe how his films feel than what they're about?

"That's very good," he says, clearly pleased with the question. "That's very good, because the things that I love in life are abstractions. I don't think a film should be totally abstractions, but I think a story that I love holds those abstractions.

"Ideas inspire me. Ideas, to me, are everything. They're all seeds, and, in a lot of ways, they're like the Vedas, the laws of nature," he says.

Does he try to infuse his films with lessons he's learned from Maharishi and Transcendental Meditation?

"No, no, no. They say, If you want to send a message, go to Western Union," he says, wryly. "Film is a different thing. I love painting, I love photography, and I love music. And you know, if it comes through there, it comes through there in an innocent way. I'm not about to make a film to sell this thing.

"I want to make films based on ideas that I've fallen in love with."

SEPTEMBER 2004

SANDRA CISNEROS

Author

We're just rough drafts.

✳

BIRTH DATE: *December 20, 1954*
RAISED: *Roman Catholic*
NOW: *A "Buddhalupist"*
ATTENDS: *Doesn't but meditates frequently, particularly before she writes*
WORDS TO LIVE BY: *"You don't have to go to the ashram or go up the mountain or into the desert to experience spirituality. It happens every day if you're open to it."*

D o the trees ever talk to you when you're all alone?" the poet and novelist asks, eyes wide and voice lilting in her genuinely sweet way. "If you asked children that, every one would say, '*Oh, yeah.* Everybody knows that!' But adults never say it."

Sounding very much like Esperanza, the young narrator of her popular and best-known work, *The House on Mango Street*, Sandra Cisneros is trying to describe her spirituality, how she sees God and the world around her. "When you're a child, spiritual things happen all the time; you have a reverence for every animate and inanimate thing, and you sense that the spirit is present in a rock or a blade of grass, you know?"

I do. As she talks, my mind wanders back to my own childhood, when spotting a ladybug crawling in the folds of my grandfather's draperies or a scrawny yard bunny hopping across a patch of grass would send me into frenzies of joy and spellbound wonder. But then we grow up, the magic

fades, and those moments of mystical transcendence, when they do come, seem at best like supranatural anomalies in otherwise ordinary lives.

Cisneros believes this happens because we've lost touch with our spirituality, the kind that is inherent in all children and is obscured when intellect intervenes and tries to explain away what instinct doesn't need to. Happily ensconced in middle age, Cisneros, a Mexican American who was reared Roman Catholic in the barrios of Chicago, has been able to see once again with a child's eye by reconnecting with the Spirit.

"As a kid, I was very much in touch with the spiritual, but adults never called it that," she says one summer afternoon, flanked by books, Mexican antiques, and assorted religious artifacts—Buddhas, Virgin Marys, and various house saints—in the saffron-hued living room of her home in San Antonio, Texas. "I don't know why Catholic school doesn't explain things better to children. I mean, they show you a little white bird and you say, 'What's that?' And they say, 'That's the Holy Spirit.' And so you think the Holy Spirit is a white bird, but you don't realize that the Holy Spirit is what fills you up when you go to a concert and tears fill your eyes, or when you sit in the sun and you just feel so happy, or when you write a poem, or when you go to church and you look at the little colored glass in the windows and you're just filled with god. That's all the Holy Spirit, but they don't tell you that." (Cisneros prefers to spell *god* with a lowercase *g* because she views the deity as something "normal and not a mighty being with a white beard, but rather 'god' as in 'love,' which is both remarkable and ordinary, and in its ordinariness, remarkable," she says.)

"If they had explained the Holy Spirit in a concrete way—that it is when a flower smiles at you, for instance—I would have understood that completely," she says. "But they never explained that to me. Later on, when I became an adult and went to theology class with the Jesuits, they told us about Maslow and his theory of peak experiences." In the mid–twentieth century, the psychologist Abraham Maslow, an atheist, posited that mystical or transcendent experiences were common for what he called "self-actualized" adults but weren't necessarily religious or theistic in nature. "When I read about it at first I didn't understand it, and then I went, Oh, yeah, that happens to me all the time! But why did he call them peak experiences? They happen all the time, especially when you're a little kid. These are everyday occurrences. These aren't things that you have to climb Mont Blanc and see the

Alps to experience. You just have to go outside to be filled with god. You can be living in the worst neighborhood in Chicago and have that experience daily, with a twig you brought home from Humboldt Park or a little pip of lily of the valley, as often happened with me. These things were filled with god, and those moments were filled with god.

"But the Catholic Church never talked about that. It wasn't until I looked at other things, other religions in the world, and I read about Hinduism and Buddhism and looked in other places, that I could find the places that intersected with my own life."

The youngest and only daughter among seven children born to her Mexican father and Mexican-American mother, Cisneros attended Catholic school and, during the school year at least, Mass on a regular basis. But she wasn't raised in what she'd call a "traditional" Catholic household. Neither of her parents was terribly pious—her mother didn't have an altar on her dresser or keep icons of the Virgin Mary around the house like her friends' mothers did. And now that she is an adult, Cisneros's spirituality is even less traditional than her mother's, a mosaic made with pieces from the religion of her youth, Eastern philosophies, and life experience.

Nestled next to the bicep of her left arm, Cisneros sports a tattoo of what at first glance appears to be either the Virgin Mary or the Buddha. Upon closer inspection, I can see that the figure inked in black is really both. "I call myself a 'Buddhalupist,'" she says, smiling conspiratorially. "I have the Virgen de Guadalupe on my arm, but she's not the traditional Virgen de Guadalupe— she's not standing on the baby, she's sitting in the lotus position on the Coatlicue, and her face looks like it can be one from anywhere. She could be from India, she's sitting like Kuan Yin, she looks a little bit native—you don't know where she comes from. I tell people I'm a Buddhalupist, because there are some things I believe that are from my Catholicism, and Buddhism is nice because it allows you to return to your roots. So someone can be Buddhist *and* Catholic. That's why being a Buddhalupist makes perfect sense to me.

"I believe all the religions are valid. I do. But I believe more in spirituality than I do in organized religions. The corruption of religion happens when it becomes my-god-is-right-and-you're-wrong. And I live in a place that is as conservative as any. We have the Christian Taliban here. I like to tell people I don't even live in the Bible Belt, I live below the Bible Belt, which is the

Bible Groin—even worse! So here I am in the Bible Groin, and my ideas are considered pretty weird and out there because I believe there is god in all of us and in each of us." Cisneros pauses briefly to consider a plate of *pan dulce* and *cochinitos*, Mexican sugar cookies in the shape of pigs, on the table in front of her. A tall glass of unsweetened iced tea sweats in her hand. "I really try to gather from all the religions and keep an open mind to try to see similarities in places that unite me even with people that are very conservative and terrify me. I still feel a sense of hope that they will find god and that they have spirituality, and that's a place that could unite us."

When she looks back on her life, several moments stand out as signposts on her journey, turning points that led her back to her spiritual roots. The first was when she was hit by a car as a graduate student at the University of Iowa in the late 1970s. "I realized there was something bigger than me," she says. Another came when she turned thirty-three and suffered from paralyzing depression.

"I was saved by such spiritual forces that my life has never been the same," she says, quietly. "I was living in Northern California at the time. I went through nine months of severe depression and almost suicide. Then, just intuitively, in my heart I felt that if I just went back to Chicago everything would be all right, even though it would mean the breakup of my relationship. I just knew, in my gut, that I had to go home. And I did go home, knowing my partner wouldn't be there when I came back because he so much didn't want me to go. But I left. And when I got home to Chicago, with my coat still on and with my suitcase in my hand, my mother said, 'There's a letter from Washington for you and I think it's good news.' So with my coat on I opened this letter—it was from the National Endowment for the Arts— saying that I was awarded a $20,000 grant. It was my second, and it couldn't have come at a better time. I was thirty-three years old and ashamed to always have to ask my family for money. I was so broke—I owed everybody money and I had taken a job I hated and this grant money saved me and saved face. More than anything, it reminded me that I wasn't supposed to be doing what I was doing. I was supposed to be writing.

"I had been in such a severe depression that my body stopped menstruating. I read the letter and I went to the bathroom and my period began. And then I wrote, with my coat still on, a letter to the NEA saying they had saved my life. I meant it with all my heart, and I thanked them," she continues, a kind of wistful gratitude flashing across her face. "I wrote it on lined paper with three holes because that's the kind of paper my mother had in the house—she's working class, she doesn't have stationery—so I wrote it on the same paper my mother would have sent to our teachers when we were sick. And I had been sick. My spirit had been sick. It had been telling me so, my dreams had been screaming at me, but I didn't know what was going on until later. And that began my conscious spiritual journey of reading about spirituality and searching around."

A friend she met while living in Sarajevo, Yugoslavia, in the early 1980s gave her a book by the Vietnamese Buddhist monk Thich Nhat Hanh called *Being Peace*. It would transform her, setting her on a trajectory toward integrating Eastern philosophy into her spirituality. But she didn't read it when she was first given the book. In fact, it wasn't until many years later, in the middle of the war in Bosnia, that Cisneros opened it up.

"I believe books don't resonate in you until you're ready to hear them. My friend bought that book for me, but it wasn't time for me to read it until the war started and I couldn't communicate with her. I didn't know if she was alive or dead. And during that time, the book just came to me by accident, in all this chaos," she says, waving her arms at the overflowing bookshelves and stacks of books here and there. "You can see how I keep my books! I found *Being Peace* when I was looking for something else. I thought, Well, here was a monk who lived during the Vietnam War and worked toward a new kind of engaged Buddhism where you could be spiritual *and* socially active. I thought that perhaps this monk who lived through a war could give me an answer about how I, as a private citizen, could do something for someone I knew who was in a war-torn country. And he did. His book made me feel that I didn't have to wait for a Rambo in a helicopter or for the president, that I could make change just by opening my mouth. And as a writer, I can do a lot more than most people if I just talk about it everywhere I go."

So she did. Cisneros gathered a group of like-minded women together to meet and silently meditate for peace in front of a cathedral in downtown San Antonio for months during the Bosnian War. The day she showed up at the cathedral all alone and stood there meditating with her peace sign, "like Henny Penny," she says, a letter from her friend in Sarajevo arrived saying that she was alive and well. "I see patterns where there wasn't a pattern in my younger life and I would have thought things were arbitrary and happened by chance. Now I see divine providence and an order to my life that gives me absolute faith in some higher power."

Cisneros's eclectic spirituality is perhaps the inward expression of what sets her apart in this decidedly traditional part of the world. Her thoroughly bohemian house on a corner lot on the border of San Antonio's elegant historic King William district is a riot of color—inside and out. In the late 1990s she painted the house a vivid purple, offending the sensibilities of some of her neighbors, who complained it failed to fit with the aesthetic of King William's grand antebellum mansions a few blocks away. Now the exterior is the shade of the inside of a ripe watermelon. "*Rosa mejicana*," she explains— Mexican pink—although she's chosen a slightly darker shade than the traditional pink of her ancestral land, anticipating that it will fade to a more subtle hue after a few years in the intense South Texas sun.

A wild array of native plants—prickly pear, cactuses, and huge magueys or century plants—lines the perimeter of the yard. And the inside of her welcoming home is dressed with a panoply of mementos (some sacred, some not) and vibrantly colored artwork by artists she and her life partner, the documentary filmmaker Ray Santisteban, know personally. Hanging alone on one wall of the living room where a larger painting is usually displayed (the painting has been loaned to a show in town) is a black-and-white portrait of Cisneros's great-grandmother.

"You have to demystify spirituality, so you fill your house with things of the spirit. And those things of the spirit can be a plant growing in a coffee can, or you can surround yourself with paintings, making your house a living altar. That's what I try to do," she says, gesturing toward the noble-looking woman in the picture. "I feel that I have to go to images of great-grandmothers who believed because my own mother was such a skeptic. My mother grew up following my grandfather's belief. He saw a lot of corruption among the clergy in Mexico during the Mexican Revolution, and so he was very cynical about religion. My mother was maybe the only one of his children who believed that, too. My grandmother, on the other hand, was very devout and meek. My mother saw that meekness as weakness and not as strength. It seems as if I've had to look beyond my mother and find these strands of the spiritual where I could.

"I've looked all over the world, and that's kind of how I've put together my Buddhalupismo," she says with a laugh. "God doesn't have a gender and really isn't a being. It's more like love. Pure love—that's how I see god. Everything else is in doubt, but pure love is real. You know how Jesus appears to some people, and that's how they envision god? Well, when they say 'Jesus,' I just substitute in my head 'Guadalupe,' and when I say 'Guadalupe,' I just substitute in my head 'love' or another image of god. Pure love came to me as a brown woman because that's someone I could open the door to."

Cisneros meditates frequently, but with characteristic free-spiritedness, she doesn't follow any particular school or method of meditation. And she doesn't practice at a designated time or place. When the spirit moves her or, more accurately, when she's looking for the spirit to move her, she turns inward.

"I use my spirituality to become unblocked, to start my writing day, to give a speech," she says in her singsongy voice. "I talk to teachers and librarians and readers and I tell them, 'This is what I do. If you don't believe and you don't have any spirituality you can substitute "spirit ally" for your own higher power, and even if you don't believe in god, you must believe in love. Love exists. So substitute it for god.' To me love and god are the same thing. It's just a different word."

There are two things Cisneros always asks for when she meditates: humility and courage. "Humility so my ego and interests can get out of the way for something bigger. And courage because when you do get that guidance, it's scary and you might not want to do what is being given you to do," she says. The moments when she is able to see the guidance clearly and catch the spiritual golden ring, "that's when we're god, that's when we're at our highest potential, but it's only for a couple of seconds. The rest of the time we're just rough drafts. If you remember that, it will keep you from being too full of yourself."

Chaos erupts momentarily as her four dogs—Berto, Dante, Lolita, and Zelda—who have been sequestered outside in the garden while Cisneros chatted in the living room, burst through the kitchen doors and rush in to investigate the stranger in their midst and lavish their mistress with affection. "This is one of the things I learned from being in my house, that the things of the spirit are in animals. If I get blocked, I just take a nap and these guys sleep with me and I wake up and it's great. This is god, too," she says, petting Dante, her Italian greyhound, on the snout. "They're like walking flowers."

Cisneros finds God everywhere—in the sublime and the mundane—

which is where the Teletubbies come in. It sounds a bit odd, she realizes, but not if you approach it from a child's perspective.

"Think of those Teletubbies, with the baby's face in the sun, but instead think of someone you love, whose face is in the sun, someone who loves you and is sending you absolute love," she says, describing how she explains meditation to the uninitiated. "Then you inhale, you just inhale their love. Picture them smiling, and when they smile, you inhale their smile, and when you exhale you send it back. Do that ten times and that's meditating. You just inhale that love," she says, taking a deep breath in through her nose, "and when you exhale," she says, exhaling dramatically through her nose, "you send it back. You can do it with other people in the room and it really gets you in the zone, it gets everybody feeling really good.

"That's it. That's the Holy Spirit. It's very simple! I don't know why religions make it so difficult."

JUNE 2005

HAKEEM OLAJUWON

Professional Athlete

Islam is not just a religion, it's a lifestyle.

✳

BIRTH DATE: *January 21, 1963*

RAISED: *Muslim*

NOW: *Muslim*

ATTENDS: *Prayer several times daily at a mosque near his home in Sugar Land, Texas*

WORDS TO LIVE BY: *"You fall into sins and mistakes—honest mistakes—but the door of repentance is always open. You can always repent."*

When most professional basketball players turn in their jerseys and end their careers on the court, they go on to new lives as color commentators, entrepreneurs, managers, restaurateurs, and scratch golfers. Hakeem "the Dream" Olajuwon, the seven-foot-tall Nigerian center who twice helped lead the Houston Rockets to national championships and was a member of the gold-medal-winning American Dream Team at the 1996 Atlanta Olympics, may be the first retired pro player to reinvent himself as a serious student of Arabic and the Qur'an.

After he retired in 2001 as the NBA's all-time leading shot blocker with 3,830 shots, people would ask him what he was going to do next, "like basketball was my only life," Olajuwon recalls as we chat in the cavernous white-toned sitting room of his sprawling home in Sugar Land, Texas, a suburb of Houston. "This was the goal. After finishing with basketball, I wanted to study Arabic. I could have gotten myself occupied again and not done this.

But I said all along: When I finish, I will go to Jordan and study. Now I have the time to go to Jordan to study. And not just me. My wife, my children, they get to have that base, too. We all study. Everybody speaks Arabic." Olajuwon says he spends more than half the year at his home in the Gulf state of Jordan with his wife and four of his five children, who range in age from infant to adolescent.

Olajuwon, who grew up in a middle-class Muslim home in Lagos, Nigeria, before emigrating to the United States in 1980 to attend—and play basketball for—the University of Houston, has structured his entire life around his Muslim faith. When he is at his Sugar Land home, which is built in a traditional Islamic style of architecture more common to Morocco than to Texas, Olajuwon (who became an American citizen in 1993) prays five times a day at a nearby mosque, beginning sometimes as early as four in the morning and ending at night before he goes to sleep. He even has a small, cupolaed outdoor mosque in his front courtyard, where he occasionally prays alone or with friends and family. All of his business meetings—he is involved in various real estate development and charity projects—are scheduled around his daily prayers. No exceptions.

"Islam is not just a religion, it's a lifestyle," Olajuwon says. "You can't just say, 'I'm a Muslim,' and be a Muslim. No. You have to study, you have to understand, you have to grow. Islam is all about practicing. Islam commands all aspects of life. You can say, 'Oh, this is a beautiful home.' This is Islamic architecture. It's not just something we built. Islam is in architecture. It's in all aspects of life."

It wasn't always in all aspects of Olajuwon's life, he admits. While he's never doubted the teachings of Islam, he did stray from them during his youth. "I grew up in a Muslim home," he begins to explain and then suddenly jumps up to move a glass of orange juice and a bottle of water that one of his household staff has just placed on the coffee table in front of me to a side table he feels is easier for me to reach. When I object, my doting host insists, "No, no, that's too far away." Even though it's nearly one hundred degrees outside, he's not having anything himself—not even water—because he is fasting. It's not a required fast, like that practiced for forty days during the holy month of Ramadan. It is an optional fast that he does once or twice a week purely out of devotion. "But even though I was raised in a Muslim home, I really started practicing Islam later on in life when I came to the

United States. Before, it was never a concern. I was living under the guidance of my parents, in a culture where everyone was more or less protected, without a concern to encourage the practice of Islam. I knew that I was a Muslim, I wasn't confused about that. But if you don't follow and practice Islam, you can't say that you're a Muslim.

"Islam teaches that once you reach the age of maturity—puberty—then you are conscious. It's not just something that I inherited, that I'm a Muslim because I was born a Muslim. No. You don't follow blindly. You have to reflect and think and come to your own conclusion. Islam urges you to grow, to look at this universe and how it is working as a unit, to see God's creation. It is not by accident. This is a sign for those who would understand. Once you are conscious of your surroundings and know that this is not by accident, then you go forward, and Islam gives you the purpose of life and defines for you why you are here and what your destination is," he says.

"One of the beauties of Islam is that it is an open book. It gives you a clear picture so you can make wise choices. 'You're all going to die and you all come back to me,' that's what God says. 'And you will be rewarded according to what you used to do.' So you try to stay in what's lawful and stay away from what's unlawful. And you fall into sins and mistakes—honest mistakes—but the door of repentance is always open. You can always repent. We say Allah is the 'most merciful of the merciful,' and Islam is very merciful. But at the same time it is strict in punishment, so there is a balance. Those who are sincere and fall into error, for them, the door of repentance is always open. The servants that fall into error and acknowledge it and go back to the door of repentance, they are promised forgiveness. Islam is very detailed about how to do this. Let's say I have a business deal with somebody and I break it and cheat, I cannot just ask for forgiveness. First I have to go back and fix any harm that I have caused anybody, ask them for forgiveness, and then ask God for forgiveness," he says. "For a Muslim, this is normal. It's like when you are playing basketball and you do a layup. Before you can do a layup, you have to know the rules—dribble, double dribble, traveling. It's just a lifestyle. It's not scholarly. It is just the duty of every Muslim."

Olajuwon was seventeen when he arrived in Houston from Lagos. While he was never a wild partier, he did lead the life of a typical college student. He had a steady girlfriend through college and into his early years in the NBA, Lita Spencer, with whom he would have a child—his eldest daughter,

Abisola—in 1988. The couple never married. In 1995 Olajuwon married an eighteen-year-old Texan named Dalia Asafi in what has been described in some reports as an arranged marriage. (Dating, as such, is forbidden in Islam, Olajuwon explains.) Asafi's father was an acquaintance of his at the local mosque. As of 2005, the couple had four young children together—three girls and a their youngest, a boy.

Olajuwon's life changed one day in about 1990 when he found out there was a mosque five minutes away from the Houston basketball arena where the Rockets play. "Five minutes away! Five minutes! I didn't even know it was there for all those years," he recalls. "When they told me I was like, Are you serious? I wanted to go right away. Mosque was not something I had been running away from. I didn't know what was available. I had been trying to understand the American culture with all the confusion about these groups who say they are Muslims. I didn't even know who was for real to begin with. You know Islam from where you came, how it should be. But when you start seeing differences, all these differences, you wonder, Where do they come from? Do they lead to the main source? So it took time."

The first Friday he attended weekly prayers at the Houston mosque is a memory that Olajuwon recalls viscerally, almost ecstatically. "When they made the call to prayer, there were goose bumps all over me. It was so emotional to hear that call again. I was like, wow, look what I've been missing! I was so close. Our practices were from eleven to one. The prayer was at one-thirty. It was perfect timing. And it's something I love. I just love it.

"The beauty of Islam is the *adan*, the call to prayer. A lot of people who travel to the Muslim world see that it is dominated by all these minarets and, from them, this call to prayer. Everybody closes down their stores and goes in the back to pray. When you drive around, you see the Qur'an everywhere, from the taxi to the stores. When people play music, the Qur'an is the music. It is the music of the Muslim. It has its own rhythmic tone, and the recitation of the Qur'an is so soothing to your soul. I was detached from that for many years here," he says.

"The people who saw me at the *masjid* that first Friday said they knew by my name that I was a Muslim. But there are lots of Muslims who don't practice. After prayer they all came up to me and said, 'We didn't know you were practicing.' I told them, 'I just didn't know the mosque was here.' They took me back to the mosque's library, and I got started again, learning again how to pray, getting books on the Qur'an, the basics. One of the brothers there gave me his phone number and said he was always willing to help me. Prayers at the mosque took only thirty minutes, but I found myself staying three or four hours talking and talking. I really had a wonderful day, coming back home again."

So began his Islamic reeducation. Olajuwon started from scratch, relearning everything from how to wash himself in preparation for prayer to memorizing passages of the Qur'an. "I wanted to make sure what I knew was correct," he says. "Islam defines a lifestyle for a Muslim, so you don't have to go out on your own to find out and make mistakes. It takes all the guesswork out of the picture." Even when it comes to his diet. Four years after his retirement from pro ball, Olajuwon is fit and trim. He still plays basketball from time to time in pickup games and takes a long walk around a track near his home every morning after returning from prayers at the mosque. "People see me now and say, 'Wow, you look like you're in shape!' Once you stop playing basketball, you naturally gain weight. But for the Muslim, nothing is left out. Even food. More than thirteen hundred years ago, the Prophet, peace be upon him, gave us a diet. If you follow it, you can't miss. The first condition is we don't eat unless we are hungry. We don't just eat because it's time to eat or because we feel like eating. You have to have an appetite. And then, when we eat, we do not stuff our stomachs, so we don't overeat. You eat one-third food, one-third water, and one-third the air that you breathe. You can eat what you want—except for food that is *haram*—but not a lot of food. It's portion control."

Over time, Olajuwon's spiritual devotion has developed past being obedient to what is required by the faith to doing that which is over and above what is expected. He says it's his way of saying thank you to Allah. For instance, *salat*, the five required daily prayers, can be said anywhere. But Olajuwon makes every effort to say them in a mosque with other Muslims. "The Prophet, peace be upon him, said the quality of *salat* in *jumaa*, in community, is twenty-seven times superior than individual prayer. There is a reward expected in the hereafter. If I make a decision knowing that I can get a reward twenty-seven times more than just the one, why would I pray at home?" he says. Every able-bodied Muslim is required to make the *hajj*, or pilgrimage to Mecca, at least once in his or her life. Olajuwon has made the *hajj* twice and has gone on the *umrah*, a lesser pilgrimage to Mecca made at a different time of the year, close to ten times.

He runs his businesses according to Islamic law, which forbids incurring interest. "Islam does not support having all the money sitting in the bank. You have to circulate the money, you have to invest. You have to take a risk," he explains. Olajuwon gives the required *zakat*—2.5 percent of his income— and more to charity.

"In Islam you never say, 'Oh, God has blessed me.' You have to look at every position in life as a test. Healthy children, a healthy marriage, wealth, fame. In the Qur'an, it says these are tests to see if you are grateful or ungrateful. How do you demonstrate you are grateful? You continue to raise your level. For example, let's say you get up in the morning at five-thirty to pray. That is obligatory. There are a lot of other deeds that are voluntary, that you don't have to do. Do it and there is a reward. You have to go to the next level, to make the voluntary obligatory. It's not voluntary anymore."

Olajuwon compares the way he lives his exceptional life as a Muslim to being an NBA player with a huge salary. "You cannot rank yourself as an average player anymore," he says. "The team expects more." And for the rest of his life, he hopes to deliver spiritual slam dunks, and not just layups. *"Inshallah,"* he says. God willing.

JUNE 2005

TOM ROBBINS

Author

Paradox is the engine that runs the universe.

✳

BIRTH DATE: *July 22, 1936*
RAISED: *Southern Baptist*
NOW: *"Cosmic lounge lizard"*
ATTENDS: *Doesn't but practices yoga now and then*
WORDS TO LIVE BY: *"We live in hell because we take ourselves too seriously."*

Have you ever licked a psychedelic frog?

Okay, so it's an unorthodox way to begin an interview about someone's spiritual life, but Tom Robbins is an unorthodox kind of guy. It's a bizarre question, I say apologetically before he can answer.

"Bizarre is my middle name," says Robbins, the novelist who for more than thirty years has mixed religion, sex, countercultural social commentary, and hallucinogens in cult favorites such as *Even Cowgirls Get the Blues*, *Still Life with Woodpecker*, and *Another Roadside Attraction*.

Considering Robbins, a famously idiosyncratic fellow with a penchant for psychedelic experiences, has crafted wild, bizarrely humorous stories involving, variously, an existentialist can of beans (aptly named Can o' Beans) as a main character, a love affair that takes place inside a pack of Camel cigarettes, and extraterrestrial beings whose earthly representatives are African

amphibians that secrete a mind-altering substance, the frog-licking inquiry is not that far-fetched.

"With your permission, I wanted to start by telling you a story and then telling you a joke," Robbins purrs in a distinctive Virginia drawl he hasn't been able to shake despite living just outside Seattle for more than four decades, before I can get my first *serious* question out.

Go for it, I say.

"It's a Sufi story," he begins. "There was a middle-aged man who had been thinking about serious things and as a result applied for an audience with a great master. And he eventually was granted the audience, but he could ask only one question. So he approached the master and he said, 'Master, my question is this: What is God really like?' And the master said, 'God is a carrot. Hahahaha.' Well, the man went away rather disappointed and felt that he had been mocked and ridiculed. He was quite upset and, of course, very dissatisfied with the answer. But he kept thinking about it, and a couple of years later, he reapplied and once again was granted an audience. He said, 'Master, what did you mean when you said God is a carrot?' And the master said, 'God is not a carrot! God is a radish, hahahaha.' Well, again the man went away perplexed, but he thought about it, and eventually he understood: You can't define God. You can't even really talk about God. Anything that you can really define or describe is not God.

"So, are we done now?" Robbins says, facetiously.

Yeah, I'll be going, I say, pantomiming a hasty departure.

"Okay, okay. So the joke is: What do you get when you cross Jehovah's Witnesses with agnostics?" he says, grinning.

I don't know, what?

"People who come to your door and just stand there and shrug."

Rim shot, please.

"And that is fairly indicative of my position," Robbins says in a more serious vein. "Because even though I have a compulsion toward the spiritual and even though I pray every night, I am at the same time an agnostic. But I will say also that I think the pope is an agnostic, Billy Graham is an agnostic, we're all agnostics, because nobody knows and nobody has ever known, including the biblical prophets. Now, there's a contradiction in there, but we should not let that deter us because paradox is the engine that runs the universe.

"The Bible itself is absolutely teeming with contradictions. But the problem with Christianity—one of the many problems with Christianity—is that the contradictions don't seem to bother the Christians. They pick and choose and say under certain circumstances, 'Jesus said, "Turn the other cheek; love thine enemies."' But then on a different day, with different motives, they will quote the Old Testament, 'An eye for an eye, and a tooth for a tooth.' The problem is not with the contradictions themselves. I don't think the Bible is any less valuable because it's full of contradictions. The problem is Christians choose one or the other. And you have to choose both. You have to hold both of those ideas in your head at the same time," he says.

"We don't have any tradition of paradox in our culture, so it's very difficult for Westerners to deal with that, which is why it's also very difficult for Westerners, no matter how well meaning, to ever achieve enlightenment in the Asian sense of the word."

Robbins grew up in what he describes as an "extremely strict" Southern Baptist environment in Richmond, Virginia, where paradox was not particularly well tolerated. Both of his grandfathers were Southern Baptist ministers, and he attended church services at least twice a week through most of his childhood. "As I became more well traveled, more well educated, more well read, I began to see the wizard behind the curtain and to see the fallacy in so many of those beliefs and the hypocrisy in so many of those beliefs, that it sent me out on a quest to find the truth," he says. "It sounds pretentious to talk about a vision quest, but I feel to a certain extent that I've been on one."

Robbins's spiritual journey has been, in the truest sense, a very long, strange trip. It began when he was a boy of eleven, and as he approaches his seventieth birthday, he's still traveling.

"I had my first two spiritual experiences as a result of Natalie Wood," he says. "When I was eleven, the local minister was this really creepy guy. My mother liked him a lot, but I just thought he was weird—wet, sweaty palms and pale skin. His name was Dr. Peters. They were getting ready to have a revival at our church in Virginia, and he wanted me to consecrate my life to Christ, and to step forward, to walk the aisle. So I did it, and I was baptized—immersed—in the Rappahannock River. I kept waiting for some kind of uplifting enlightenment experience. I thought I would feel really different and it didn't happen. I felt wet and that was about it.

"A few weeks later, our family drove to a town about twelve miles away, to a movie theater which showed films that were a little bit more recent than the ones shown in our little town. And it was a film with Natalie Wood as a child actress. Somehow that movie touched me so deeply that on the way home, in the dark backseat of the car, I had this oceanic experience where I felt that we were all one, that I was part of the oneness. I felt everything that I thought I would feel after being baptized. I suppose in that little half-baked eleven-year-old brain of mine, that's where this spiritual quest began, when I realized there was this *feeling*, but it didn't come from church."

Robbins says he had lost interest in Jesus at an even earlier age, also as the result of a movie. "When I was growing up I bought into the idea that Jesus was what it was all about, that he should be my hero and my ideal and my savior. And then, at probably age six or seven, I saw my first Tarzan movie, and Jesus could no longer cut the mustard. Johnny Weissmuller just completely wiped him out." Everything about Weissmuller's Tarzan appealed to Robbins. "The freedom, swinging between the earth and the sky in an absolute liberation. Not wearing many clothes. Being in a totally exotic environment. Communicating with the animals. Diving into those lucid pools. Just everything about it—even the yell, which I can still do. I've been kicked out of a number of bars over the years for doing my Tarzan yell. He captured me in a way that Jesus obviously had not."

None of this sat particularly well with Robbins's parents, who shipped him off to a military school when he started seriously rebelling in high school. "It was a Southern Baptist military school. We were literally marched to church every Sunday morning. But the following year I went away to college, and I've scarcely been in a church since," he says.

In college, Robbins began reading about Zen Buddhism, German mysticism, and various traditions of Eastern philosophy. "A lot of it made sense to me, but it was all intellectual, whereas the Southern Baptist teachings had somehow wormed their way into my emotions. Zen and these Asian systems of liberation, which I identified with more, I could only process on an intellectual level. That is until that fateful day in 1963 when I ingested three hundred micrograms of absolutely pure Sandoz lysergic acid diethylamide thirty-five," he says, fondly.

The first time Robbins dropped acid in Seattle, more than forty years ago, was the best day of his life, "the one day in my life I would not exchange for any other," he says. "During the eight hours that I spent in the same chair—

I got up once to go to the bathroom and that was like the Odyssey—all of it made sense to me on a cellular level. Not only these concepts of Zen Buddhism and Taoism and Sufism but also the Einsteinian concepts, the theory of relativity, suddenly were as real to me as this tabletop. I mean, the cliché of having your mind blown was really apt," he says.

There are Indians in Mexico who live in the hills above Oaxaca who explain his experience in a slightly different way. "They say about Christians, 'You white people talk *to* God. We talk *with* God.' In other words, they get answers. It's not a one-way conversation; it's not just a monologue," he says, adding that he's had that kind of dialogue with the divine only when he's been in a psychedelically enhanced state.

Does he still dabble in drugs? "The kind of drugs that I've taken one does not dabble in," he says as a big wiseass smile spreads across his thin goateed face. "You get in your little canoe and you push it out on that vast dark ocean and just hope you get back safely. It's not something that you do lightly, and it isn't necessary to do it very often. I'm still mining nuggets from that first experience. Psychedelics may be our only hope. It's the only thing that may be standing between us and the destruction of the planet."

If that's true, then I'm out of luck, as I've never taken any psychedelics, I confess.

"Well," he says, pensively, "as I wrote once: It's never too late to have a happy childhood."

We're sitting in the lobby of New York City's historic Algonquin Hotel, not far from a table where Dorothy Parker and Robert Benchley used to convene their fabled Round Table luncheons in the 1920s to debate the issues of the day and critique culture. This probably isn't quite what they had in mind, I think, as Robbins continues explaining the connection between altered states and spirituality.

"The whole goal of these Asian systems of liberation, which is really what Zen is, is the obliteration of the self. Patriarchal religions—Christianity, Judaism, and Islam—are used to prop up the ego, to inflate the ego. Whereas our whole relationship with the divine should be to merge with the divine, and you can't merge with the divine as long as you have ego. You should get rid of the self, and that's what happens in a psychedelic experience—the ego disappears. And that's why it's so associated with the feeling of ecstasy. That's why orgasms are so popular. At the moment of orgasm, you don't know who you are. You lose yourself. You don't know your address, your job description, your name, your race. And people crave that. They crave this loss of ego, but they don't really know how to go about doing it, so we go about it in crude ways.

"There is a sense in which a crack house is a temple. People are going there to smoke crack and, even though they don't know this consciously, to obliterate the self and the ego, to reach that level, that plane of ecstatic participation in the divine universe," he says, smiling.

In 1971 Robbins—who has several generations of loyal readers, rivaled in their devotion perhaps only by Deadheads, Trekkies, and Red Sox fans—published his first novel, *Another Roadside Attraction*. It's a story set largely at Captain Kendrick's Memorial Hot Dog Wildlife Preserve, where the roadside attraction is the mummified body of Jesus Christ, which has been stolen from the Vatican by a couple of countercultural characters, and which they intend to destroy as a way, more or less, of saving society from itself. The novel, which was clearly heavily influenced by the author's discovery of hallucinogens and adherence to Timothy Leary's call to "turn on, tune in, and drop out," presents his persistent belief that if Western society could rid itself of Christian traditions and embrace a higher consciousness, the world would be a much happier place.

Robbins's novels are told in complex sentences laden with his particular brand of metaphor—a favorite of mine from his 2000 novel *Fierce Invalids Home from Hot Climates* describes "a mist-bearded Saturday morning, gray as a ghoul and cool as clam aspic." The plots, which sometimes unfold using the metafiction technique, in which the author, as himself, interjects an explanation or a point, are complex, often ridiculously far-fetched, sexy, and packed with ideas from various spiritual traditions meticulously researched by Robbins.

"I've been asked why I write as much as I do about religion and about sexuality, and I say, Well, because those are the two things that people on this planet are most interested in," he explains. "And they are very much intertwined, entangled. Religion is so entangled with sexuality that it's almost impossible to separate. They're often confused. They often overlap. There's a great deal of sublimation going on on both ends, but that's really what it's all about.

"One of the reasons I've been attracted to Tantric Hinduism is that Tantra is the only philosophical system for liberation that takes sensual energy, which is the most powerful energy that we humans possess, and actually uses it in a spiritual way. Tantra harnesses it and uses it as rocket fuel to blast off into the godhead. So if you come up on a Tantric saint, he would probably be playing a sitar, smoking hashish, drinking wine, there would be beautiful paintings on the wall, beautiful fabric everywhere, at least one and probably more clothed or unclothed women around him, with whom he would have repeated intercourse. All of that. But he would be using that in a spiritual way. It's just so beyond comprehension in our culture."

Certainly writing is an intrinsically spiritual activity for him. Almost every act in life can be spiritual if the intention going into it is correct, Robbins says. He labors over his novels—on average he releases one book every five years. He's written eight novels and one collection of short stories and essays over a span of thirty-five years.

"I was on a panel once with John Irving, and he said he would never begin a book if he didn't know how it was going to end," Robbins says. "I just looked at him in disbelief and said, 'John, I can't believe you're saying that! Isn't that like having a job in a factory?' Well, ya know, I guess it works for him. But I have to surround the act of writing with surprise and discovery and even terror in order to do it every day. I have to let it marinate down there in the green ooze at the bottom of my brainpan and then squeeze it out a little at a time, like a tube of toothpaste.

"It's a journey," he says. "It pleases me when people say that my books are a trip, or a journey, because that is literally what they are."

Enlightenment is Robbins's chief pursuit. Twice he's had what are called "satori" experiences, or glimpses of Nirvana, while he was entirely sober. They lasted only a few seconds each. The first occurred while he was driving in a blizzard in Seattle in 1964, and the second years later while he was watching yet another movie, 1991's *The Fisher King*, starring Robin Williams. "I understood how the universe was put together, what held it together. There was nothing I didn't know during those one to three seconds," he says.

Robbins abandoned faith in a traditional, personified God years ago. "I'm a pantheist *and* a monotheist," he says, explaining that he believes a divine force infuses everything in the universe and therefore God is everything and everywhere. Over the years, as people have tried to affix a religious label to this notoriously private man, he has been described as pagan, neo-pagan, Druid, Buddhist, Hindu, Tantric, and Zen. Robbins says he's all of those and none of them at once because, essentially, they're all the same. And he doesn't believe in heaven and hell in the biblical sense, preferring to think of them as spiritual states that exist here on earth.

"Heaven is a small, porous, flexible ego and hell is a big, stiff ego," Robbins says. "If you live in your ego, then you're livin' in hell. Now Jesus himself said in the apocryphal Gospel According to St. Thomas—a book that is very much at odds with the four that were included in the Bible—'Heaven is spread upon the earth but men cannot see it.' In other words, open your eyes!

"We live in hell because we take ourselves too seriously. If there's any one message that's permeated my literary output, I guess that's it: Stop taking yourself too seriously, which is not the same thing at all as living a life of frivolity. There is nothing whimsical or frivolous about it," he says.

"When I fall out of grace, which is a great deal of the time, sooner or later I realize it's because I'm taking myself too seriously."

For the record, no, Robbins has never licked a frog, psychedelic or otherwise. But if the opportunity presented itself, he wouldn't necessarily decline.

SEPTEMBER 2005

JOHN MAHONEY

Actor

Be charitable. That's the greatest virtue.

✳

BIRTH DATE: *June 20, 1940*

RAISED: *Roman Catholic*

NOW: *Roman Catholic*

ATTENDS: *Mass at several Chicago-area parishes, "whenever the Spirit moves" him*

WORDS TO LIVE BY: *"God is the personification of love and forgiveness. He constantly forgives you and constantly loves you."*

She was squishing my heirloom tomatoes, and I wanted to slap her. The sullen, vaguely menacing clerk at the greengrocer was roughly bagging my purchases, including the two perfectly ripe beauties I had carefully picked for dinner. When I handed over my credit card, I even had asked, nicely, if she wouldn't mind, please, putting the two tomatoes on top. She ignored me. When I reached into the bag to move the pretty yellow-and-red-striped one, she grunted and shoved the bag at me. It was hot, she was inexcusably rude, and I was about to lose my cool. But a single thought suddenly stopped me: What would John Mahoney do?

So instead of being ugly back at her, I smiled, picked up my bag of slightly molested groceries, said thank you, and held the door for another customer on my way out.

I'd like to think it's what John would have done. He is truly the kindest man I know. We've been acquaintances for a number of years—he lives a few blocks from me in Oak Park, Illinois, an artsy, historic suburb (birthplace of Ernest Hemingway, we like to brag) just west of the Chicago city limits— and his unfailing magnanimity is well known in our community. But it wasn't until we had a discussion about his spirituality over lunch at a local Italian joint a few days before the tomato incident that I came to realize that being charitable is, for John, an act of faith. And it should be for me, too.

Most people know John as the dad—Martin Crane—on the television show *Frasier*, a role he played for eleven years, until the sitcom ended in 2004, and for which he won an Emmy. But he is also a Tony-award-winning stage actor, a member of Chicago's renowned Steppenwolf Theatre Company since 1979, who was leaving for London not long after we spoke to begin rehearsals for a six-month run in David Mamet's latest play, *Romance*. John also has appeared in a dozen films, including *Moonstruck* (he was the guy who had the drink thrown in his face by an angry date) and *Say Anything* . . . , in which he played Ione Skye's controlling father, the nemesis of John Cusack's iconic Lloyd Dobler.

Of course, those are just characters, and most aren't anything like the real John Mahoney. "I'm more spiritual than anything else, and Christianity is probably the most important facet of my life," he tells me, after returning from the salad bar with a small plate of vegetables and cottage cheese. "I try to live my life in a way that is definitely spiritually based. I pray a lot. It's the first thing I do when I get up in the morning, and it's the last thing I do before I go to bed. I have a little mantra that I say probably twenty or thirty times throughout the day: 'Dear God, please help me to treat everybody— including myself—with love, respect, and dignity.' That's why it's important for me to be liked.

"If people like me, it means I'm treating them well and it's sort of proof that I'm doing the right thing," he says, interrupting himself momentarily to thank the waitress when she brings his cup of chicken soup to the table and to ask her gently when my artichoke ravioli might be arriving. "I try to be charitable. I think that's the greatest virtue. I was always taught that it is the greatest virtue, and I feel that. I try to be very loving to people, and I try to be very patient with people, which is my biggest failing. I'm a very impatient person. I work constantly on that.

"I'm not sure who to pray to for that. I don't know who the patron saint of patience is," he says, laughing.

Later I did a little checking around and, surprisingly, there doesn't appear to be a patron saint of patience. But there are two patron saints of actors: Genesius and Vito. Both were martyred in 303—Genesius was beheaded and Vito boiled in oil. I suppose you could argue that both knew a little something about patience and long-suffering.

When John talks about the importance of being kind, his mind drifts back to a time well before he was an actor, a vocation he chose to pursue full-time at the age of thirty-seven. Born in Manchester, England, the sixth of eight children, John emigrated to the United States when he was nineteen, joining the Army for three years before becoming a citizen and enrolling in Quincy College, a Franciscan school in downstate Illinois. He worked his way through college as an orderly in a local hospital.

"I must have given a thousand enemas and catheterized a thousand people. I just think that somehow being around all that sickness and illness, yet seeing people's resilience and faith, I noticed that the people to emulate were the people who loved, and loved God, and loved their fellow man, and weren't selfish," he says.

"Charity is more important than telling the truth. I think sometimes the virtue is making sure you don't hurt anybody's feelings, as opposed to patting yourself on the back saying, 'Oh, well, I had to tell them the truth,'" he says, as he begins to tell the story of a patient who was in the last days of her battle with cancer. "She was in excruciating pain. She had gray hair but had always wanted to have red hair, so one day the nurses said, 'Would you like us to dye your hair for you?' When they finished, it looked kind of carroty, but she was thrilled that before she died she was going to have red hair. She just loved it."

But then, her daughter showed up at the hospital for a visit and threw a fit, telling her mother that her hair looked ridiculous and raising holy hell with the nurses for making her mother look like a clown. "One of the nurses said, 'Your mother's dying. That's what she wanted. Why are you so cruel? Why are you saying that to her?' And the daughter said, 'Well, I can't lie to her, can I?' Yes. She could have. It would have been much more charitable to say, 'Oh, how pretty!' even if you hated it. If I go to see a play and somebody's not very good in it, or it's not their best work, I would never tell them that. I mean, why? All you're doing is being proud. You're congratulating yourself for always being truthful." John's raspy voice sounds genuinely pained. "When they asked Jesus what the greatest virtue was, he said it was to love God with all your heart and soul and to love your neighbor as yourself. Sometimes to love your neighbor, you have to tell a lie. And I don't think there's anything wrong with that."

John's focus on kind living evolved over time. "I was very, very self-centered when I was young," he says. "I thought the world revolved around me. It even affected my work when I became an actor. I used to think about how great I had to be and how wonderful I had to be on that stage instead of honoring the playwright or honoring the screenwriter and becoming a part of something that was wonderful."

While he can't put an exact date on it, John believes his mind began to change when his heart did, around the time he had what he describes as an "epiphany" in a Roman Catholic church in downtown Chicago around 1975. "I was in the Loop, and I went into St. Peter's and went to Mass, and it was just about the most emotional thing that ever happened to me. I don't know where it came from, I just had a little breakdown of some sort, and after that, made a conscious effort to be a better person, to be a part of the world, and to try to revolve around everyone else in the world instead of expecting them to revolve around me.

"I think maybe it was the intercession of the Holy Ghost," he continues. "I've always prayed to the Holy Ghost for wisdom and for understanding and knowledge. I think he answered my prayers when I stopped in the church that day. My life was totally different from that day on. I saw myself as I was, and I saw into the future and saw what I wanted to be. And I sort of rededicated myself to God and begged him to make me a better person. It wasn't fear of hell or anything like that. I just somehow knew that to be like *this*, like what I was, wasn't the reason I was created. I had to be better. I had to be a better person. And I think I am now. I like myself," he says, breaking into one of his patented head-back-eyes-closed-mouth-open laughs.

"I'm pretty much in a spiritual state most of the time. Even when I'm out drinking with my friends, and even when I drink too much, God's never far from my thoughts. I'm not a freak, asking 'What would Jesus do?' and stuff like that. I don't think things like that. I don't pride myself on being able to do what he did anyway. We don't really know. I just try to live a good life."

Before John goes onstage each night, he says a prayer. "'Most glorious Blessed Spirit, I thank you for all the gifts and talents that you've given me.

Please help me to use all these gifts and talents to their fullest. And please accept this performance as a prayer of praise and thanks to you.' I always say that," he says, adding that occasionally it leads to special spiritual inspiration. "It's only happened to me about three times, where I was totally struck by divine intervention, where it was the most rewarding thing I had ever experienced, where I felt totally at one with the actors, with the playwright, and I couldn't do anything in that part that was not right. The way I crossed my legs, the way I folded my arms, whatever. I was just totally engulfed by the character. It was one of the most glorious feelings I've ever had, but I've only had it about three times."

The first time, he was playing a flamboyantly gay character in the play *Loose Ends*, directed by Austin Pendleton. John says he was doing it over the top, and Pendleton told him just to play it straight. "I started doing it the other way, and BOOM! That was it! There was an actual feeling that fused through me, where I just knew I was inspired. Truly inspired." Another occasion John was in what he might call the Holy Spirit Zone was when John Malkovich directed him in Harold Pinter's *No Man's Land*. (It was Malkovich who invited John to become a member of Steppenwolf in 1979, not long after Mahoney started acting professionally.)

"Once again I was too fussy and doing too much. And he told me, 'I want you to double through this, forget the pauses that are written. Just go—*vroom!*—right through it.' And I said, Okay, and I did. And about three-quarters of the way through, BOOM! I was suffused with inspiration, and it became a joy to do because everything was right."

We're finishing up lunch, and our conversation about faith is winding down. John hurries out for a couple of minutes to feed the meter where his car is parked a block away. When he returns, he's got something else he wants to tell me.

"I was just thinking how wrong it is to second-guess God. Everything I've ever wanted in my life, I got. Everything—except a wife and family," he says, with a hint of sadness in his eyes I'm not used to seeing. "But had I had a wife and children I probably would be dead by now."

He's not exaggerating. In the late 1980s, John was diagnosed with cancer. He says if he hadn't been so happy with his life as a full-time actor, he probably would not have had the will to fight the disease. He'd made the leap of faith several years before the diagnosis, when he left a job he hated as an editor in Chicago. "I was finally doing the one thing that I wanted to do. I was gloriously happy and joyful for the first time I can remember. I was just walking down the street, clicking my feet in the air, thinking, I'm a working actor in Chicago. I get paid for this and I love it!

"And then I got struck with cancer. I was determined, because my life was finally so great, that I didn't care. I was going to go ahead. I had a colon resection, and I'll tell you something that very few people outside my life know: I had a colostomy. I've had it for almost twenty years now. The doctors at the hospital said they were amazed at how fast I recovered. I was out of the hospital in a week, and the following week I was in Paris wrestling Harrison Ford under a table shooting a movie. I was so thankful for the life I had, and I've had almost twenty glorious years since that," he says. "I see that when the one thing came along that would finally fulfill me as a human being—acting—I was able to do it because I wasn't married with children. There would have been mortgages and tuitions and things like that, and I never would have been able to just throw away my job to get seventy-five dollars a week at Steppenwolf. I had to sell almost every piece of furniture I had. I was sleeping on the floor. Sold all my records, all my books. But I was so happy. I finally understood why God withheld a wife and children from me.

"I've achieved remarkable success, and I think it all goes back to my faith, especially after I became an actor and realized that was God's plan for me and surrendered myself to it joyfully," he says. "It enabled me to shrug off the disappointments because I figure the only reason I didn't get a part was that something better is awaiting me. Unless there was a plan for me, God would not have let me quit my job at thirty-seven to become an actor where at any given time 95 percent of the union members are out of work. So I might be disappointed I didn't get a part, but I'd think, Forget it. There must be something better up ahead. And there always was."

John Mahoney's God is a kind God. But that's not the God he knew as a child. "My original idea of God was an extremely vengeful, powerful God. Love never entered the equation," he says. "If I had children, what I would mostly want them to understand is exactly the opposite of what I was taught when I was a kid. I'd want them to know that they will always be forgiven, that they will always be loved, that they will always get a second chance, a third chance, a fourth chance, and a fifth chance and however many chances it takes. I would want them to know that, unless they are really, really vicious and mean and totally horrible, that they *are* going to heaven. They don't have to worry about a thing. God will always love them and forgive them. That's what I'd really want them to know," he says, smiling so warmly it brings tears to my eyes. I want to jump up and hug him.

"Yes, you make mistakes. And yes, you do things that you shouldn't do, but you will be forgiven, and you will be loved, and you won't be loved less. You will be loved just as much as you were before you made the mistakes."

Even if you squish the tomatoes. On purpose.

JULY 2005

JOHN PATRICK SHANLEY

Playwright

I have no beliefs. I have assumptions.

✳

BIRTH DATE: *October 13, 1950*

RAISED: *Roman Catholic*

NOW: *Nothing in particular*

ATTENDS: *Doesn't*

WORDS TO LIVE BY: *"There is a part of people that is wordless, and that is probably the most central part of their existence, their lifeline to the race, the planets, and the stars—and that is spirit. And it is beyond words."*

John Patrick Shanley is having a thirty-five-minute kind of a day.

He's seated at a long conference table, autographing a pile of hardbound copies of his play *Doubt*, for which he has recently won the 2005 Tony Award for Best Play and the Pulitzer Prize, with a royal blue felt-tip pen. His white T-shirt with a big red dot and black Japanese letters ("I have absolutely no idea," he tells me when I ask what they mean) is rumpled, his shock of silver hair is not. And he is wearing an expression that is somewhere between beleaguered and exasperated. "This is what my life has come to," he says, deadpan, as he inscribes the last script and closes its cover, his startlingly azure eyes flashing darkly, an indication that he is absolutely *not* having a good day. "I'm just . . . Oh, you don't even want to know," he mutters.

A few hours earlier he had called to change the venue for our meeting from his apartment in Brooklyn Heights to the offices of the Dramatists Guild in Times Square. "It's supposed to be ninety-three degrees today, and I don't have air-conditioning here—personal foible," he told my voice mail. I could practically hear him sweating. He has no air-conditioning at his Brooklyn apartment for the same reason he doesn't own a dishwasher: Because his mother—"an hysteric," he says—ran the washing machine and vacuum cleaner nonstop for most of his childhood and he can't stand the noise of anything motorized. So he sweats, but it's quiet. And quiet is what he could really use this day, which means he should probably be meditating rather than talking to me. But what can you do?

"If emotions get too loud, I have to meditate," he explains. "I should definitely meditate today. I don't know if I will or not—it's been months since I meditated—but this would be a hell of a good day to do it."

What, exactly, has brought on his current disquietude he never explicitly says. But here are some of the things on his mind on this biblically hot afternoon: The new play he is writing. The heat. Smells. The bombings of London's Underground. Catholic doctrine. Fundamentalists. His Arab neighbors. Tony Blair. Napoléon. The *New York Times* editorial page. His father's funeral. Terrorists. The Irish Christian Brothers. His sons. Gnosticism. And a lack of high-minded discourse.

"Usually I meditate because I am experiencing anxiety about different things. When I meditate I realize it's really none of those things. It usually means that there's something I need to do, something that needs to be addressed that I'm not addressing. And then when I meditate, I find out what that thing is," he says. "I close my eyes, I concentrate on my breathing. I sit in a comfortable chair and I hear a lot of noise. I think of the many things that I have to take care of, and I see them, and I let them go. I have all these thoughts and feelings and I let them go. I remember to concentrate on my breathing— it's amazing how many times you forget. I breathe in through my nose and out through my mouth. And this will go on until I finally get to a place where all the voices stop. There's usually one thing down there under everything else, powering all the voices, and it's the one thing I have to do or say out loud.

"I look at my watch before I start, and I can tell when I finish, by looking at my watch, what kind of shape I'm in by how long it takes me to touch down," he says. He looks at his watch. So, how long is a good time? "About ten minutes," he says. And a bad time? "Thirty-five minutes." How about today? "Oh, I think this would be thirty-five—easy."

Shanley probably needs to pray, too, which, he believes, is a different thing than meditating. "I have a great respect for prayer," he tells me, "because it works." How does he pray? I ask him. There is an extended, awkward pause as the playwright tries to decide how to answer me. "I don't have anything to say about that," he growls in his thick Bronx accent and then bursts out laughing. "That's . . . ya know . . . private."

Fair enough. There's not much Shanley holds close to the chest when it comes to religion or spirituality. His Pulitzer Prize–winning play *Doubt* dives right in, examining complicated issues of faith and belief, with equal parts dark humor and pathos. The ninety-minute play follows four characters—a priest, two nuns, and the mother of a young schoolboy—as they all confront the possibility that the priest is a sexual predator. The opening lines, delivered in perfect Bronx dialect by the Irish actor Brian F. O'Byrne, who plays the priest, Father Flynn, as he stands in embroidered liturgical robes on the steps of St. Nicholas Catholic Church's altar, are an apt synopsis of the play, and, perhaps, of what Shanley thinks of religion: "What do you do when you're not sure?"

Shanley doesn't give the audience an easy answer. In the play, which is set in the working-class Bronx in 1964, Sister Aloysius, the stony principal of St. Nicholas's school, played by Cherry Jones, believes Father Flynn has molested the school's only African-American student but can't prove it. When the curtain falls after ninety minutes, the audience (some of whom write to Shanley at the e-mail address he lists under his bio in the *Playbill*, thanking him, criticizing him, asking him things) leaves the theater with more questions than answers: Did the priest do it or not? How do you know what's true? Can you be faithful and have doubts at the same time? Do you trust your instincts or rely on facts alone? Is it better to impugn an innocent man than to risk harming an innocent child? What is innocence? What is redemption? What good is faith? Does religion have the answers? Does religion have any answers? The playwright leaves it up to someone else to decide.

"I guess because of things I see going on in the world, I would start by railing against what I don't like, which is, basically, all organized religions, because they all seem to have been created out of fear," Shanley replies when I ask how he might describe himself spiritually. "They are people huddled together against what they don't know and trying to tell themselves that they *do* know something. Religions are a shield against having an actual, personal experience of the divine. As soon as you try to nail down what your spiritual experience is, or capture it in language like a tiger in a cage, it begins to die and not be what it was. I believe that my experience really doesn't translate to anyone else's experience. You're born alone and you die alone and you have this relationship with the universe and it's yours and yours alone. At different times in my life I certainly have felt I could learn from other people's experiences or aphorisms. But the longer I live, the more I feel that it is the one area that is truly personal and is not extrapolatable to others. It's a natural human desire to learn from your fellows, but in this area, it seems to me the best guidance is to stay away from other people.

"I have no beliefs. I have assumptions. And I'd like to get rid of them, but you need a whole bunch of them just to get through the day. I've had all kinds of experiences. Are they explicable? No, they're not explicable. Have I experienced extraordinary events that can't be explained by rational Western thought? Yes, I have. Do I see in those events a special significance? No, I do not. Do I see that these are the things I can rely on to explain why I have some sort of spirituality? No. That's not why I have some degree of spirituality," he says, impressively interrogating himself. He's clearly on a tear I dare not interrupt. "Wisdom memorized is not wisdom anyway. You have to live your life and discover what is good and what is bad, what is right and what is wrong for you, within the context of your life.

"One of the reasons I'm curmudgeonly on this subject at the present time is that there just were the bombings in London. And these people, I am sure, have beliefs that are like the fiftieth Xerox of an experience someone had a thousand years ago. And I have no respect for that. We're living at a time when organized religions are really just not doing a good job. The Catholic Church with their kind of anti-revolution thing this week, and the Catholic Church with their don't-use-condoms-against-the-AIDS-epidemic-in-Africa thing, the Catholic Church and their continued justifications for forced celibacy made by men who have never had sex . . ."

While he has few kind words for any sort of organized religion, Shanley, the youngest of five siblings raised in a intensely Irish Catholic family, seems to save the most vitriol for his religion of origin. He and Catholicism have had a combative relationship, dating all the way back to grammar school.

His short biography in the *Playbill* for *Doubt* recounts part of the stormy history:

He was thrown out of St. Helena's kindergarten. He was banned from St. Anthony's hot lunch program for life. He was expelled from Cardinal Spellman High School. He was placed on academic probation by New York University and instructed to appear before a tribunal if he wished to return. When asked why he had been treated in this way by all these institutions, he burst into tears and said he had no idea.

Many of Shanley's dozens of plays, such as *Danny and the Deep Blue Sea* and *Italian American Reconciliation*, and screenplays, such as the 1987 Oscar-winning *Moonstruck*, feature deeply flawed Catholic characters whom he treats with unfailing candor and affection. "Everything has the potential to be constructive," he says of Catholicism. "But, ya know, the Catholic thing, I departed from that shortly after I hit puberty. It's very good when you're a child, but at a certain point you realize the schema doesn't really cover anything like what you're experiencing in life with the moral choices you have to make or the things you have to do or not do."

He admits, however, that when he told his Catholic Christian Brother teachers he didn't believe in God, it wasn't really true. "It was a provocation," he says. What was his earliest idea of what God was like? "I wasn't allowed to have it. I was told what it was before I even had the concept. I was not allowed to be the inventor of my mythology. I had a mythology foisted on me, and, from an early age, I was aware that I had to find it for myself, that I had to find everything out for myself. I had to find my own philosophy, I had to find my own connection to this world and this experience of life."

Clearly he had a hard time with many of the Catholics who tried formally to educate him. But what about his parents? What did he learn from them spiritually? "My father was a very religious man. He slept with rosary beads under his pillow. He went to Mass several times a week. And he *never* talked about it. I have so much respect for that," he says, with a laugh. "They have all these codified rules and regulations in the Catholic Church, and I know he didn't know what half of them were. He didn't bother his head about that. He had his talismans, his methods of focusing his meditation, and he used them to pray. I think I could make some pretty good guesses about what he prayed for, which would be fairly simple things having to do with his family, and that's it. That was the guy. He was a very simple, powerful person who had a direct connection to the earth, and I think that's what saved him.

"My mother ostensibly was religious. She was certainly raised Irish Catholic in Brooklyn. But she didn't have the same connection to anything," he says, drily. "My mother was extremely intelligent, but she was an hysteric, and I don't think she had a clue about her feelings."

Emotions ruled Shanley's world for most of his life. He lived in an "aquarium of emotion." He did everything by intuition alone. But as he entered middle age, that began to change. "The longer I go on, the more I have come to envision my emotions as being like children on a bus that I am driving," he says. "I think emotions are affected by spirit, and I think the analytical brain is affected by spirit, but I don't think spirit is either one of those things. Very often that is the big mistake I see being made—that spirituality is really emotionality in disguise.

"I don't think that emotions are the most evolved part of the person. There is a part of people that is wordless, and that is probably the most central part of their existence, their lifeline to the race, the planets, and the stars—and that is spirit. And it is beyond words." When does he feel closest to that spiritual part of himself? "Man, not lately. Not today."

Shanley is raising his sons, Frankie and Nicky, whom he adopted as newborns with his second wife in 1992, without any formal religious training. "Oh, God, no. No no no no," he says, when I ask if the boys are being reared Catholic. "They are being raised to be thinkers, to think, to ask questions. There is no sanctified area, but they're good boys. They're respectful. They have an innate decency—more than I did, certainly. I had to go out and reinvent the wheel because I had everything foisted on me, and so I went through periods of incredible depravity as a result of being in the wilderness.

"I'm finding it a difficult world to live in at this point because I'm not finding the kind of companionship that I need among my fellows, because I don't feel there is enough interesting conversation going on. I think that's because it's a highly emotional time. I need that toga thing," he says.

That *toga* thing? "When I was a boy, I read *Dialogues* of Plato. I was living in the Bronx, and I was like, *This is it*. These are the kinds of conversations I want to be having. There they are! I was, I don't know, fourteen or something. And I was so relieved to see that these conversations were had and were being had, probably, still. But I'm just not hearing those conversations. I'm not hearing anything like the Socratic method going on around anything. Everybody's all worked up about something, and I am, too."

A lot of us are pretty stressed out and scared, I say. "Yeah, well, I'm more warlike than that," Shanley retorts. "So I'm not afraid. I'm very pissed off. About a lot of things."

I hope this isn't one of those loathsome conversations—the *non*toga kind—that lately he's been having too many of, apparently. "Actually, by letting me rail, I feel a little better," he says, smiling and giving me a two-handed handshake as he heads south on Broadway into the teeming, cacophonous masses of Times Square tourists, in search of some quiet and peace of mind.

A few weeks later, I e-mail him to find out if he ended up meditating that day and, if he did, whether he managed to come in under thirty-five minutes.

"Our conversation *was* my meditation that day," Shanley replies. "It lasted about sixty minutes and made me feel a whole lot better."

JULY 2005

THE REVEREND AL SHARPTON

Activist

"Jesus" is the password.

✳

BIRTH DATE: *October 3, 1954*
RAISED: *Pentecostal Christian, specifically Church of God in Christ*
NOW: *Baptist Christian*
ATTENDS: *Bethany Baptist Church in Brooklyn, New York*
WORDS TO LIVE BY: *"The goal in life is to seek holiness. Very few actually achieve it, but I think that's the goal."*

At the age of four, before he had learned how to read or write, Al Sharpton preached his first sermon. When he was nine years old, he went on the road with the great gospel singer Mahalia Jackson as "The Wonder Boy Preacher." And by the time he was ten, he was an ordained minister in the Church of God in Christ. There is scarcely a time Sharpton can recall when he wasn't a Christian, or a Sunday in close to fifty years that he didn't stand in the pulpit of a church—somewhere—and preach the Gospel.

"I'm the most myself when I'm in the pulpit—most fulfilled, most natural, most who I am," he says one morning in the dining room of the Regency Hotel on New York City's Park Avenue. It's a power-breakfast kind of place. In fact, the hotel claims to have coined the term "power breakfast." On this particular morning, various politicos and power brokers are strategizing over their bowls of oatmeal and berries. Sharpton's a regular here (he lives a few blocks away), and the hostess, who calls him simply Sharpton—as in "Hey, Sharpton, there's a reporter waiting for you at your table!"—escorts him to his regular spot, a large booth against one wall from which he can survey the entire restaurant.

The minister-activist-politician, who is dressed in an impeccably tailored charcoal gray suit and a shirt with monogrammed French cuffs, stops to gladhand a few similarly attired men on his way to and from the table, and a few others stop by during his breakfast of two eggs over easy (no toast, no potatoes) to say hello, thank him for his support, or ask for a favor.

"I'm a very spiritual person, a very religious person. I would venture to say that my religious convictions are the core Al Sharpton. That's who I start as. I approach my public life, be it my activism or my political involvements or social policy involvements, based on my religious convictions."

Despite an unsuccessful yet high-profile bid for the presidency in 2004 and the accompanying makeover that left him looking every inch the elder statesman, Sharpton still is perhaps best known for the garish track suits and James Brownesque pompadour he wore for years. He's probably better remembered for championing the racially charged case of Tawana Brawley, a fifteen-year-old black girl from a small town near Poughkeepsie, New York, who in 1987 claimed she had been raped by six white men, than for his rousing speech at the 2004 Democratic National Convention. But none of that, he insists, represents the real him, the soul of the man. "My first calling has been preaching, and throughout my career—including when I ran for president—I would always preach in a church or two on Sunday. That's just me," he says plainly, not boastfully, as if stating a simple fact, like his height or his shoe size. "If I had two hours to live, I would find a small storefront church with about twenty people and preach. That's just who I am."

Some of his earliest memories are of church. The Sharpton family joined Washington Temple Church of God in Christ, a Pentecostal church in Brooklyn led by the charismatic pastor Bishop Frederick Douglas Washington, when he was three. Young Alfred Jr. joined the junior ushers' board, a group of children who would help people to their seats and hand out bulletins in the sanctuary. On the one-year anniversary of the junior ushers' board formation, the children were asked to put on a special program to celebrate.

"They asked the kids what they wanted to do," Sharpton recalls. "Ronnie Dyson, who wound up being a pretty big singer in the seventies—he was in

Hair and sang 'Aquarius'—he was in the church with me and was about a year older than me, about five. Ronnie wanted to read a poem. My sister wanted to sing. I said I wanted to preach—I don't know why. I used to go home after church on Sundays and put on my mother's bathrobe, and I would repreach the sermon that the bishop had preached that Sunday, almost verbatim, to my sister's dolls. That was my first congregation, really, my sister's dolls. And they were probably the most cooperative audience I've ever had. They never complained," Sharpton says, laughter and a bit of happy nostalgia interrupting his otherwise sober demeanor for a few moments.

"Anyway, so I said I wanted to preach, and all the other kids laughed. But the adult adviser—Hazel Griffin was her name—said, 'Don't laugh. Bishop Washington started preaching as a kid. Maybe he's been called to preach, too.' And she brought me up to see Bishop Washington, and he encouraged me, and I preached at the anniversary. There were about nine hundred people there." The scripture for his first sermon was taken from the Gospel of St. John, fourteenth chapter, first verse: "Let not your heart be troubled. Ye who believe in God, believe also in me."

"I talked about how there is no reason to be troubled in this world and to have your faith in God. The general theme was that we're troubled about more than we should be if we really have faith. Of course, that advice took on new life as I got older. It was easy for a four-year-old kid to say that," Sharpton says, laughing again. "It became a little more difficult at fourteen or twenty-four or forty-four. But it was cute at four. It was more confessional at forty-four."

In 1964, right around the time he was ordained a minister while still in grammar school, life turned immensely more complicated when Sharpton's parents split up and he moved with his mother, Ada, from the relative comfort of working-class Hollis, Queens, where his father was a successful contractor who bought a new Cadillac every year, to the housing projects of Brooklyn. While he doesn't discuss the details of his parents' divorce on this day, he has talked about the painful episode at length in the past. His father, Alfred Sr., had an affair with Sharpton's eighteen-year-old half sister (Ada Sharpton's daughter from a previous relationship), ended up getting her pregnant, and then took off, casting the rest of the family into poverty.

"I ended up going deeper in my faith. Church was my only life. I was at church almost every day. I did a lot of reading the Bible, and I preached a lot, because it helped with income for the family. Whatever free-will offering I got when I preached I gave to my mother to add to her welfare check," he says. "I think it made faith even deeper for me. Ironically, my other sister, who was three years older than me, it had the opposite effect on her. She rebelled and didn't believe anything anymore."

In the Pentecostal tradition, people become "born again" when they realize their sinful ways, repent, and give their lives back to Christ. But Sharpton was only three when he joined the church, well before what, in theological terms, is known as the "age of accountability," when a child has the self-consciousness to realize the difference between right and wrong and, therefore, the ability to sin. So Sharpton started preaching sermons to help save souls before he "got saved" himself?

"Exactly," he says, "which is why, as you grow older, you go through re-conversion experiences. At three, when I joined the church, there was no real accountability to have, but when I became a teenager—maybe not as much as others did because I was in the church and everybody knew me as a preacher—but I did go through life's challenges and temptations. And then, as I got older, I continued the cycle. I've seen a lot of people who grow up in the church and become rebellious of having done so, and who then become almost irredeemably wayward. That never happened to me. I went through challenges and changes, but I was never shaken at all in my faith and in my beliefs.

"I was a teenager in the sixties and seventies, and a lot of things changed for me. Culturally there was the whole hippie movement and, at the time, the pot movement. You reach puberty, and you've got girlfriends and all of that. That was a challenge. I never smoked pot, but all of my friends did. I wanted to date like everybody else, and I did. So I think that became the challenge for me in my teen years," he says.

So sexuality or, as the Baptists might say, "sexual sin," was his stumbling block? "Sexuality and all the forces of my peers," he says. "One reason I don't think I ever got into pot and drugs and all of that is because at that age I also joined the civil rights movement. So all of my peers were activists. Going out for us was picketing the A&P or sitting up discussing whether the Black Panther Party or Operation Breadbasket was the best route to take. That's what we did. The seventies was a time of real social revolution, so the scene wasn't the discos and clubs of today. They might have existed, but they didn't attract us."

When he was about twelve, Sharpton met the Reverend Jesse Jackson and quickly became the New York City youth leader for Jackson's Operation Breadbasket, an organization dedicated to improving economic conditions in the black community that distributed food to the poor in a dozen cities. Jackson and Sharpton have been great friends—and some might say rivals—ever since. Sharpton refers to Jackson, who is thirteen years his senior, as one of his chief mentors. Around the time he met Jackson, Sharpton also met the man he now calls his father, the musician James Brown. He says Brown's son was involved in the youth group he was running, and the two teenagers became friends. When Brown's son was killed in a car accident, "James Brown kind of adopted me, because he knew his son and I were close," Sharpton says.

Brown took Sharpton on tour with him as a kind of gofer, but the young preacher eventually became his road manager, a position he held from 1973 to 1980. "Brown became like a father figure to me who insisted I live the life of a monk, let alone a minister," says Sharpton, who in 1980 married Kathy Lee Jordan, one of Brown's backup singers. The couple has two teenage daughters.

"If I was on the road with Brown, I had to stay in the hotel he stayed in, stay in my room, and he would almost select my girlfriends. He was very adamant that he had promised my mother that I would not go wayward on the road, and he enforced it. So even though I knew the entertainment world, I was not *of* the entertainment world—and not by any choice of my own. He promised my mother that he'd make sure I was never on drugs, that I never lost my head, and that he'd take care of me himself. And he did."

What is sin? "Sin to me is the conscious disobeying of what you know to be God's will," Sharpton answers without hesitation. "Knowing something is against the will of God and doing it anyway is a sin. I don't think unknowing trespasses are sin, even though the acts might be sinful." Can ego, then, be a sin? "Absolutely, because you are putting yourself and your personal needs in front of what you know to be God's will and, in some cases, in front of God himself, depending on how far your ego takes you."

How is it possible, then, to lead a holy life? "It's very difficult. You know the old Southern Baptist song? 'If I never reach perfection, Lord, you know I've tried, I tried.' I think the goal in life is to seek holiness. Very few actually achieve it, but I think that's the goal. The challenge in life is to seek that in everything you do. And you grow in stages."

Holiness is kind of like greatness, Sharpton explains, launching into an anecdote about Muhammad Ali and Ludwig van Beethoven that would fit perfectly into a sermon. "When I was a kid in the seventies, I used to run around with Ali every time he was in town. Because I was well known in the civil rights movement, I got to know him. One day, I was somewhere with him, and I said to Ali, 'You always say you are the greatest. What made you great?' And he said, 'I'll tell you the truth, Sharpton, I wasn't great when I beat Sonny Liston for the first time in '64. I said I was the greatest, but I hadn't reached greatness yet. I wasn't even great yet when I won again in '74 after three years being out of the ring protesting the Vietnam War. When I became great is when Ken Norton—an unknown guy—broke my jaw. Everyone, all the fans, turned to jeering me, and somehow I found the strength to fight on anyhow. Greatness is when you overcome adversity.'

"A composer like Beethoven became great when his works were distinguished as different from any others," Sharpton continues. "But when he got to a different level of greatness, even different from what Ali told me, it was when he lost his hearing and he wrote the Ninth Symphony and he couldn't even hear it. When he performed the Ninth Symphony, he couldn't hear the cheers of the crowd. At the end of the performance, they had to turn him around to see the crowd's reaction.

"At some level, I think greatness is when it doesn't matter anymore what anyone's reaction is. It's when you work out your own soul's salvation. That's the level we have to reach in our own spiritual life, when it is totally oblivious to work and ego. I used to say that I fought for many victims of racial violence or racism, discrimination or sexism or police brutality, and they never thanked me. An old minister said to me one time, 'If you're still at the level that you need gratitude, then you haven't prayed enough yet.' And he's right. You've gotta fight yourself until you get beyond the need for adulation and applause if you're really doing this because it's your ministry and your work. And that's all growth. And it doesn't go by age, it doesn't go by time, it goes by who you are and how far you grow spiritually."

Is he there yet, at that egoless level of greatness? "No," he says, smiling. "I'm better than I was, but I'm not where I need to be." He prays a lot, so, at least according to that old minister, he's on the right track. "Before I go to bed at night, I get down on my knees and pray. I get up in the morning, and I may pray lying in bed. I pray walking, riding, it doesn't matter where. Prayer to me is an incessant conversation with God, all the time. The more you live and develop a prayer life, you pray about different things. I don't just pray, 'God, I want this situation to go through,' or 'I need this deal.' You pray for people. I might walk down the street and see somebody crippled and pray for them. Like that. I'm in constant prayer. I believe God answers prayer, God answers prayer based on his own decision and also on the purity of the request and, sometimes, on his mercy for the one who makes the request. I believe that."

Beliefs can be tricky, especially when you're a politician. Sharpton isn't shy about calling himself a Christian or talking very personally about Jesus Christ. "Jesus is the lens in which we see God," he says. "I absolutely believe Jesus existed, and I believe the constant conversation with him is our way in. It's sort of like if you have a computer. It could be the finest, most up-to-date computer in the world, but if you don't know the code, you can't get it to work. You gotta know the password. And I think 'Jesus' is the password."

Much to the chagrin of politically conservative Christians who also believe they know the password, Sharpton is equally forthright talking about his spiritual conviction that women should have the right to have an abortion and homosexuals should be allowed to marry legally, even if he doesn't personally agree with abortion or homosexuality from a moral or scriptural standpoint. During his presidential campaign, Sharpton went toe-to-toe on more than one occasion with conservative Christians who questioned how he could call himself a Christian—an ordained minister no less—and be pro-choice or pro-gay.

"The most passionate arguments I get are from other Christians, because if you get a true believer who disagrees with you, they are really passionate and just can't understand how someone can be a minister and a true Christian and disagree with them," he says. "I have certain convictions, and certain things that I don't agree with personally. But I also don't believe I have the right to impose them on anyone. Part of my problem with the conservatives is that I might not even disagree with some of what they say, but I do disagree that we have the right to make that into social policy. That's where I draw the line."

That line, in Sharpton's eyes, is a decidedly spiritual one. It's about Jesus, free will, redemption, and grace. "The whole spirit of condemnation is troubling," he says. "Jesus met the woman at the well to save her, not to condemn her. And they are condemning people and trying to enforce it with laws, which takes away free will, and which is also, by the way, not converting people. At all. If I behave because I have to, or because if I don't I'm going to jail or I'm going to be penalized, that's not something that gives me access to the gates of heaven. I don't think you ever get there out of fear. You may submit out of fear, but you don't ever get to grace and love out of fear. When the woman was caught in adultery, the tradition, the law, was to stone her. Jesus stopped the stoning. Jesus stopped the stoning and gave the woman an alternative in life. She chose to stop, but she couldn't have made that choice if they had stoned her to death."

Sharpton admits his greatest spiritual struggle is with, simply, himself. "I'm just trying to be better, trying to be more, a growing Christian, and trying to get beyond the temptations of vanity and ego," he says. "The more you submit to what your calling is and give the glory to God, the more perfect your work will be."

And, while he might never reach perfection, as the song goes, he's trying. Lord, he's trying.

JUNE 2005

ANNIE LENNOX

Singer-Songwriter

I'm on my own journey.

✳

BIRTH DATE: *December 25, 1954*
RAISED: *No religion*
NOW: *"Seeker"*
ATTENDS: *Doesn't*
WORDS TO LIVE BY: *"Ask yourself, 'Is this kind? Am I being kind?'"*

The final track on Annie Lennox's 2003 album, *Bare*, is a plaintive, haunting song with a perplexing title: "Oh God (Prayer)."

"Where are you now?" Lennox asks the deity. "If there was ever a soul to save, it must be me."

Strange sentiments from someone who doesn't really believe in God.

"The word *God* always troubles me," says Lennox, the singer-songwriter and half of the band Eurythmics. "The word has so many connotations and, for me, quite negative ones quite often. Very often it connects with something organized and something fundamentalist, and that bothers me. There's something even Victorian about it, you know? But if I really have to own up to the word, the best use of it is like this: If we look into the world of nature, it has a life force. So if you say God is a word to describe the life force that has created all, and creates and maintains the energy, the source of all living things, I'll go with that."

Curled up with a bottle of water on the settee of her suite at a Philadelphia hotel, Lennox is on the first day of a four-week break from a summer tour with Sting, and she's relaxed, bright-eyed, smiling.

She doesn't buy into what she says is the popular idea of a judgmental, wrathful God. "For me, brimstone and hellfire is unacceptable. I can't accept it. I won't accept it," she declares. "If there is a God, let's say, an intervening—not interfering—an intervening, benign, compassionate being somehow that intervenes with our hellish experiences, then surely he wouldn't be backing up the preachers who are going, 'YOU ARE GOING TO ROT IN HELL-FIRE!'

"I think God would be going, 'Let's go and calm down. Take it easy. You don't need to be making people afraid like this.'"

So what did she have in mind when she wrote that song?

"It came from a place of deep despair and anguish," she says. "It was just this little tiny voice. At times you can be in a hellish place, and they talk about prayer. I don't know if my prayers have ever been answered.

"Sometimes, you know, in despair, people who are nonbelievers think, you know, if only you could have an answer, if only the 'hand of God' would intervene and immediately pull you out of your hell. I don't know. I have no experience of that."

Still, the song is a real prayer.

"It's a prayer for nonbelievers. It's an unanswered prayer. But the little hope is that the answer might come."

Lennox dwells in paradox. It's her home turf, the place she's most used to, she says.

"Maybe now you have more a sense of who I am. And you're probably thinking, 'Quite complicated,'" she says with a velvety Scots accent as she smiles easily, as if to say, *And you're absolutely right.*

"I've always said that opposites coexist. Beauty with great sadness. I love the yin-yang symbol. This black shape nestled against the white one, and together they create this whole."

When asked to describe herself spiritually, she says, simply, "Confused." It's not a glib answer. In the days leading up to an interview about her spiritual life, she thought a lot about it.

"I haven't anything conclusive to say to you about the subject," she says, smiling again. "But that is my state. My state is seeking, and I haven't yet come to an arrival point. And it's a little late, because time is running out, and if I don't come to an arrival point soon, I'm leaving the planet and I will not have understood anything. But I will have had a hell of an experience on the way."

Confused. Complicated. Searching. Unanswered and unfinished. Such is Lennox's spirituality.

Born in Aberdeen, Scotland, on Christmas Day 1954, the singer has always considered herself an outsider.

"I'm an only child, so that kind of facilitated that sense. So, looking back on the last almost fifty years now, my journey has been to try to define self. Because, although I am a woman and an artist and female and a singer and a mother and a this and a that, still, who am I? It's the question. It's the basic philosophical, spiritual question. What am I? What am I doing here?

"I've looked into various groups, books, organized religions, and I've never easily identified with groups. This is why I said to you I'm from the outside. This hesitancy of mine to belong to one thing or another, to strongly identify with one group or another, has possibly held me back in my quest to find the answer to that question."

Lennox was not brought up with any religion, although she did occasionally attend Sunday school at a Church of Scotland parish. It was the thing to do socially at the time, she says. "At the school I went to, the year was defined by the Christian traditional festivals. So, you know, Christmas, Easter, all the usual things. But I had difficulty connecting with religion. It just didn't speak to me at all. Christian religion has never spoken to me. That's how it is. It's not wrong, it's not right. It's how it is. It's how I am," she says. "I've never sat well with it."

What she has sat well with is music. It's one of the ways she's tried to answer the existential questions that continue to occupy her. "My mother used to say that I would sing myself to sleep in the cradle," she says. "It's been a way to explain the question to myself, to explain it to other people. If I were to define what I do as an artist, that's what I do. I connect with people in an emotional, spiritual, intellectual sense through the vehicle of music, through the word and the sound . . . It sounds ridiculous, but there's an element of something shamanistic in it."

As a child, Lennox played piano and flute, eventually earning a scholarship at the age of seventeen to the prestigious Royal Academy of Music. But she didn't quite fit in there, as her love of Motown-style music conflicted with the restrictive classical training. She left and, while she was waiting tables in London in her early twenties, met the musician Dave Stewart, with whom she would eventually form Eurythmics.

Lennox and Stewart shared a sense of otherness, of being outsiders, she says. "I started to explore that, really, when I met Dave," she says. "It was like, Well, who are we, then? Because we understood each other, we understood that we both felt like outsiders and that we had something to say about that, musically. And that was our vehicle, that was our raison d'être. Oh, well, if we're not that, we're this. So let's be renegades, and let's create something outside of that, that we belong to."

She's a nonconformist artistically, socially, and spiritually, she'll readily admit. It's not some kind of political statement. It's just her way.

As part of Eurythmics, she cultivated a trademark androgynous style—nearly buzz-cut hair, severe makeup, and men's suits—that bent gender stereotypes. One often repeated story says that, back in those days, MTV executives asked her to produce her birth certificate to prove she was a female.

Lennox's style has morphed and softened over the years. On this particular afternoon, she's dressed casually in a tank top and Army green slacks, her hair is short and blond, and she doesn't appear to be wearing a stitch of makeup. Her manner is at once warm, gentle, and intense.

Eurythmics melded rock 'n' roll, rhythm and blues, and New Wave sounds. Their lyrics were often ethereal but sometimes decidedly not. The duo went their separate ways in 1989, reuniting in 1999 for an album called *Peace* and a tour benefiting Amnesty International and Greenpeace. In the intervening years, Lennox has released several solo albums, winning a number of awards for her solo work, including an Oscar, a Golden Globe, and a couple of Grammys.

One of Eurythmics's earliest hits, 1983's "Sweet Dreams (Are Made of This)," may describe aptly Lennox's own existential journey twenty years later.

I travel the world and the seven seas, everybody's looking for something . . .

"Things are never what they seem when you start on this journey of looking for the answers and the clues," Lennox says. "The world is full of contradiction. It's full of saintly sinners or sinners who are saints. You know?

Looking around, I've explored things, and I've seen, you know, that many so-called spiritual teachers are absolute blackguards in every respect, and I find it appalling. But it is what it is."

Lennox eschews labels. And there isn't one that accurately describes her spiritually anyway.

The closest might be Buddhist. She's studied Buddhism and says it has helped her try to quiet her hyperactive mind. "I'm sort of in Dante's Inferno in my head."

While she has been fascinated by Eastern thought and metaphysics since she was a teenager roaming the bookstalls of Aberdeen, one traumatic event helped focus her attention on her most elemental spiritual questions.

"To be frank with you, my biggest turning point—and it's very, very personal—was losing my first child," she says, speaking of her son, Daniel, who was stillborn in 1988. "That was an extraordinary turning point because all of a sudden I had a huge aha moment. It was like, Oh, you're not in the driver's seat. Life—you have to bow down to it. For all your dreams and aspirations, actually, anything can happen. The flickering candle that can go out in any moment is life."

Lennox, who lives in England, now has two adolescent daughters—Lola and Tali. Their father is Lennox's second husband, the Israeli filmmaker Uri Fruchtmann, from whom she has recently split. (She also was briefly married to a German Hare Krishna devotee in the mid-eighties.)

The singer is not rearing her children in any particular religious tradition. "I felt from my own experience that if you try to force an issue with children and make them believe some dogmatic view, they will either rebel or they will conform to it. And I don't agree with that," she says. "I think you are on this planet to find out for yourself. To taste it and see, you know? And that doesn't mean to say that I'm irresponsible about it or that I'm laissez-faire in some way, or that the issue isn't important. I believe you teach your children through your own example, good and bad."

The spiritual figure she most respects is the Dalai Lama, whom she's met on several occasions, including a private meeting in the late 1990s in Dharamsala, India. Lennox says she wanted to ask him personally if there was anything she could do to help Tibetan causes.

"He's someone you instantly feel you want to do everything for," she says. "He's the one person on the planet that I've met—and it sounds so facile and trite because everybody quotes the Dalai Lama—but there is something authentic. It's his authenticity as a human being as well as a spiritual teacher and the extraordinarily powerful noble diplomat."

Something the Dalai Lama teaches is an ethic by which she tries to live her life. "He says, 'If you have compassion, if you have kindness, basic human kindness, then maybe you're on the right track.' And I just find that so direct and simple and easy to understand. So you can ask yourself, 'Is this kind? Am I being kind? What am I being here?'"

In December 2003, Lennox, long active in social justice and human rights issues, traveled to South Africa, where she performed with Dave Stewart at an AIDS benefit concert in honor of Nelson Mandela, the man she refers to with awe as "the other one, the other great sage."

"We spent time there looking at the AIDS genocide, which is so appalling and so disgraceful," she says. "There's such a fuss being made over all kinds of things here, and yet when it comes to Africa, it's just decimated in every way, shape, and form. I do know that, in the not-too-distant future, I'll be given something to do there. I have to. It's essential."

While music will always be a significant part of her life, Lennox feels a yearning, perhaps a calling, even, to do something more.

"I haven't been involved enough," she says, a look of grief momentarily darkening her eyes and erasing the smile from her face. "In my heart, I believe I'm an activist of some description. I'm trying to build a platform to try to make myself more effective in the long run. And I will do it. It's my dream."

In the meantime, Lennox is pursuing peace—of mind and spirit. And she's not dismissing the notion that, after a lifetime of being an outsider, she might someday be ready to belong somewhere religiously.

"Part of me hankers after it," she says. "There's something in me that would like to have an arrival point. Now, whether that's me joining up and signing on the dotted line as some kind of practitioner, maybe it is. I often envy people who can do that."

Lennox is fairly certain of one thing: She's still searching for something.

"You've asked me these questions, and I put up my hands and say, 'Yes, I'm a very confused person,'" she says, without the slightest edge or hint of frustration in her voice.

"There's no point in following me. If anyone had thought I had any so-lutions to anything, ever, I don't. Because I'm busy asking the questions my-self," she says. "I'm on my own journey here, and it isn't a clearly defined one. But it is what it is."

JULY 2004

SEAMUS HEANEY

Poet, Nobel Laureate

BIRTH DATE: *April 13, 1939*
RAISED: *Roman Catholic*

M y husband and I fell in love reading Seamus Heaney poetry aloud to each other. "Oysters." "The Otter." "A Drink of Water." "The Haw Lantern." The divine artistry of the poet's words, at once earthy and transcendent, dripped off our tongues. They were sexy. And sacred. We opened our wedding invitation with a verse from "Station Island."

In 1995, the Swedish Academy awarded Heaney the Nobel Prize in Literature, declaring his poems to be works of "lyrical beauty and ethical depth, which exalt everyday miracles and the living past." Amen. Whether he's writing about the sectarian Troubles in Northern Ireland, farming, or the contours of a lover's body, Heaney's poetry elevates my soul. Which is why, if there was one person I wanted to interview for this book, it was Seamus Heaney.

I wrote him a gushing letter. And he responded posthaste by fax from Dublin. I'm sorry, he said, with the kind of charming self-deprecation that

the Irish have mastered, I have to decline. His own spirituality, he confessed, is an arena in which he feels woefully inarticulate.

Instead, bless him, he offered the most marvelous of consolation prizes:

A FOUND POEM

Like everybody else, I bowed my head
during the consecration of the bread and wine,
lifted my eyes to the raised host and raised chalice,
believed (whatever it means) that a change occurred.

I went to the altar rails and received the mystery
on my tongue, returned to my place, shut my eyes fast, made
an act of thanksgiving, opened my eyes and felt
time starting up again.

        There was never a scene
when I had it out with myself or with an other.
The loss of faith occurred off stage. Yet I cannot
disrespect words like "thanksgiving" or "host"
or even "communion wafer." They have an undying
pallor and draw, like well water far down.

2005

JONATHAN SAFRAN FOER

Writer

Belief is like a muscle.

✳

BIRTH DATE: *February 21, 1977*
RAISED: *Jewish*
NOW: *"Not particularly practicing" Jewish*
ATTENDS: *Only High Holy Day services at synagogue with his family*
WORDS TO LIVE BY: *"When something is hard, it doesn't mean that something is wrong."*

T he little girl at the table behind him has a blue tongue. Her lips, also, are bright blue—New York Mets blue—and so is part of her chin, several fingers on her right hand, and the small mountain of cotton-candy-flavored ice cream she's digging into. Conversely, Jonathan Safran Foer's tongue is a regular, fleshy color, and the cup of espresso ice cream that is slowly turning to soup in front of him after he's taken a few disinterested bites, is beige. "I really didn't want it," he says. "I just wanted something cold."

We were to have met at the Grand Canyon, a diner a block away from the ice cream parlor near his home in Park Slope, Brooklyn, but Foer, the celebrated young author, called about an hour before our appointment to say he had scouted out the diner and it was too crowded and noisy. In fact, there were only a couple of customers at the Grand Canyon when I arrived out front to meet him, and it was practically library quiet. Our new rendezvous locale, Maggie Moo's Ice Cream and Treatery, by contrast, was about as peaceful as a five-year-old's birthday party. Kids all hopped up on frozen goodness and overstimulated by the circus-colored interior, darted from table to table, parents shouting after them to sit down before they got ice cream all over themselves. (Too late.) The milk shake machine whirred intermittently, the jangling front door banging open and shut as a wailing chorus of "I WANT CHOCOLATE!" and "I DON'T LIKE CHERRIES!" filled the room.

But this is where Foer wants to be—for reasons I don't think he really understands himself—to talk about spirituality. "God is kind of like ice cream," he says as we walk in and proceeds to posit something about neither one being particularly good for you. Sometimes you just get a craving.

Actually, we are here precisely *not* to talk about God. At least that's what we had agreed upon, more or less, before meeting. "I don't believe in God. Or I don't think so," Foer had said in an e-mail a few days earlier. "Which precludes conversations that lead from that question. Or maybe not."

We choose a table in the back of the parlor, where he thinks it'll be quieter. There is a large yellow stuffed-animal duck on one of the three chairs around the table. "The duck will save our seats," Foer says as he heads toward the counter to place his order.

"THEY TOOK OUR TABLE!" a pigtailed girl howls a few seconds later.

"Oh, were you saving these seats?" Foer, a bit cowed, asks the exasperated-looking mother.

"Didn't you see the duck?" she says.

We move to a small table in the front window, Foer ambivalently fetches his ice cream, and we start our conversation *not* about God. "Nobody would ever ask me about religion or God. It's an entirely taboo subject," he says. "It would be like asking a woman who is three months pregnant if she's pregnant. You think you might have reasons for asking, but it would be completely inappropriate to ask." Foer's wife, the novelist Nicole Krauss, whom he married in 2004, is, in fact, expecting their first child, he tells me. At the time of our conversation, she's about four months pregnant.

"I was talking about this with my wife and explaining your project and some of the questions you might ask." (If you believe in God, what do you think God is like? What does God require of you, of any of us? What do you wish you knew spiritually that you don't already? What are you searching for? What have you found so far?)

"She was saying, 'Well, God! What would you say to some of those?'" he continues. "And it struck me, because they are some of the most basic, big-themed questions that there could be, and she's the person who knows me best in the world, but she wouldn't have known my answers. In large part that's because I wouldn't have known my answers right off the bat.

"I don't know why that is. I bet you it's easier for someone who really believes to have answers to questions than for someone who doesn't necessarily believe. Believing gives you confidence. Not believing doesn't give you confidence."

A lot of people might expect Foer to exude confidence. By the age of twenty-eight he has published two novels—*Everything Is Illuminated* (2002) and *Extremely Loud and Incredibly Close* (2005)—both critical and commercial successes. His first novel has been released in more than two dozen countries and has been made into a movie, directed by Liev Schreiber and starring Elijah Wood. The foreign rights to his second novel have been sold in at least a dozen countries and the film rights to Scott Rudin, producer of films such as *The Life Aquatic*, *The Village*, and *Orange County*. But there is no swagger to Foer; his demeanor is unassuming and thoughtful. He thinks out loud, but he also thinks before he talks. Raised Jewish in Washington, D.C., in a family just religious enough to attend synagogue services on High Holy Days and to send him to Hebrew school once a week, he is in the midst of editing two new books. One is a collection about animal suffering and human responsibility, the other a modern Haggadah—the text used during Passover Seders that recounts the biblical story of the Exodus of the Jews from Egypt. He also has started writing a new novel. ("It's terrible. I mean, really awful," he says. I don't believe him.)

He's about to become a father. And he's got more questions than answers.

"I'm somebody who, as a Democrat and at least an agnostic (I'm probably just an atheist), doesn't feel good about not having straight answers. That's how I think the world works—straight answers," he says. "Where I live and the kinds of people I know, God is a subject that never comes up in conversation. In part I think it's taken for granted that you wouldn't believe in God. That's not to say that nobody I know believes in God. It's just taken for granted that they wouldn't because a belief in God is unreasonable, it's illogical. It's very much against the grain of the ways in which we were educated and the ways in which we've organized our lives. We don't expect someone else to pay our electricity bill for us. We know that if we want to continue to have electricity in our apartments, we pay the bill. It's the same with everything else: The world follows rules that make sense. Why would we make one grand exception for the biggest question when everything else we do abides by logic?

"Right now I think it's easier than ever not to believe in God because there are so many negative role models of people who do believe in God. How many of the problems in the world right now can be traced to people believing in God? I know that on the other side of the coin is: How many of the good things in the world are traced to believing in God? I am not so sure the good things have to do with God anymore. And it's not that the bad things do either, really, at the end of the day. But at least the bad things are more explicitly done in the name of God than the good things are," he says.

"I don't believe in God. I don't think my parents believe in God. My grandparents were maybe a little closer to believing in God. But at some point, someone in my family believed in God, and this Jewish set of values supposedly organized around that belief got handed down. It's like how they say that when the sun dies it continues to heat the earth for ten minutes. Even though I don't believe all of the values that were set forth, they reached me and informed my life. But I don't think that has anything to do with God."

But that depends on how you define God. "There is a way of describing God so that I believe in God," Foer concedes. "I just think it's not the way most people would talk about God."

Try me, I say.

"I remember when I was a kid I would ask my dad constantly, 'Do you believe in God? Do you believe in God?' I was obsessed with it. I went to Hebrew school once a week, where we did talk about it. Once when I was in nursery school, before I started kindergarten, we were in the car and I asked my father about it. I said, 'In Hebrew school they teach us that God is everywhere. Is that true?' And he said, 'If you believe in God, that God exists like a being in the Torah, then God is everywhere.' And I said, 'Does that mean that God is in the car with us right now?' And he said yes. I said, 'Is God in my closet?' He said yes. 'Is God in the dirty clothes hamper?' Yes. 'Is God in my penis?' Yes. 'Is God in my butthole?' Yes. I was raised to ask questions like that, the funny ways when you draw logic to its end. In any case, I asked my dad if he believed in God, and he said, 'If you mean, am I amazed by the laws of physics and that we live in the one universe that seems to have worked, where gravity is such a number that human life can exist? I believe those things, but I don't believe there's any human kind of force that's involved in guiding the world or who you can have a personal relationship with.'"

When he recounts this story, Foer sounds an awful lot like Oskar Schell, the nine-year-old protagonist of *Extremely Loud and Incredibly Close*. Oskar, a bright, eccentric, socially awkward boy who likes to ask questions—all sorts of questions of all sorts of people—loses his father in the September 11 terrorist attacks on the World Trade Center. Oskar's father, Thomas Schell, a jeweler, was having a breakfast meeting in the Windows on the World restaurant at the top of one of the towers when the planes hit. His death propels Oskar on a quest across New York City's five boroughs to find out more about his father and how he died. In the process, he uncovers family secrets and tries to make sense of what everything means. All of it. Life. Death. Love. Hate. Evil. Good. I can't help but wonder if Oskar and Jonathan are the same soul.

"I was a little bit like him," Foer says after thinking for a few moments. "I had all sorts of weird outfits. Nobody is really quite like him, but then everybody you write is you to some extent. If it's not you, who is it? If you're not creating these characters, then who's creating them?"

In his first novel, *Everything Is Illuminated*, one of the main characters, also named Jonathan Safran Foer, travels to Ukraine in search of a woman he believes saved his grandfather from the Nazis. It's another quest to answer what turn out to be, for the most part, unanswerable questions. "When you write one book, anything that's in the book can be kind of a coincidence. But when you write two books and you start to see patterns, then you have to wonder. In both of my books, there's a kind of search. I don't know why I did that. People walk around with these ideas of who they really are, and some of them sound really nice. But they're not necessarily true. I could say I wrote about searching because there are certain things missing from my life and writing is a way of safely looking for them, or looking for metaphors for them. On the other hand, maybe it's just a nice form in which to write a story.

"People always jump to the most poetic explanation. I'm sure you're getting a lot of that. It's very easy to say the thing that sounds most satisfying, when usually a lot of the time you don't know why something is the way it is, or something is the way it is for a thousand different reasons."

While the events of September 11 led Foer to change the direction of the novel he was writing at the time, they did not alter his spiritual course. He didn't rush back to temple. He didn't start praying regularly. "I told my family members I loved them for the first time in a really long time. Like my older brother. I mean, you have no occasion to say it to your older brother. And we said it. It was like a kind of prayer in the sense that we were pausing life and stating something that was true only once we said it," he says. "It's like the reason I think wedding ceremonies are nice. You stand up in front of people and say something. Situations like that feel to me like prayer—saying something out loud when it's not sufficient for something to stay inside of you."

There have been times in his life when, despite not believing in a personal God, Foer has prayed. Most recently he found himself praying on the day of his wedding to Krauss, "just, basically, not to fuck it up," he says, laughing. "I didn't believe my prayer was being listened to by anybody. I prayed in a way that's very similar to the way I write. I had something I wanted to announce. I had something that couldn't be kept inside of me and that, in some way, needed to be expressed to be made true. Somehow."

Krauss also has published two acclaimed novels. Her second, *The History of Love*, was released a month after her husband's *Extremely Loud and Incredibly Close*. Foer believes he probably has learned more spiritually from his wife than from anyone else. The greatest lesson she's taught him? "When something is hard, it doesn't mean that something is wrong," he says. "I really used to believe that a situation that was sad or frustrating or angering was an expression of something wrong. Now I think a lot of times it's an expression of something being right. But it took me a long time to take that in, and I ruined a lot of things because I didn't understand it. I would get clammy when something was difficult or run away from something instead of just incorporating it, accepting it as it is, as part of that seasonality of success and failure. There's a whole picture we're looking at that's bigger than a conversation or a day or a week or a month."

Foer believes in ideas. And he believes in believing. And he's having not a few fresh spiritual ideas as he awaits the birth of his child. "It's a very religious moment in this sense: I'm believing in something I have no physical interaction with. We had our second sonogram the other day. Suddenly you see something on the screen moving, and you say to yourself, 'Wow, that was just an idea I had.' It's an idea I really believed in, and it's amazing to me that there's a physical reality there. We were just talking about that and then there it is. There's this funny movement from the moment of conception to the moment of birth. The moment of conception is entirely an idea and belief, not grounded in any kind of reality except what you can imagine," he says as a redheaded boy about four years old creeps up behind him to see what we're doing. Foer doesn't notice him. "You project ideas. It's almost like Nicole's belly is a movie screen and you can see what the fetus might look like, and then you see it as a kid, and then as the kid grows up to be an adult, and you watch the whole movie play out.

"At the beginning it's really just up here," he says, touching the top of his head. "As you move closer and closer and closer to birth, there are more infringements on reality, which make you believe less. Once you see a sonogram, the first picture of the baby, you have to believe much, much less than you did before because there it is—you can see it! And when you hear the baby's heartbeat, you don't have to believe that there's a heartbeat because you hear it or you can see it. The moment it's born, at that point, there is no more believing. It's an actual physical being. But I think there's a residue of belief. I think that's the reason parents act the way they do around their kids."

Foer tells a story about how his father's voice cracks and he gets emotional anytime he talks about his family—Jonathan, his mother, or his two brothers. It's a trait the young author has inherited. "I'll come home from the grocery store, and I'll say 'I got milk' or something, and my voice will start to get all crackly. I was trying to explain to Nicole the other day, it has to do with being part of a family, being part of something bigger than me, something that I contribute to. It's a running joke now in the house. I'll say, 'Nicole, I got us movie tickets for tonight,' and she'll say, 'Oh, are you going to start crying now?' But things like that set me off, when I'm momentarily aware of the change, momentarily aware of the world that is so much bigger than me and that I contribute to. It's not an awareness of my smallness. It's an awareness of my bigness. Bringing home milk: If you think about it, it's an incredibly powerful thing. It's providing sustenance for someone you love, who loves you. It's providing the same sustenance that people have been drinking for tens of thousands of years. Those things we just can't escape."

The reason Foer thinks parents often act unreasonable with their children—unreasonably angry over silly mistakes or unreasonably happy over seemingly insignificant accomplishments—is essentially spiritual. "It's just this residue of having had to believe in something for so long. You just can't shake it," he says. "The child will never be just a child to you. It will probably always have a religious or spiritual aspect. Literally. It is literally something you have had to believe in. It's also probably a reason so many new parents become religious. In addition to the idea of wanting to impart a tradition and a set of ethics, you also suddenly have practice in believing in something. And belief is like a muscle. The more you do it, the better you are at it."

AUGUST 2005

MARK MORRIS

Dancer, Choreographer

I'm sort of an amateur *of religion. I'm a fan.*

✳

BIRTH DATE: *August 29, 1956*
RAISED: *Nominally Presbyterian*
NOW: *Atheist*
ATTENDS: *Doesn't*
WORDS TO LIVE BY: *"If believing in something helps you get along better with people, or helps you heal yourself, hooray. Hooray! I'm not against it for other people."*

A barefoot Mark Morris, dressed in a bright green camp shirt and a long orange sarong, folds his burly six-foot-two frame onto a couch in the living room of his apartment in Manhattan. Sipping a screwdriver that he's mixed up for himself, he begins to tell me a story which, given that he is probably the preeminent choreographer of his generation, is, not surprisingly, about dance.

"I was in Bali a couple of years ago, in Ubud. I love it there. I wanted to see music and dancing. That's why I go—there's always music and dancing going on. Even the hotel shows are great there.

"Now, this trip happens to coincide with the rededication of the temple there that takes place every ten years. I ask, 'Is there any good dancing going on?' And they say, 'Oh, I don't know. Probably not. But try over there.' Because they don't think the rededication is something that would interest me. But I start to walk, and the next thing, I'm following a thousand people

walking to the temple. And soon I'm packed in with fifteen hundred Balinese in the open court of the temple, and it's humid, and there's music playing, and there are women with offerings on their heads like this"—he stands to mimic a woman gingerly balancing something on her head—"and I'm freaking out because it's so incredible. There are several different pavilions in the court, open but with roofs, and in one there's a puppet show—a shadow puppet show on a tiny screen—that's religious *and* pornographic *and* political, all at the same time. The puppets are like fucking, then the god shows up (from what I can tell, because it's all in Balinese), and hundreds and hundreds of people—little kids and grandmothers—are watching it, screaming and laughing. This goes on until three o'clock in the morning.

"I wound up going every night for the five nights I was there. At 11:00 p.m. I would go to the temple dressed in full formal Indonesian attire—Balinese attire—in a sarong and then a formal sarong over that and then a sash and a hat; you had to have long sleeves, too.

"The night after the puppet show there were like seven or eight different gamelans—different orchestras—playing everywhere. It's pouring rain and two o'clock in the morning and people are smoking clove cigarettes and there are these witch dances where everyone stabs themselves with knives and goes into a trance. It's entertainment—and the most sacred day of the decade. It's fabulous, amazing.

"While this is going on, people are carrying offerings to the temple—fresh fruits and flowers and objects that they've spent a year making just for the festival. They're just used for one day. That's one of the things I love about it—everything is disposable. It's burned or you put it in the water and it floats away . . . Like the kites they burn in Tibet . . . So, every once in a while somebody would put down an offering"—he stands up again, striking a pose to demonstrate what comes next—"and there's a gamelan playing and there are these old gals in sarongs and zoris, and everyone just kicks off the sandals, and they all start doing this dance. This ninety-year-old gal is dancing like this," he says, throwing a hip in one direction and a foot in the other while he snakes his hands gracefully in the air around his head. "And there are two twenty-year-old girls on cell phones who notice and go, 'Oh, look, we know this one,' and they put down their purses and phones and join in. And suddenly there are, like, twenty women doing this dance and talking. Then it's over—and they pick up their stuff and go. It's like, Oh, I know this dance—the god Rama. That's one of my favorite ones. Let's do it. I know the guys are waiting for us on their motorcycles, but let's just do this one dance and then we'll go.

"That, to me," Morris says, settling back into his couch, "is fabulous!

"I've been to many fabulous, fascinating religious spectacles all over the world. I'm interested in them. They're so detailed and so thought out, and it's created such a history for itself. There isn't a boring creation myth. They're all fascinating—*all* of them. And they're all true. Or, you know, none of them is true. I think none of them is true, but they're true if you believe them. I just can't get into them. Well, maybe I'm not supposed to. Maybe they're just not for me?"

Here are some ritual experiences he's witnessed and also deemed "fabulous": Native American corn festival rituals at a pueblo in New Mexico; a high-church Eastern Orthodox wedding ceremony in Skopje, Macedonia; the wanderings of a female guru around rural India as devotees prostrated themselves in the dirt at her feet. "That was *amazing*," he says.

And spiritually moving?

No. "I don't think of myself as spiritual in any way," Morris says, in a lilting, singsong voice with a timbre somewhere just north of Harvey Fierstein's. "I think the whole notion of spirituality is suspect. I'm probably more aware of religion than most people because I'm *interested* in it, but I have no religious belief whatsoever."

It is hard to express how strange it is to hear these words, because here in Morris's apartment, everywhere you turn there is a spiritual figure or icon. The walls, tabletops, and shelves are crammed with crucifixes, Christian saints, statues of Lord Shiva and the Hindu elephant god, Ganesha. "I like Ganesha," Morris says. Then he points to a couple of framed prints of Christ and several crucifixes of varying styles and sizes. "There's a bunch of Jesus stuff because I had some a long time ago and it accumulated and I like it. That's some of the older stuff . . ." Then: "Look at these incredible caskets over here." Behind us, leaning low against the wall of an alcove near tall bookcases crammed with books—including copies of the Bible and the Qur'an—are two framed dioramas that resemble small baroque caskets.

What are they? I wonder aloud.

"I don't know," he says, with a laugh. "Guilt-producing things for children? I don't know. But they're beautiful, aren't they? Somebody died and somebody had a sale and they gave them to me."

Over the framed mini-caskets is a portrait of Jesus rising above a tractor-trailer painted in garish colors on black velvet, the kind of artwork you might find at a truck stop gift shop or for sale by the side of the road in Tijuana. "Beautiful, isn't it?" Morris says when I ask about it.

"Those on the bookshelf over there are from India," he says, continuing the odd artistic tour of his modest apartment, with two pictures of Christ painted on linen. "They're from Manipur. They're blue like Krishna, but it's Jesus. They paint them for tourists because the Indians aren't Christian. But then, if you're painting God it should be blue because that's how they know Krishna to be. Cool, isn't it?"

I wasn't entirely surprised to find religious icons in Morris's apartment. His tour de force, 1988's *L'Allegro, il Penseroso ed il Moderato*, is an exhilarating dance choreographed to the words of John Milton and the music of George Frideric Handel, two men whose work is replete with overtly spiritual themes. Morris's huge music collection includes two hundred Bach church cantatas—"They're the best music ever written," he says. And for years, Morris dedicated his performances "to Maxine Morris," his mother, "and God."

So when I first arrive at Morris's apartment and look around a bit, I think it is safe to verbalize an assumption. "Well, I guess I don't have to ask you if you're spiritual," I say.

"Really?" he says, looking startled. "Why would you say *that?*"

I gesture around the room. "All the religious icons."

"They're not icons," he says blithely. "They're just things that I like. I like the way they look.

"Look," he says, "these objects I have, I love that people grant them power, and one of the reasons these objects I have are beautiful and dramatic is because of the meaning they've accrued over a long period of time. It's a gorgeous-looking, fabulous thing, this mirrored cross hanging over there or that green plastic crucifix, or the beautiful terra-cotta one there. I LIKE them.

"But I detest and despise pretty much every branch of Christianity. I pretty much feel that about most religions. So there." He laughs, aware of how categorical he sounds, and he proceeds to rail against the Catholic Church, and "Bible-thumping morons," and a host of other affronts. Then he softens for a moment. "Look, if believing in something helps you get along better with people, or helps you heal yourself, hooray. Hooray! I'm not against it for other people. And if being told 'Thou shalt not kill' works for you—if a fear of what God will do to you if you *do* kill keeps you from stabbing someone, then hooray. But as far as I'm concerned, very, very, very few people who I've met in my life are actually functionally, deeply, nonhypocritically religious. I haven't seen religion make many people better people.

"I suppose that at one point, probably until maybe fifteen or twenty years ago, I would have considered myself—as everyone does who is scared not to be religious—an agnostic. And then I considered myself a pantheist. Being a queer, I was thinking that paganism would be interesting. But that's just nonsense, really. Praying doesn't hurt anybody, I'm sure. The concentration helps. But as far as religion goes: zero. I'm an atheist."

But what about "Thanks to Maxine Morris and God" in the Mark Morris Dance Group programs?

"I dropped the God part maybe ten years ago because people were thinking I was a spiritualist," he says. "My mother, who is now sort of senile, used to sign letters 'Love, Maxine Morris and God,' which I thought was great." He giggles. "Really, she would sign cards, 'Happy Birthday. Love, Maxine Morris and God.' But at a certain point I felt it was getting too much attention and that people believed something about me that wasn't true. It's much easier to have a soft religious point of view—like, everything is fine, and I believe it all. But I don't believe. I really don't."

Still, while Morris may declare himself "repulsed" by religion, it clearly fascinates him. A voracious reader, he's studied Hindu and Buddhist texts, the Bible, the Qur'an, and the Book of Mormon. He's read all twelve of the apocalyptic Christian Left Behind books, he used to watch the New Age TV show *Touched by an Angel* devotedly, and he's ever so slightly obsessed with the Latter-day Saints.

"I'm sort of an *amateur* of religion," he says, carefully articulating the word in its correct French pronunciation. "I'm a fan. It's interesting to me, but *yuck*, it gives me a bad taste in my mouth, and if I can avoid being in a church, I will."

AUGUST 2005

JEFFREY SACHS

Economist

We're all in this together.

✳

BIRTH DATE: *November 5, 1954*
RAISED: *Secularly Jewish*
NOW: *Secularly Jewish*
ATTENDS: *Doesn't*
WORDS TO LIVE BY: *"What can be done to improve the lot of all of us in some way? That, for me, is the point."*

A tsunami in the Indian Ocean kills more than 275,000 people and displaces more than a million others—most of them poor villagers—in at least a dozen countries.

Hurricane Katrina destroys the lives of more than a thousand around New Orleans, where a third of the residents live below the poverty level—$18,850 for a family of four.

In sub-Saharan Africa, where 25 million men, women, and children are infected with HIV, AIDS kills 6,300 people every single day.

All of these natural disasters—be they meteorological or medical—have a single shameful factor in common: They disproportionately affect the lives of the poor and the otherwise disenfranchised.

We are living in distressing times. War. Pandemics. Famine. Earthquakes. Tsunamis. Hurricanes. Terror. Indifference. Never before has a minority of the world had so many resources and a majority of it so few.

Welcome to Jeffrey Sachs's world.

One of the leading macroeconomists in the world, Sachs, director of the Earth Institute at Columbia University and a special adviser to United Nations Secretary-General Kofi Annan, believes wholeheartedly that the world can be saved, the sick can be healed, and extreme poverty can be eradicated in our lifetime. But he's not looking for any help from divine intervention. If the world is to be saved, he says, we're going to have to do it ourselves.

"We have in our capacity the chance to reduce suffering sharply," says Sachs, author of an ambitious plan to rid the world of extreme poverty by the year 2025. It's a scheme he outlines in detail in his book *The End of Poverty: Economic Possibilities for Our Time*, which came out in 2005.

"It shouldn't be the case that some people die because they have nothing while others luxuriate in unimaginable surplus of material goods. There is a very good reason to help the poor: You may be poor yourself. You may be a stranger in a strange land, as the Jewish tradition says. Your children may be poor, your grandchildren may be poor. If the poor aren't taken care of, not only will tragic things happen to them but your own life may be at risk because of terrorism or because of the spread of disease or because life itself has been devalued, so why should anyone care about your fate?

"Now *should* carries a lot of baggage and a lot of meaning. It could mean 'should' in an ethical sense, it might be 'should' in a sense of justice, it might mean 'should' in a practical sense of what's going to work for producing good outcomes on the planet. I happen to view all three of those dimensions as pretty much the same. But *should* for others is what God would say, a purely theological perspective. Christian social teaching is what Jesus said, that when you feed the least of these you feed me. So for some it's a matter of doctrine. For some it's ethics. For some it's right and wrong and justice. For some it's utilitarian pragmatism of how we're all going to get along on a crowded planet," he says.

"And I think it's okay that there are many different ways to view the same thing. I tend to take the view that three of those four ways of looking at things— the way of ethics, the way of justice, and the way of pragmatism—are really, in a deep way, the same. Others disagree with that, but that's how I view the issues of ethics and justice as systems that work to produce the outcomes that we would like to find compatible with human life on our planet. So I take a kind of pragmatic approach to this."

Sachs is the chief architect of the United Nations' Millennium Development Goals, a multilevel strategy to eradicate poverty and hunger in the poorest countries of the world and to provide basic education and health care for all children by 2025. In order to accomplish those ambitious goals, the world's richest nations would need to contribute about $150 billion of assistance each year. It sounds like a huge amount, but it is actually less than one percent of the gross national product of most industrialized countries, including the United States. Currently, the United States contributes only about two-tenths of one percent of its gross national product to foreign aid—proportionately the least of any industrialized country in the world.

In *The End of Poverty*, Sachs says his plan is simply a forecast. "I am not predicting what will happen, only explaining what *can* happen," he writes. "Currently, more than 8 million people around the world die each year because they are too poor to stay alive. Our generation can choose to end that."

It's surely a noble cause, a righteous endeavor about which Sachs is irrepressibly optimistic. "I think all of these things are worth fighting for," he says. "My whole belief in life is that we make of it what we do. I don't much like the idea of fate. I like the idea of choice, and I like the idea of action, of acting upon one's knowledge and judgment and values. I don't sit back and say, Oh, in the end it's all going to work out well. It's going to work out how we make it work out."

A few days before our conversation in his Earth Institute office on the third floor of Columbia's Low Library, he had returned from one of his frequent trips to Africa, where he met with local villagers and world leaders alike. "In the last three weeks, I've been to villages in Kenya, in Ethiopia, and in Senegal, as well as to meet heads of state all over the world and to try to get some money out of them to help the poor with all the frustrations that are attendant upon that," says Sachs, a man with a boyish face and sleepy eyes who speaks in the measured tones of a professor. "I meet people—not just ideas. I meet people in villages who open their hearts and their houses and their huts and who share their experiences with me—people with the most radiant smiles, people with almost nothing. It doesn't mean I'm not frustrated, but I have to say I find what I do exhilarating. There is nothing like making human contact across cultures and feeling this common link of humanity."

Sachs grew up in what he describes as a "generally secular" Jewish household in suburban Detroit. While he had some religious education as a child and was bar mitzvahed, his family had a deep skepticism toward any kind of religious orthodoxy. "Theology never interested me. But ethics interested me very much, and I guess it's gone that way ever since," he says, adding that he rejects the notion that ethics arise from any particular theology or religious doctrine. "I find personally the links to theology, meaning the questions of God, a completely different matter. And for me, of much less concern. People have different motivations for who they are and what they do. Theology means different things to different people, so I think it's extremely important to connect meaningfully with other people, to try to inhabit their world and their way of thinking.

"I'm a big believer in the interconnectedness of humanity. I'm not dismissive of other people's beliefs, desires, wants, cultures. And I do think that at the core there really is an ability for deep, shared understanding. For me, that won't run through any one single theological text, that's for sure. I don't believe a Jewish text or a Christian text is going to reach and solve the problems connecting with the Islamic or Buddhist world or Hindus or any other part of the world. And yet I am quite confident that there are ways to connect, and it's extremely important to do so. I'm just skeptical that any single religious tradition is going to be the way to do that."

That may well be, but most religions do have that please-take-care-of-the-poor theme running through them, I say.

"And we do pay attention to that," Sachs counters. "There are a lot of common ethics across all of the great religious traditions. That's extremely important. There's also a lot of us-versus-them in a lot of religious tradition as well, which interests me considerably less, I must say, and which has been the source of a lot of grief in the world. But there is, of course, a lot of shared ethics, and it is the basis for understanding each other better. It's important not to be dismissive of other people's traditions, that's for sure."

On the wall behind him are rows of framed pictures of Sachs with an array of world leaders, many of whom he has advised formally and informally about the intricacies and ethics of modern economics. There are three pictures of him with Pope John Paul II, who consulted the American economist before writing his historic 1991 encyclical *Centesimus Annus* (The Hundredth Year) in which, after the fall of Communism in Eastern Europe, he urged capitalist nations to fix injustices in their own systems. "Here I am, some Jewish kid from Detroit, speaking with the pope about an encyclical he was preparing," Sachs says animatedly. "It was quite an experience! And I think it was a wonderful encyclical."

While he doesn't believe in God, at least not in any traditional sense, and is not religious himself, Sachs says he does draw inspiration from the faith of others. "I learn a great deal from Christian social teaching. For instance, the whole Catholic Church emphasis on the preferential option for the poor is obviously something I believe very much in, and a lot of Christ's teachings about the poor I find profoundly moving and profoundly important. But I've also learned from Buddhists, and I've learned from rabbis and learned from people in villages whose religion I don't know," he says.

"I find the exciting part of life—probably my main driving belief—that we should learn in life, and there's an incredible amount to learn. The more understanding there is and the more we are able to live together, the more we can enjoy our short time on this planet. I've yet to find anyplace in the world that doesn't offer something to teach. If you're open to it, it's a marvelous continuing education."

The battle—and it is a battle—to rid the planet of extreme poverty is based on a single conviction at the very core of what Sachs believes, ethically, spiritually, or otherwise: the essential equality of all people. "The evidence strongly shows that we are all Africans," he says. "We left Africa seventy thousand years ago. We share roughly a common gene pool. We're all in this together. And so ethical and moral standards conform very well to what biology tells us about ourselves. These distinctions that are so much at the center of global controversy, war, hatred, and other things are really in a deeper sense rather preposterous and superficial obstacles to understanding one another.

"We should try to understand these issues not from what's right for the United States or what's right for me in particular but what's right for a human community trying to figure out what to do on this planet. Then add to that the fact that we are all the same biologically and that we have common ancestry not so far back, and that we have the same human nature, the same challenges, the same struggles. When we combine those things, for me it leads to a lot of implications about why we shouldn't leave the poor to die."

When it comes to his belief in our collective responsibility to intervene on behalf of the least of those among us, the professor can conjure the zeal of a preacher. Sachs is hard to ignore, says Bono, the rock star, activist, and friend of the economist since the two began working on the Drop the Debt campaign in the late 1990s, urging the world's richest countries to forgive the stultifying debts of their poorest neighbors. "There is a wildness to the rhetoric but a rigor to the logic," Bono wrote of Sachs in the foreword to the economist's book. "God may have given him a voice with an amplifier built in, but it's the argument that carries the day. He's not just animated; he's angry. Because he knows that a lot of the crises in the developing world can be avoided."

One thing Sachs cannot abide is a peculiarly American notion that the plight of the poor stems from their own moral failures. "One of the things I fight against is the strong view in our society that has its own religious and cultural roots that says the poor have themselves to blame," he says, gaining momentum. "That basic statement is, scientifically, incorrect. But it is part and parcel of the kinds of belief systems that pervade the world and that are actually distinctively American on the particular issue of poverty. America stands out almost uniquely in global society in attributing poverty to the shortcomings of the poor rather than to the structural conditions in which they live. Africa's plight has been variously viewed as a function of being black or being heathen, being pagan, being corrupt, being immoral, being libertine, being savage, being subhuman. Our wonderful civilization has attributed all of these reckless notions to Africa and used those also to condone, excuse, and justify every kind of barbarism on the side of the West imaginable over the last five hundred years. Mass slaughter. Mass slavery. Imperial rule. Colonial domination. Neglect of the AIDS pandemic. It's all been part of a set of beliefs that have their own basis in deep misunderstandings."

His mind wanders to the Indian Ocean tsunami, which had wreaked its havoc a few months before our chat. Some people wrung their hands, asking how God could let something like that happen or, more troubling to Sachs, what the people in the countries devastated by the tsunami might have done to deserve it.

"When the tsunami hit, there was absolutely zero theological reflection on my part. I don't ask the questions Why did God let innocent people die? or Why was somebody saved when somebody else wasn't? Those are completely outside my way of understanding these issues. It was a seismic event, and poor people were living in vulnerable areas, and they died tragically.

When I sat down with my colleagues—seismologists who explained to me how the fault line worked in the Indian Ocean—they helped me to understand the physical forces at work. And I could help them understand some of the socioeconomic reasons why the poor die more than the rich when natural hazards and natural events like this occur," Sachs says.

"There was no theological import for me in this, just lots of heartrending tragedy and lots of questions about early-warning systems and preparedness and relief and things we ought to do as a society to reduce the risks of suffering and to ameliorate suffering and to respond," he says. "What can be done to improve the lot of all of us in some way? That, for me, is the point."

MARCH 2005

LAURA ESQUIVEL

Author

When we unite our bodies, we worship the divine.

✳

BIRTH DATE: *September 30, 1950*

RAISED: *Roman Catholic*

NOW: *An eclectic Christian*

ATTENDS: *Nowhere regularly but likes to go into churches when they're empty; meditates daily*

WORDS TO LIVE BY: "La esencia del espíritu es el amor. Esta energía es luminosa, amorosa, y nos que connecta uno al otros." *(The essence of the spirit is love. It's a luminous, loving energy, and it connects us to each other.)*

St. Benedict, in his famous Rule, admonished his monks to "let everyone that comes be received as Christ." He meant that every guest who arrived at the monastery should be greeted with sincere charity and welcomed with genuine acceptance. No faking it. Hospitality, according to St. Benedict, is a spiritual practice, an act of worship.

I can't help thinking of Benedictine hospitality as I arrive at the gates of Laura Esquivel's home on a quiet, tree-lined street in Mexico City after a long flight from Chicago. She sent her driver to pick me up at the airport and, since he doesn't speak any English and my Spanish is embarrassingly inept at best, she also dispatched one of her nephews who speaks some English to keep me company on the thirty-minute drive to her home. She's so thoughtful, I'm thinking, as I look up the front steps to see her standing in the doorway, arms outstretched and smiling, as if I'm some long-lost relative instead of a reporter she's never met in her life.

"Welcome, welcome," she says, engulfing me in a big hug. "I am so happy that you have come," she goes on as we enter her spacious home. It is bursting with color, festooned with folksy artwork, and—oh, yes—incredibly inviting fragrances are emanating from her kitchen, the room, she tells me later, that is the most sacred space in the house.

I breathe in deeply, trying to sniff out hints of chocolate. Esquivel is, after all, the author of the novel *Like Water for Chocolate* as well as the screenplay for its film adaptation. It is one of the most sensual movies of all time, in which cooking sequences were shot as if they were steamy sex scenes (for that matter, the film's love scenes are presented in an equally delectable way).

We sit down at a table in a quiet alcove just off the kitchen and sip hibiscus-flavored fizzy water as we begin our conversation about spirituality. Another of her nephews, an artist who is illustrating her next book, serves as our translator. Esquivel, who was born and raised in Mexico City, speaks excellent English but feels she can communicate her ideas with more nuance in Spanish. Interestingly, while her nephew translates her answers to my questions, she rarely breaks eye contact with me. It's as if she wants me to know that this is between us. It feels intimate.

"Primero que no, yo me considero un ser espiritual . . ." she begins. "First of all, I consider myself a spiritual being. A spirit that is part of a universal spirit. I am not a separate entity or separate spirit from it. And the essence of the spirit is love. It's a luminous, loving energy, and it connects us to each other. For me, God is the same thing. I think of God as a loving energy."

Her spirituality is decidedly eclectic, but she is comfortable giving herself a religious label nonetheless. "I consider myself a Christian. Not as one adhering to the Christian religions but adhering to this person who was love, and I strive to understand what could have been Christ's state of mind," she explains. "That Christ-like state of mind is what allows you to come to real forgiveness. Real forgiveness is nothing else but an extension of love and an absence of judgment. That is very important to me, and I don't think all Christians follow that. I can't believe in a religion where people supposedly talk about love but are really talking about hate and the absence of forgiveness. Jesus' true teachings, when they are listened to, are precisely those of real love—unconditional love—and forgiveness. There has always been confusion about whether we are spirits or a body, so the body becomes a vehicle of evil or sin, a means by which we can lose grace—the grace of divinity. We turn the body into a receptacle of sin and not of God or of that loving energy."

In Esquivel's world, physical passions, be they for food or for lovemaking, are not out of step with deep spiritual devotion to God, the force of loving energy. They are, she explains, intimately intertwined. The way she describes food and sex in conversation and in her works of fiction, including *The Law of Love* and *Between Two Fires: Intimate Writings on Life, Love, Food and Flavor*, has a sacramental quality to it.

How can sex be worship?

"I believe our bodies have to be the means by which we can extend love properly. To make love—to really make love—using the body while being totally connected spiritually can be a very enriching, fortifying experience. There are those who would make a case for sex being bad, or a way of separating us from God, but I don't agree with them. When we unite our bodies, we worship the divine. It is only our intentions and what we think about the body that would make it sinful," Esquivel says. "I believe that the contact of the bodies is a song. In truth, it is a song and a praise to God. The union is a ritual, a true ritual, a ceremony through which we are being made conscious and reach luminous, loving states. It's not a question of romance; it's a question of ritual. That's why I always make my love scenes so intense with flowers and incense and candles—making it worship in every sense."

Like Water for Chocolate, Esquivel's most famous work, is the story of Tita De la Garza, a young woman living with her family in Mexico at the turn of the twentieth century, during the Mexican Revolution. Tita is the youngest of three daughters who live in fear of their cruel widowed mother, Mama Elena, who has proclaimed that, as is her family tradition, Tita will never marry because she will have to take care of Mama Elena until her death. The story is set by and large in the De la Garza home, where Tita spends most of her time in the kitchen (where she was born) with the loving family cook, who teaches her all kinds of magical recipes. Tita falls in love with a young man, Pedro Muzquiz, but the tyrannical Mama Elena forbids their marriage, forcing the young man to marry Tita's older sister, Rosaura, instead. The love between Tita and Pedro never dies, and she channels her passion into her cooking. When people eat what she's made, they feel what she feels—whether it is joy, despair, or lust. In one of the more memorable scenes, Tita makes a dish from the petals of roses Pedro has given her, and her passion for him causes others who eat the meal to flush with lust. So much so that her middle sister, Gertrudis, rides off into the night naked on the back of a revolutionary's horse.

In the end, Tita breaks the cycle of her mother's cruel control, and her love for Pedro is at last requited. When they make love more than twenty years after they first fell in love as teenagers, Pedro is so consumed by passion that he has a heart attack and dies. Tita takes her own life, and their literal love shack goes up in flames around them.

"Love has always been present in my work as a transforming energy," Esquivel says. "Like in *Like Water for Chocolate*, where loving energy is transmitted through food and everyone who comes in contact with the food is changed. The changes are internal. My intention with *Like Water for Chocolate* was to show that real change in society does not take place externally, in the public eye. In that story, outside the house there was the Mexican Revolution. It was supposedly going to change everything for Mexico, but the real change in my novel comes in a space where apparently, to the outside world, nothing was happening—the kitchen! The real revolution takes place when Tita puts an end to and destroys a castrating tradition in her family and stops it from being transmitted to new generations. All of those castrating traditions go against loving energy.

"It's true for each one of us. Real change comes from within, starts on the inside and then goes outside. I come from a generation, in the sixties, that truly believed it was possible to change the world. Our disenchantment was very big. Change in society will not come from changing a political candidate or a president from a single party or country. Because if the next person still has the same ideas, it will never change. You can't speak of democracy if there are people who are dying of hunger. Real change will come from people who are very conscious of the fact that their well-being comes from everyone else's love. Governments and economists have a very clear understanding of economic globalization, how if the stock market in Tokyo falls, then it will fall in New York as well. But they don't grasp the idea that if one person in the world is suffering, we are all suffering."

Esquivel was raised in a devoutly Catholic home. But two events that occurred when she was a young adolescent led her spiritual path away from the church. The first happened when she was ten years old, on the occasion of her grandmother's eightieth birthday. There was to be a huge family Mass in her *abuela*'s honor, and everyone had to go to confession the day before. "When it was my turn to confess with the priest, he asked how long it had been since my last confession, and I answered, 'Three months.' He was out-raged by this and started yelling all this terrible stuff at me—to a ten-year-old girl who was well behaved and everything—that he would not accept my confession because it was outrageous that it had been three months," she re-calls passionately. "I came home with this terrible, heartless feeling, and I was crying, and my mom told me, 'Okay, we'll go to another church.' And I just said, '*No!*' The next day everyone went for communion. Everybody except for me.

"At that moment I came to realize something that I continue to write about today, which is that God knows that I have not committed sins and God knows that I have communion with him even if I'm not standing there with everyone else. That led to a falling out between my ideas of love and the practices of Catholic priests. I made a strong distinction between my God and that vengeful, judging God they talked about."

The second event, which set her on a spiritual road headed east, was when her older brother came home one day and announced that he was no longer Catholic and had decided instead to practice the Baha'i religion. Their mother and grandmother and aunts all cried hysterically. Not Esquivel. "For me, it was interesting and shocking, and I asked him to take me with him to his meetings. And he did. It was amazing. The idea of the Baha'i religion is to take the best out of all the world's religions to create one that unifies instead of divides us. Because God is only one," she says.

While she didn't become Baha'i herself—and her brother eventually abandoned Baha'ism as well—Esquivel began studying Eastern philosophies, immersing herself for a time in Mazdaznan. It is a religious movement that began in the United States in the early 1900s incorporating elements of Hinduism and Christianity but emphasizing belief in one god, Mazda, the creator. Mazda manifests himself in three persons—the Father, the Mother, and the Child. Mazdaznans believe that the world can be improved (and made suitable for God) through the power of breath, and their practice involves a variety of breath control exercises, rhythmic praying, and chanting. Esquivel says she still practices the breathing exercises each morning and meditates daily using a number of mantras—one of her favorites is "I bow to my eternal being." She also prays the rosary regularly. But in her own way.

"I do the Hail Marys and the Our Fathers, but I substitute the word *mistakes* for *sins*. I say, 'Pray for us who have made mistakes,' instead of 'Pray for us who are sinners,'" she explains. She doesn't believe in sin, really. "God does not judge," she says. "I offer my fears, and I ask for help for seeing the world through the eyes of God and not through the eyes of my body. And I ask for help in destroying my fear, because I know that fear is not true. I believe strongly in the power of prayer. It brings me a lot of peace and faith. My purpose every day is to become an instrument for God to extend his love. The only thing that can keep me from doing that is my own ideas and my own fear."

Esquivel makes her own rosaries. She is eager to show me some of her handiwork and disappears upstairs for a few minutes to retrieve a collection of rosaries hand-strung with beads of different shapes and sizes. One is made from black and yellow dried corn kernels instead of round beads. Another has a dragonfly where the crucifix would be. Yet another has a silver charm of a man and woman intertwined in place of a cross. She never puts a crucifix on the end of her rosary beads.

"I don't want to think about the pain," she says. "I don't like that idea of the pain and how Jesus died for us. I don't believe in that. I think he really died in another state of mind, loving all the time. Not suffering. So I always look for objects that awaken in me love and passion and wanting to adhere to this loving energy, instead of an image that suggests pain and suffering."

"Now," Esquivel says, getting up and walking toward doors of her sacred kitchen, "we are going to eat."

My heart leaps.

Squash soup the color of aspen leaves. Sweet green peppers the size of my hand stuffed with cheese baked in a flaky crust. And fillet of beef marinated in garlic, oil, and a fistful of cilantro, rubbed with dark, bitter, rich chocolate and baked until all the juices run together. Gathered around the table with us are her husband, two nephews, and one of their girlfriends. They smile at me and watch as I take my first bite, almost as if they are waiting for something to happen. Perhaps an imperceptible change.

We finish our meal—it's unbelievably delicious—and it's time for me to go back to the airport. Esquivel calls her driver to get the car and then hands me a little package. It's one of her handmade rosaries. Silver and turquoise beads the same shade as the India-inspired silk outfit she's wearing, with a glittery silver cross on the end. "This is my gift to you," she says, closing it in my hand.

That and so much more.

MAY 2005

SHERMAN ALEXIE

Writer

I believe in God, but every day is a struggle to get there.

✳

BIRTH DATE: *October 7, 1966*

RAISED: *Roman Catholic, evangelical Protestant, and agnostic*

NOW: *Catholic/agnostic*

ATTENDS: *Six to eight times a year attends Mass at a parish in Seattle with his wife and sons*

WORDS TO LIVE BY: *"I don't always feel loved by my wife or sons or brothers and sisters, so why should God be any different?"*

I f you're looking for dream catchers, smudge sticks, vision quests, and a kind of in-touch-with-the-Great-Spirit, ancient-native-earthy spirituality, the author Sherman Alexie wants you to know you've come to the wrong Indian. But if it's an off-the-reservation, begrudgingly agnostic, formerly vaguely evangelical, recovering Roman Catholic trying to make sense of God and this crazy world that you're searching for, he's your man.

Alexie and the Creator have a complicated relationship. "God is an absentee father," says Alexie, the award-winning, prolific Native American writer of novels, poems, short stories, and screenplays, including the 1998 film *Smoke Signals*, as he sits in the freshly painted offices of his company, FallsApart Productions, in Seattle. "I believe in God, but every day is a struggle to get there. I feel like God is just out there, not paying attention, and yet it seems instinctive to reach out to God. My dad was an alcoholic who left us a lot, too, and I loved the hell out of him. If God made us in God's image,

then God is pretty damned complicated. I don't always feel loved by my wife or sons or brothers and sisters, so why should God be any different? I mean, I pray. Generally laying on a couch mumbling. It's always late at night. I'm an insomniac, so most of my prayers take the form of 'Please God, let me sleep,' and then they become other things. I'm not a disciplined pray-er. I'm mumbling. I mumble through life. I guess it sneaks up on me, the stuff you see or feel or are reminded of—good or bad. I never know when I'm going to feel the need to pray.

"I was reading the Sunday *Times* yesterday and there was this article about retirement homes for chimpanzees. I was just reading along—it was cute and funny and interesting. And then there was this scene described where this woman who had been a researcher dropped off her chimps on this island and came back nineteen years later. When her boat was docking on the island, her chimps ran out of the crowd and ran to her. Nineteen years later they remembered her! I'm lying there on the couch reading this, and I just burst into tears. My first thought was I don't think I've ever loved anybody as much as those chimps loved her. So it made me feel inadequate. I was crying and praying, 'Teach me to love as well as those chimps just did.'"

Many of Alexie's stories in the sixteen books he's published as of 2005 have deeply spiritual content. Sometimes it's overt. Sometimes it's subtle. But it's always there, pulsing just below the surface. At least that's my take on it as a reader. "My stories feel desperate," he says. "At least to me, they feel desperate. They feel like prayers. And I don't think prayers get answered very often, if at all. I always feel like I'm screaming at the sky and all I hear is echoes back."

Often his stories revolve around the sometimes humorous, ever-pathos-filled struggles of modern American Indians on and off the reservation. They seem to be at least partly autobiographical. Alexie was born and raised on the Spokane Indian Reservation in Wellpinit, Washington, about fifty miles northwest of Spokane. His mother, a Spokane Indian and born-again Christian, was "various kinds of Protestant," he says. "Mom went from thing to thing. She's very traditional Spokane—a ceremonial person, a powwow person—but she moved from Presbyterian to Assembly of God to the church in somebody's living room. She rolled around on the ground more than a few times and tried to speak in tongues but could never manage it." His father, a Coeur d'Alene Indian, was Catholic for most of his life. "The surest part of me has always been my dad. He was the only one of his generation to go to Catholic school on purpose. The Coeur d'Alenes, my father's tribe, are very Catholic. My great-great-great–et cetera–grandmother was the one who had the vision of white folks showing up, precontact. She had this vision of three crows with white-feathered necks showing up. And then here come the Jesuits!"

What was her name? "Mary."

Both of his parents were alcoholics. "Loving people, decent people" is how Alexie describes them. "As screwed up and alcoholic and unemployable as they were, they treated people with dignity." And they gave their son a lot of latitude spiritually. "They didn't force me into anything." He walked away from any kind of organized religion—Catholic, Protestant, or Native—when he was twelve. "The thing that did it for me is when the churches on the rez—the Catholics, the Presbyterians, and the Assemblies of God—all got together and had a book burning. On a rez! On a reservation!" he says indignantly. "In the late seventies and early eighties there was that sort of popular wave of burnings. It was rock music albums and books. My rez really got into it. The Assembly of God leader at the time was really charismatic. And I loved books. I loved music. And they were burning Pat Benatar! What the hell's wrong with you? You're burning Pat Benatar! I grabbed my books and ran home and thought, That's it. I wasn't exactly atheist, but I certainly wasn't going to buy into a God that allowed that to happen.

"I was unclear on the concept of free will. A twelve-year-old Indian growing up on the rez, you don't have free will. You start understanding free will when you have a little bit of privilege. No privilege, no free will. And so I turned away from everything, any organized religion, whether it was tribal or Christian. From the age of twelve until I met my wife, I never set foot in a church."

Alexie's wife, Diane Tomhave, whom he married in 1994, is a member of the Hidatsa Indian nation and a devout Catholic. She has a master's degree in theology and is actively involved with a parish in Seattle. Their young sons are being reared Catholic. "I'm Catholic by name, baptized and unconfirmed," Alexie says. "By proxy, I'm more Catholic than I would be otherwise, I think, because I married a person who is more Catholic than I am. But I still have no use for church. I have no use for the pope, this one in particular. I love Jon Stewart's take on him. He said, 'Is it just me or do you get nervous when there's a German guy on a balcony with hundreds of thousands of people cheering for him?'" he says, breaking into a loud giggle. "I had the dim hope the new pope was going to be somebody brown. I mean, there are plenty of people just as conservative as Benedict XVI that are brown. It could have been a major move, but . . .

"So my own church I'm suspicious of. I hate that women are so relegated to secondary and tertiary status. I love Eucharist. I love the ceremonies. But I can't practice them in my own church in Seattle because I have fame here. I can't stand up in front of a crowd here to take Eucharist because I'm being watched and I know I'm being watched. I don't go to Mass often enough to where I'd alleviate that, to where I wouldn't be 'new.' Our church is a very popular one for guests and tourists, so there's always someone new to recognize me. Every time I go to church I have to deal with 'Oh, I'm a big fan!' I don't want to hear that shit in church. Nobody comes up to a plumber and says, 'I really like your pipes!' At least not in church.

"I'm completely suspicious of any reason why people gather together," he says, by way of explaining why his spirituality is hard to label neatly. "I'm just as suspicious of Native spirituality. It's become incredibly fundamental. I think in our assimilation into the dominant culture we've assimilated into fundamentalism. It's funny that liberals are so into Indians, because Indians themselves are so conservative. I mean, pro-gun, pro-war, anti-choice, anti-gay. There's no separation of church and state on the rez. You pray for everything.

"So my liberalism doesn't fit with the old religions I'm part of—Catholicism and my tribal religion. But, on the other hand, I hate liberal religions even more—the ceremonialist religions that hold you completely unaccountable, that are all about self-help and not about helping others. So in some sense I feel adrift, isolated. I'm the kind of person who, if I weren't so suspicious, would probably wind up in a cult or something," he says, laughing uproariously. "I think that's what happens, that people just feel so left out. They don't fit in the religions they grew up in, the age-old religions in their cultures, and they can't buy into the sort of self-help crap, but they still have a desperate need for a church. So then David Koresh shows up in Waco, and *hey*, there you go! The tribal spiritual stuff I completely walked away from. In a sense, I walked away from my tribe. That was sort of the beginning of knowing I'd have to leave the rez if I was going to have a chance."

Alexie left the reservation as a teenager to attend Reardan High School, a public school in Reardan, Washington, where the only other Native American was the school mascot. He excelled in sports and academics alike, graduating with honors and as a basketball star. He has a twenty-foot jump shot and still plays regularly—"old-man rat ball," he calls it—with the same group of guys he's been playing with since he was in his early twenties. One of the times he feels the most spiritual is when he's shooting hoops. "We're good enough that sometimes we're great," he says of the old-man squad. "Click click click, and you know where somebody's going to be before they even know they're gonna be there. You'll throw a pass and they'll be there. I go completely mindless playing basketball." Similarly, he says, he goes "bodiless" while he's writing. "I guess in those extremes is where I feel connected—when I'm completely mindless or completely bodiless." Connected to what? "Connected to whatever is out there. What was it Lawrence Durrell said? 'I like to work late at night because there are fewer people competing for the ideas.' I think in the process of creation, we're closest to God. So if I'm writing a poem or making a free throw, I'm creating and giving birth. That's when it feels most like God."

But don't get the idea that he's somehow more spiritually attuned because he's indigenous, he says. "My good friends do that to me, and they don't even realize they're doing it. I'll get e-mails, like one from a friend recently who said, 'I had a dream about you the other night, that you were telling me stories, and I realized that what you were saying was right and therefore I'm divorcing my husband.'" Wow. That's a lot of pressure if your friends think you're appearing to them as some sort of spirit guide, I tell him. "I know!" he responds. "I wrote back and said, 'You know, I'm not in the marriage counseling business and I like your husband.' I didn't say it, but I like him more than I like her. I mean, I'm just a goof."

In my experience, often it's the goofiest among us who are also the wisest—and the bravest. I tell him as much and about how I was poleaxed by the short story "Can I Get a Witness?" which was in his 2003 collection *Ten Little Indians*. It raised spiritual questions about September 11 that I'd not thought of before. Subversive ideas. Dangerous, important ideas. "Can I Get a Witness?" is the tale of a unhappily married woman who goes out for a long lunch at a Seattle mall that ends up being attacked by a suicide bomber. She's blown into the street but survives and decides just to disappear instead of going back to the family and the life that have left her feeling empty. She wonders aloud—

speaking the unspeakable—about how many people in the September 11 bombings at the World Trade Center might have done the same thing, and how many horrible people might have died in the attacks whose families were happy they never came home again.

Most people don't mention "Can I Get a Witness?" to Alexie. A lot of them hated it. He got nasty letters calling him things like "perverted evil bastard." What was going on with him spiritually when he wrote it? "I was pissed at Katie Couric," he tells me, smiling but, I can tell, absolutely serious. What did Katie do? "Once again, someone in a position of power was just being completely and unnecessarily banal. That morning of 9/11, when it happened, I was driving to the airport here in Seattle to catch a flight to Los Angeles for a gig. I was listening to the radio when it happened. So I went back home and sat down in front of the TV with my wife. And Katie Couric must have used the word *innocent* seventy-eight times that day. It's a bullshit word. That word has absolutely no meaning whatsoever. None. The idea of innocence—it's so lazy. There is no intellectual ambition in that word, and Katie kept saying it all day, all day. The script was being written. Heroes and victims. Nothing in between. What it did was turn everybody in the Trade Towers into metaphors, not human beings. Calling them innocent dehumanized them just as much as flying a plane into their building did. They were complicated and tense human beings. I was sitting there ranting at the TV. At one point they were worried thirty thousand people were going to die. How many people were in those buildings? A hundred thousand? I don't know. And among all those people you don't think there was a murderer? You don't think there was a dad in there that used to go home at night and sexually abuse his daughter? It comes out later that one of the firefighters who died actually had two families. And one woman actually did disappear. She was gone and then she just showed up. I'm sure there are at least a couple of people who just walked out of the ash and kept going.

"That day, I just kept getting enraged. Number one, I was enraged at fundamentalists, period. Ours. Theirs. Anybody's. I fundamentally hated all fundamentalists that day. All of them. But it wasn't just fundamentalists. I was pissed at everybody that day. I'm still pissed at everybody. I'm pissed at me," he says.

There's another short story in *Ten Little Indians* called "What You Pawn I Will Redeem," which elicits a vastly different response from readers and seems to arise not from the author's anger or dismay but from a deep well of hope. Alexie says it's received the most passionate reaction of anything he's written. Many readers found the story intensely spiritual and profoundly moving. It is the tale of a homeless Indian who sees his grandmother's pow-wow regalia, which had been stolen fifty years earlier, in the window of a pawnshop. The homeless guy makes a deal with the pawnshop owner that if he can raise a thousand dollars in twenty-four hours, he can buy back his grandmother's ceremonial robe. "The story is his quest, his meandering quest, to get the thousand dollars to get it back," the author says. In the end, he doesn't come up with the money, but the pawnshop owner gives him the regalia anyway.

What did Alexie intend for the story to mean, spiritually? "I don't know," he says, and then, a few minutes later, he interrupts our conversation to tell me: "As we're talking now, I think I just realized that the pawnshop owner in the story is God."

Could his mission in life be to tell stories like that?

"Yeah. But I think my mission is to ask questions and flail and thrash about. People interpret that as having answers," he says, with a laugh. "I think I'm just a spectacular thrasher."

JULY 2005

The God Factor / SHERMAN ALEXIE

HAROLD RAMIS

Director, Actor, Writer

No matter how much I seek, there wouldn't be an answer.

✳

BIRTH DATE:*November 21, 1944*

RAISED: *Jewish*

NOW: *"Buddh-ish"*

ATTENDS: *Nowhere regularly*

WORDS TO LIVE BY: *"Yes, we're alone in the universe, life is meaningless and death is inevitable, but is that necessarily so depressing? It just puts the burden on us to fill our lives with joy and wonder and weirdness and adventure—whatever it is that makes your heart pound, your mind expand, and your spirit soar."*

So, I tell them I'm a pro jock, and who do you think they give me? The Dalai Lama himself. Twelfth son of the Lama. The flowing robes, the grace, bald—striking. So, I'm on the first tee with him and I give him the driver. He hauls off and whacks one—big hitter, the Lama—long, into a ten-thousand-foot crevasse, right at the base of this glacier. Do you know what the Lama says? Gunga galunga . . . gunga, gunga-galunga.

So we finish the eighteenth and he's gonna stiff me. So I say, "Hey, Lama, how about a little something, ya know, for the effort?" And he says, "Oh, there won't be any money, but when you die, on your deathbed, you will receive total consciousness." So I got that goin' for me . . . which is nice.

—Carl Spackler (Bill Murray) in *Caddyshack*

Of the American Film Institute's list of the 100 Funniest American Movies of All Time, Harold Ramis has four: *Ghostbusters*, which he cowrote and in which he played Dr. Egon Spengler; *Groundhog Day*, which he cowrote, directed, and produced; *National Lampoon's Animal*

House, which he cowrote; and *Caddyshack*, which he cowrote and directed (and which I can pretty much quote to you verbatim). He's also written, directed, or acted in *Analyze This*, *National Lampoon's Vacation*, *Stripes*, *Back to School*, *Meatballs*, *Orange County*, *Baby Boom*, *Multiplicity*, *Stuart Saves His Family*, and *Bedazzled*. I've seen all of them. At least three times.

For many people of a certain generation (mine), Ramis represents the gold standard of funny. His movies are cultural talismans against the blues, fictional worlds much like our own but where wiseassery is both a requisite and an art form. They gave us a common language of humor and a litany of inside jokes whose punch lines have become mantras. "Cinderella story . . . it's in the hole!" Ramis's work has received accolades from fans and critics alike over the years. One bit of praise that he is particularly proud of came from an unlikely source after the release of his 1993 film *Groundhog Day*. A Buddhist newspaper ran a story about the film with a headline that read: "Greatest Buddhist Movie Ever Made."

"That was cool," Ramis, who calls himself "Buddh-*ish*," says, grinning. "It's a movie that doesn't mention the Buddha or Buddhism once, and yet it kind of lays out what it's about." For the unacquainted, *Groundhog Day* is a modern-day morality tale about Phil Connors (Bill Murray), an egotistical weatherman at a Pittsburgh television station who's sent to Punxsutawney, Pennsylvania, to cover the annual Groundhog Day festivities. And to see, of course, whether Punxsutawney Phil, the groundhog, will see his shadow or not. Phil Connors—who obnoxiously refers to himself as "the talent"—gets stuck in a time warp and repeats the same day, Groundhog Day, over and over again. At first he uses this cosmic hiccup to work his way through the seven deadly sins, but he finds that ultimately unfulfilling. He tries to kill himself several times but always wakes up alive the next morning or, rather, the same morning. It's not until he focuses on helping others and improves himself as a human being that Phil breaks out of the loop and into the next day—and the rest of his life. That's karma, baby.

Were the Buddhist undertones in *Groundhog Day* intentional? "Well, Danny Rubin, who wrote the original screenplay, has investigated Buddhism, too, although he would never claim to be a Buddhist either," Ramis says. "But you know, I saw articles that asserted the movie had a deeply Christian point of view. And more Rosh Hashanah and Yom Kippur sermons were preached on *Groundhog Day* than any other movie in history, I'm sure, because I kept getting them from rabbis. A lot of psychological and psychiatric journals did pieces on the movie, too, and the Jesuits wrote and said, 'This perfectly expresses the Jesuit point of view.' So clearly we touched something that was more universal than anyone knew."

Ramis was raised in a Jewish home in Chicago, where he attended Hebrew school—he was school president, he tells me—finished early (they double-promoted him), and attended an Orthodox yeshiva for six months. "Something I've been saying lately is that every child is a fundamentalist, you know?" he says, smiling. He has an almost constant grin and an infectious chuckle that burbles underneath practically everything he says, much like Russell Ziskey, the character he played opposite Murray in *Stripes*. "It's a way adults keep us safe, by giving us concrete things to believe in: God is good. God loves you. Policemen are good. The government knows what it's doing. Our army is right. These are simple, right-wrong, good-and-evil-based notions. My grandparents were European Jews. My father's family came from Russia with no discernible religion whatsoever, although he was Jewish in culture and association. My mother's parents were Orthodox Jews from Poland. But my father, because he had no religious tradition, never enforced anything in our home. All of my mother's family had kosher homes, they attended synagogue almost daily. My grandfather went daily, maybe twice a day, morning and night. There was no question I would go to Hebrew school four days a week after school and synagogue on Saturday from the time I was seven to thirteen.

"I felt very Jewish except that I couldn't wait for it to end. I knew that after my bar mitzvah I wouldn't have to do anything. And I didn't. I had this bar mitzvah, I was like a stellar Hebrew school student, did the program perfectly, and then never went back, basically," he says. "There was no philosophy. There was no investigation of what Judaism was about other than this kind of rigid legalism, these six hundred and thirteen laws and everything prescribed: *This is the way you do it.* I couldn't tell what was real, what was traditional. I worried about it. When I was a little kid, I worried that if I was flipping channels and saw a Christian or a Catholic evangelical program, I had to flip past it really fast, that somehow it was a sin if I even landed on it for a moment or heard a word of it. I knew that I was never to kneel, never to get on my knees in front of anyone or anything. I don't know if anyone ever said it explicitly, but I thought, you know, these would be really *wrong* things to do. I had a friend once—I must have been ten. It was Saturday and I had a headache and he said, 'You know why you have a headache?' And I said, 'Why?' And he said, 'Because you didn't go to *shul*.' So there were notions like that floating around."

Ramis's eldest son, Julian, decided not to have a bar mitzvah when he turned thirteen, and Ramis didn't press the issue. "I would like him to have some kind of a marking ceremony. My dream is that he'd have three or four one-hour conversations with important spiritual thinkers," he says—a rabbi, a Buddhist teacher, and "a really hip Christian," if he can find one. Recently, he attended the bar mitzvah of the son of a close friend. A few days before the ritual, Ramis was at their house having dinner and asked the bar mitzvah boy if he knew his Torah portion. The kid said he had it down. "And I said, 'So what's it about?' He said, 'What do you mean? I don't know, it's in Hebrew.'" This made the former Hebrew school star pupil Ramis insane, so he went and pulled out a copy of the Torah and told the family what it meant. Unfortunately, it was one of those, well, *difficult* passages. "It's Moses and Aaron defining the requirements for priesthood: You can't have a blemish, you can't have a scar, you can't have a deformed testicle, you can't be a dwarf, you can't have a limp. I mean, this is literally all in there, and they're cracking up as I'm reading it. So I used it to make a toast at the bar mitzvah, I said, 'Aaron, I was very moved and inspired by your haf Torah, especially the part about the deformed testicle.'"

Ramis encountered Buddhism in California in the 1960s, after graduating from Washington University in St. Louis. "I was kind of always proud to be Jewish, and I'm not sure how that translated into spirituality, but no one addressed 'spirituality' as such as an issue until the later sixties, when it suddenly became a major issue as alternative religions came to prominence and the Transcendental Meditation movement hit campuses really big. My ex-wife was really into those explorations. If I was 2 percent spiritual, she was 98 percent spiritual," he says. Ramis's first wife, Anne, whom he wed in 1967 and with whom he has a daughter, Violet, born in 1977, is the quintessential spiritual seeker. "She had an astrological chart done that showed she was like 90 percent air and the rest fire—no earth and no water. I was totally balanced among all the elements and exactly balanced among all the planets." How lucky for you, I tell him. "Well, in a way," he says. "But astrology never meant anything to me predictively, just more as a projective device. But it certainly described her. She led me or dragged me or introduced me to different ways of looking at the spirit or the soul. She believed in past lives and actually did reincarnation therapy."

Did he look into his past lives? "No," he says, laughing as the strand of prayer beads wrapped around his wrist taps the tabletop. ("They're supposed to remind me not to eat carbs," he says. "It's about mindfulness, you know. It's not just carbs anymore. It's about everything.") "I did look into all this stuff," he continues. He and Anne read a book called *Psychic Discoveries Behind the Iron Curtain* that mentioned a Bulgarian professor of "suggestology," which they found intriguing. So during an extended visit to Greece, when they were "young hippies," the Ramises took a side trip. "We went to Bulgaria to meet this guy, Georgi Lozanov, the professor of 'suggestology.' He had a language institute where, using 'suggestology,' he would teach the equivalent of four years of a language in like three months or something. We went to him and said, 'We would like to learn French at the institute.' And he said, 'Fine, but we teach it in Bulgarian, so you'll have to learn Bulgarian first.' It was dumb. We didn't do it," Ramis recalls with a laugh.

He's been surrounded by Buddhists, or at least people who are Buddh*ish*, for years. One of his friends from college relocated to San Francisco after they graduated in 1966, moved into the San Francisco Zen Center, "became a shaved-head, robed monk, and stayed there for twenty years." Ramis's second wife, Erica Mann Ramis, whom he married in 1989 and with whom he has two sons—Julian, born in 1990, and Daniel, born in 1995—also lived at a Buddhist meditation center for several years. And Erica's mother lived at a Korean Buddhist meditation center for thirty years.

"I've always been kind of a dilettante," Ramis says. "But watching other people on their journeys forced me to think reactively about it: Well, what do I believe? You don't believe in past lives, so if you don't believe in the continuity of the soul, what do you believe in? I never was able to give myself over to another human being as a spiritual trainer or leader. I could never affiliate with an organization, any doctrinal organization. I could never have a guru or a spiritual teacher because I always believed it was so personal. It seemed to me logically impossible that there could be a concrete answer to a spiritual quest—by definition—and so anyone who said they had an answer was immediately suspect.

"I'm right now convinced that no matter how much I seek, there wouldn't be an answer. It's like when you're lost in the woods, instead of running you should just sit down," he says. "Nietzsche said something like—and I'm wildly paraphrasing—'Look for me, and when you find me, then leave, abandon me.' It's like once you get what I'm saying, drop it, move on, and don't believe a word of it, ya know? You have to pay lip service to other people's faith or religious choices, it's the polite thing to do. But I don't buy any of it. And I find it perplexing and disturbing that it's actively divisive, that religion is used like a wedge to divide people, and, frankly, there are some beliefs I have no respect for, that, quite the opposite, I have contempt for." Which beliefs? "Almost all faith-based belief," he answers, seriously. "Just to button up this notion that my spirituality is an evolution, if I had to say what I've arrived at, I would say that I believe that everything is part of a miraculous ongoing creation. And that's all I know."

Every year the Ramises send out holiday cards with a quotation or a verse Harold hopes will give their friends and family a moment to pause and reflect on. One recent holiday greeting contained a poem Ramis wrote. As we sit twenty-two floors above Chicago's Michigan Avenue in the Cliff Dwellers Club, a private arts club where Erica Ramis is a member, this exceptionally funny man recites his very serious poem to me:

"The ancients watched the winter solstice
The sun shrinking from the Earth
The shortest day, the longest night and then the new year's birth.
But what the ancients couldn't know
Now clear to those with eyes to see
That summer here is winter there
And day to you is night to me.
It all depends on where you stand
Six billion different points of view
I'll honor yours if you'll honor mine
And then with grace we'll see this through."

"It's all about point of view and our failure to recognize other people's right to be—to be who they are or what they want to be. That all ties in to spirituality. I don't understand people who claim faith or religion or spirituality and then use it to abuse," he says. That doesn't, however, preclude his sharing his own beliefs with others. But he does it with irreverent aplomb. A few years back Ramis had a pamphlet printed up that he calls "The Five-Minute Buddhist." It's an eight-and-a-half-by-eleven-inch piece of paper, folded lengthwise in three parts, like a Chinese take-out menu except that where the egg rolls and crab rangoon would be listed there are the Four Noble Truths, and over on the other side, right about where the mu shu or kung pao chicken would be, there are the Five Hindrances: sensual lust, ill will, physical and mental languor or torpor, restlessness and worry, doubt and skepticism. Across the bottom there is a quotation from the Vietnamese Buddhist monk Thich Nhat Hanh: "The miracle is not to walk on the water. The miracle is to walk on the green earth, dwelling deeply in the present moment, feeling truly alive." He's had copies of "The Five-Minute Buddhist" laminated. "Well, you don't want that to evaporate," he says, pointing to the shiny copy he has just handed me. "It should last forever now." Ah yes, but remember impermanence, Harold. It's the First Noble Truth.

Perhaps part of the appeal of Buddhism for Ramis is that it's nontheistic. He doesn't believe in God, at least not in the personified God of, say, Judaism or Christianity. "God as we used to think of him is not looking out for us, you know," he says. "And if he is and knows what's going on in each of our lives at every moment, he's certainly having fun with us in a certain cruel way. I could never believe in a God that played those kinds of games with us, the God who hears every prayer and knows everything we do and has control over every minute aspect of the universe. Well, why is he fucking around with us like this? What kind of a God is it that feels the need to torture us in that way when, with the wave of his symbolic hand, he could make it all good? What's the sense of that? It doesn't make sense to me," he says.

This reminds him of a line he regretfully had to cut from *Bedazzled*, a film he directed in 2000 in which Brendan Fraser plays a nerdy guy named Elliot Richards, who sells his soul to the devil, played by a minxy Elizabeth Hurley, in exchange for seven wishes. One fulfilled wish finds Elliot transformed into a famous novelist. "In the scene, a girl is falling in love with his brilliance and she says she's read his book, *Always Toujours*, and loved it. And he says, 'Oh, it's just a little exercise in existentialism.' And she says, 'Little to *you*, maybe.' And he says, 'Well, I don't know, every time I reread Sartre, I wonder why does the existential dilemma have to be so damn bleak? Yes, we're alone in the universe, life is meaningless and death is inevitable, but is that necessarily so depressing?'" Ramis says, chuckling as he recites the lines from memory. "And then—this is the part I had to cut, which I love—he says, 'It just puts the burden on us to fill our lives with joy and wonder and weirdness and adventure—whatever it is that makes your heart pound, your mind expand, and your spirit soar.'

"It's good, isn't it?" he says, his ubiquitous giggle bubbling to the surface again.

The whole time we're talking, I keep thinking about something the author Anne Lamott once wrote: "Laughter is carbonated holiness." I think she might have been quoting her pastor, but I'll attribute it to her anyway. It's an interesting notion. And if it's true, Harold Ramis is surely a holy man.

So he's got that going for him . . . which is nice.

JUNE 2005

RUSSELL SIMMONS

Entrepreneur

We get what we give.

✳

BIRTH DATE: *October 4, 1957*
RAISED: *Christian ("Episcopalian, I think")*
NOW: *"Aspiring yogi"*
ATTENDS: *Meditates daily and practices about two hours of strenuous, spiritualized Hatha yoga every day. Usually at the Jivamukti Yoga Center in New York City.*
WORDS TO LIVE BY: *"Stop doing shit that's hurtful. Feel good about doing shit that's not hurtful and practice that."*

This little light of mine, I'm gonna let it shine, this little light of mine, I'm gonna let it shine . . .

As a rousing version of the gospel song blasts through the dimly lit yoga studio in lower Manhattan, the Godfather of Hip-Hop is standing on his head, eyes closed, feet swaying to the music, humming to himself.

Perhaps sensing my desperate struggle to maintain balance in a backward neck stand on the mat next to him, the Godfather, otherwise known as music impresario Russell Simmons, opens his eyes and flashes an upside-down grin.

"Just keep smilin' and breathin', lady," he says, mischievously. "Just keep smilin' and breathin'."

Let it shine, let it shine, let it shiiiiiiiiine! . . .

It's his fault I am in this battle for balance. A couple of hours earlier, in the middle of an interview, Simmons hauled me off to the ninety-minute

Jivamukti yoga class he takes every day. He hadn't asked if I'd wanted to go. He'd proclaimed it to be so.

"You'll come with me," he had announced, adding that he had workout clothes for me in the chauffeur-driven SUV waiting outside the midtown offices of his conglomerate, Rush Communications.

Simmons is a devoted yoga convert. With an almost evangelical enthusiasm, he'll expound on the spiritual and physical benefits of a regular yoga practice to anyone who will listen, willingly or otherwise. And his zeal is understandable—yoga transformed his life.

The mellow Eastern spirituality of yoga is worlds away from the roughneck streets of Hollis, Queens, where Simmons and his brothers, Joey (better known as Reverend Run) and Danny, were reared. As a young man, Simmons, whose nickname is "Rush" because of his frenetic personality, was a petty hustler, reportedly selling marijuana and fake cocaine on the street before discovering the rap music upon which he would build his multimillion-dollar empire. In the late 1970s, after a brief stint in college studying sociology, Simmons began representing several emerging rap artists, including his brother Joey and the group Simmons would christen *Run-D.M.C.*

Building on the success of the group, Simmons and producer Rick Rubin founded the Def Jam record label in 1984, signing such seminal rap/hip-hop artists as L.L. Cool J, Public Enemy, and the Beastie Boys. With Def Jam setting the course, rap and hip-hop exploded in the mid-eighties, making Simmons one of the most successful African-American entrepreneurs in history.

He diversified, founding Def Comedy Jam as a vehicle for black comics and launching the careers of stars such as Bernie Mac, Chris Rock, and Jamie Foxx. In 1992, he also created a successful men's clothing company called Phat Farm, which eventually spawned a women's line, Baby Phat, run by his wife, Kimora Lee Simmons, whom he married in 1998. He has produced films, including Eddie Murphy's hit *The Nutty Professor*, started a hip-hop magazine, *One World*, and formed several charitable organizations focused, variously, on arts funding, voter registration, racial harmony, and AIDS awareness.

In 1999, Simmons sold Def Jam to Universal Music Group for $100 million, but the enormity of his success hasn't slowed him down one bit. At any given moment, Simmons, living up to his nickname, moves from one business deal to another like a hummingbird. He's juggling new sneaker designs for Phat Farm, an MTV reality show about Run's family that he's producing with Diddy (a.k.a. Sean Combs), a charitable project in Jamaica where he wants to help build a school, and his latest passion—a yoga infomercial.

One afternoon in his forty-third-floor office at Rush Communications, two cell phones ring incessantly and assistants hustle in and out with papers to sign, while he fields calls from Diddy, Doug E. Fresh, and Reverend Run on the speakerphone. Run, as Simmons's younger brother is known, is an ordained minister at Zoe Ministries, an eclectic nondenominational ministry based in Harlem. "They're a bunch of weirdos," Simmons says of Zoe Ministries. "Look at them," he says, handing over an eight-by-ten photo of Reverend Run and his mentor, Bishop Bernard Jordan. "They're weirdos. They both got capes on."

Mid-conversation and mid-lunch (a committed vegan, he's sipping lentil soup from a take-away cup and a concoction of choline powder with water that's supposed to help improve his memory), he calls his assistant on the speakerphone. "Can I go to a four o'clock or do I have to go to two?" he asks, referring to a class at the Downtown Jivamukti Yoga Center.

"No, you have to go to two, that's the only time you can go today," the assistant says. "I mean, you can skip it if you want to."

"No, not likely," he says, and hits a button to disconnect her.

Yoga is the focal point of Simmon's day. It stops him, aligns him, makes everything clear again. "It's like when you're in a car accident and all of a sudden, everything moves slow, and suddenly you're in this space. That's what it's supposed to feel like, the idea that you see everything," he explains. "It's all God then. There's no fear, no nothing. You're just there. No future. That's what happened to me after the first class. I wasn't too worried about nothin' for a minute. And I thought that was special. I've been chasing that ever since. That's the high."

Simmons's friend Bobby Shriver, the Kennedy cousin and producer-brother of California's First Lady, Maria, took him to his first yoga class in Los Angeles more than a decade ago. "I went there because there were so many hot girls," Simmons admits. "It was like, me, Bobby, thirty-five girls, and two gay guys.

"I got addicted right away," he says, referring to the yoga, not the hot women. "I came out saying, 'If I keep doing this shit, I'll lose all my money.' Because for one second, I felt that I wasn't . . . you know . . . The anxiety was gone. And I thought that was the driving force of my life."

According to Shriver, the Simmons he knows today is a different man from the one he took to that first yoga class. "At the time, he didn't know how to drive a car, he ate about four hamburgers a day, he didn't have a girlfriend, and he was trying to get into the movie business—he'd *say* he was in the movie business. That was his general state. After he started going to yoga and doing his practice, he got a girlfriend whom he later married, he bought a house, which he had never done before, he learned how to drive a car, which he'd never done before, and also lost, I think, forty pounds."

Clearly, Simmons has made a lot of external changes, I say.

"Yes, but as you know, there are no external changes," Shriver retorts. "Russell as we know him today—the before-and-after picture, as Arnold [Schwarzenegger] would say—in Russell's case is as dramatic a picture as can be, the difference between when he didn't have a practice and when he did. Those external things don't change without the internal things changing first."

While Simmons was raised nominally Christian ("Episcopalian, I think"), he never liked religion very much. "I don't *not* believe. I believe in all of them," he says of the world's major religions. "But I never had faith in anything that I couldn't see.

"Yoga has really helped me feel more comfortable with the idea of being present, the simplest idea of spirituality, the power of now."

Does he believe in God?

"The idea that God's inside you, that's the basic idea," Simmons says. "Collective consciousness. God's the imagination. God made the earth and then later he built it. That realized human being rap. That yoga rap. *Samadhi.* Nirvana. Heaven on earth. That thing. That's about as close as I can get to an idea of it. It's not a guy sittin' on a corner."

While he has studied various yoga, Buddhist, and Hindu texts—he peppers his conversation with Sanskrit words or phrases almost as liberally as he does with profanity—and practices a highly spiritualized form of yoga where meditation and chanting are central, Simmons also finds spiritual inspiration in other places. "One of the people who is inspiring to me is Minister

Louis Farrakhan," he says, referring to the leader of the Nation of Islam. "I see him as a person who really promotes love. He said something in his speech at the Million Family March that was very inspiring to me. He said to the Muslims that Muhammad was not a Muslim, that Christ was not a Christian, that Lord Buddha was not a Buddhist, that Abraham was not a Jew, that they were all people who were one with God and that they all had the same message."

The Million Family March wasn't the first time Simmons encountered Farrakhan or his teachings. Growing up in Hollis, he says, "There were black Muslims or, like, heroin addicts on the corner. That was it. They were one or the other."

Simmons, chairman of the Foundation for Ethnic Understanding, a multicultural, interreligious group run by Rabbi Marc Schneier and dedicated to stamping out bigotry, is all too aware of Farrakhan's reputation as an anti-Semite. "The minister's speech about love and the oneness of all religion and goals and people, that we're all spiritual people living in a physical life and all that rap, that's a good rap," he says. "We want to sell that. We don't want to sell his anti-Semitism rap."

When I tell Simmons it sounds as though he has had his consciousness raised, he laughs. "I don't know about my consciousness; it's kind of *low*," he says. "I'm evolving. I'm trying to learn, I'm trying to have a better heart, I'm trying to give more, trying to find effective ways to give more."

Later, as his tricked-out SUV (among its many amenities is a fax machine), driven by a man he calls Brother Kenny, a black Muslim from Hollis, hurtles downtown toward the Jivamukti studio, he tells me, "The idea of selling stable happiness, lasting happiness, is the thing that we all want to promote. We want to be able to do that. We get what we give. Giving is based on what we get. It's a karma thing. And when you get free of that other thing, like the receiving thing, you receive more. Your personal happiness is based on what you give the world."

Simmons says he gives away a portion of the profits from his many business ventures in an effort to give something back, to pay it forward, if you will. He and Kimora Lee want to design a line of high-end yoga-themed jewelry. "Diamond *ohm* symbols and all that shit," he says. "I want to try to connect all my businesses to something good, so with the diamond business, I'll give a third of our profits away to kids who are suffering in conflicts around diamonds. We'll sell conflict-free diamonds, donate a piece of what we do in the Simmons Jewelry Company. That's an example."

Simmons has more than a few earthly toys, including a 49,000-square-foot home in Saddle River, New Jersey, that he shares with Kimora Lee and their young daughters, Ming Lee and Aoki Lee. What about the Buddhist idea of nonattachment? I wonder aloud.

"Nonattachment, I'm not interested in that," he says, explaining his take on one of Buddhist philosophy's pillars. If a person focuses on detaching her- or himself from the physical world and its pleasures, he explains, that is often all the person ends up wanting. "Not needing anything is a state of yoga, a yogic state. The full union with God is the state of not needing anything."

Is he close to that?

"Fuck no. I'm a needy person. But I'm a little better than I was. Sometimes. Sometimes I'm better than I was," he says with uncharacteristic coyness.

Simmons's approach to spiritual transformation is at once simple, transcendent, and earthy. "Whatever dirty shit's going on in your mind, let it go," he says. "Try to practice it for a while, and then one day you'll wake up and say, 'I'm not interested in that.' Start practicing good things. It's the practice. Practice yoga. Be a *practicing* Christian, a *practicing* Muslim, a *practicing* Jew."

When a barefoot Simmons steps nonchalantly through the threshold of the Jivamukti studio, his yoga mat tucked under his right arm, he is transformed. First, he sits in the lotus position in a quiet corner surrounded by about a dozen other practitioners, and chants for a few minutes before the instructor delivers a short sermon. When she's finished, Simmons picks a spot at the front of the studio, unfurls his mat, and begins his practice, folding his long, lanky frame into perfectly aligned Downward Dog, Warrior I, and Warrior II poses.

His moves are almost balletic, gentle, graceful. Simmons is remarkably flexible and appears entirely blissful. A giant smile spreads across his face, even in the most difficult of poses. (Think upside down, feet behind his ears.) Meanwhile on the mat to his right, it's all I can do not to groan audibly as I wipe the sweat from my eyes and try not to throw my back out.

He is kicking my ass, in a karmic kind of way. When we emerge from the dressing rooms a few minutes after class, he's still smiling. I feel a certain sense of clarity that I didn't possess earlier in the day and tell him as much.

"Blissed out!" Simmons says. "That's what we want to do, to go all day long and be blissed out."

How long does this bliss usually last?

"Until a car horn blows, or someone yells, or whatever the fuck is going on. Try to keep it with you," he says earnestly, like a streetwise Master Po. "Try to keep it with you for life."

"I want to *live* yoga," Simmons says, reaching for his cell phones and a bottle of water as he climbs back into the SUV so Brother Kenny can rush him back uptown for more meetings and mayhem.

DECEMBER 2004

MICHAEL GERSON

Speechwriter, Policy Adviser to President George W. Bush

I'm a mere Christian.

✳

BIRTH DATE: *May 15, 1964*

RAISED: *Orthodox Presbyterian*

NOW: *Episcopalian*

ATTENDS: *The Falls Church in Falls Church, Virginia*

WORDS TO LIVE BY: *"Every human being that you meet is eternal and infinitely valuable and more valuable than anything else."*

H e is the man many people credit—or blame, depending on their perspective—for putting religion back into popular political discourse by helping President George W. Bush infuse his rhetoric with his faith. Michael Gerson, Bush's chief speechwriter from 2001 to 2005 and current adviser to the president for strategic policy and planning, is the man who writes the lines that become history.

"An angel still rides on the whirlwind that directs this storm."

"Our nation must rise above a house divided."

"This nation is peaceful, but fierce when stirred to anger."

"Our boys had carried in their pockets the book that brought into the world this message: 'Greater love has no man than this, that a man lay down his life for his friends.'"

"Every man and woman on this Earth has rights, and dignity, and matchless value, because they bear the image of the maker of Heaven and Earth."

"States like these, and their terrorist allies, constitute an axis of evil, arming to threaten the peace of the world."

"Many have discovered that even in tragedy, especially in tragedy, God is near."

Those are a few examples of Gerson's more memorable handiwork from Bush's inaugural speeches, State of the Union addresses, and a message delivered on the sixtieth anniversary of D-Day. For Gerson, writing for the president is an exercise in big ideas, political and spiritual—lofty theological notions of good and evil, blessings and responsibility, grace and courage. He mixes in Bible verses alongside literary references and passages from political rhetoric of the past, when a president mentioning his faith in public speeches would not have been fodder for news stories. Such thinking comes naturally to Gerson, who, like his boss, is an evangelical Protestant Christian. They speak the same spiritual language.

"We're not sitting around discussing theory but working it out as we work together," Gerson says as he sits in his orderly office in the West Wing of the White House. "I love the history of American political rhetoric. I've studied presidential rhetoric in the past, and I like to root our rhetoric in what has come before. And a language of moral aspiration with religious references is very much a part of our tradition. But I've seen it now from a slightly different perspective: At certain points it's not just part of our tradition, it's a necessity of presidential communication, particularly in those circumstances where you are having to deal with unjust suffering. And we've had to deal with it too much. Whether it's 9/11 or a shuttle exploding or soldiers dying, the president of the United States can't say that separation is endless and there is no hope. He uses language that I believe is rooted in our history, that separation isn't final, that there is a love stronger than death. It's interesting that, at those moments, we don't get any criticism for that. It comes afterward, when the moment has cooled."

The spiritual content and context of the speeches he's written for Bush are often designed to provide "comfort in mourning and in grief," Gerson says. "That's part of it. And part of it is just a recognition of the fact that faith—the variety of faith in American life—is a source of comfort and compassion. It's one of the main sources—not the only source but one of the main sources—that drive people to help their neighbors and contribute to the goodness of the country. By recognizing that, the president is recognizing a fact. I think there is also an element of recognizing that faith is one of the sources of social justice in America, that it's behind abolition and child labor laws, the civil rights movement, and a lot of other things," he says, being careful to add that faith in America is not identical to any one political party or ideology. "It actually stands in judgment of every party and every ideology. It's necessary to have a moral ideal that stands above the existing political and social order, that says it needs to be better, it needs to be different.

"I've always liked Martin Luther King's statement where he said, 'Churches are not the master of the state, churches are not the servant of the state, churches are the conscience of the state,' to remind it, to remind those who govern, of their moral responsibilities, particularly to the weak," he says. As he's talking, Gerson, who has a youthful, doughy face and floppy Hugh Grantesque hair and is wearing small wire-rim spectacles—his look and demeanor are somewhere between professorial and prep-school chess club president—is stabbing the covered end of a pen into the side of his broken-in nubuck oxfords over and over again. It appears to be a nervous habit of which he's fairly oblivious. He's quite persistent about it, though, stabbing and shoving, stabbing and shoving the defenseless pen between his heathered gray sock and the side of the shoe through most of our hour-long conversation.

"If we were to exclude faith from our common life," he continues, speaking in his gentle, ever so slightly halting manner, "we would remove one of the most important and consistent sources of social justice in American history. But, as I said, you have to be careful, because it's not identical with any party, not identical with any single ideology. It shouldn't be used by political forces, but it has to inform our political life in order to have some statement that people who are weak need to be valued, that people who are in need need to be cared for, and it's played that role throughout our history and will continue to do so in the future."

Gerson, who was ranked number nine on *Time* magazine's 2005 list of the "Twenty-five Most Influential Evangelicals in America," grew up in St. Louis in the conservative Orthodox Presbyterian Church. He attended Wheaton College, the evangelical Christian school outside Chicago whose alumni include the Reverend Billy Graham, Speaker of the House Dennis Hastert, and, well, me. While he was about six years ahead of me at Wheaton, we had similar spiritually formative experiences at an institution dedicated to blending faith and reason in all disciplines. "The fact of the matter is, Wheaton had a significant influence on me for two reasons: One of them is that very strong belief that, at their core, there is nothing inconsistent between faith and the right application of reason, that the faithful don't need to fear knowledge. And that's the truth behind 'All truth is God's truth,'" he says, quoting a line from Dr. Arthur Holmes, a professor of philosophy with whom we both studied. "Wheaton is a school that understands that the Christian faith is about more than personal piety, it's about social justice. Wheaton was founded on abolitionism and educating women early and a notion that there was a vision of justice, which I think is evangelicalism at its best."

It was during his last year at Wheaton that one of the editorials Gerson wrote for the student newspaper, *The Record*, caught the attention of the Nixon yes-man Charles Colson, now one of the leading voices in American evangelicalism (number 5 on *Time*'s list) and head of Prison Fellowship, a national ministry that works with inmates, ex-inmates, and their families. Colson persuaded Gerson to come work for him instead of pursuing a graduate degree in theological studies at Fuller Seminary in California, where he already had been accepted. Gerson did not feel a calling to the ordained ministry but had planned to pursue an academic degree and eventually teach at the college level. But God, it seems, had other plans for him. After a few years working with Colson, Gerson went on to serve as policy director for Senator Dan Coats of Indiana (a fellow Wheaton graduate), as speechwriter and policy adviser for Congressman Jack Kemp, and as a speechwriter for Senator Bob Dole during his 1996 presidential campaign. He worked for two years as a senior editor at *U.S. News & World Report* before then Governor George Bush tapped him in the spring of 1999 to be chief speechwriter and senior policy adviser for his first presidential campaign. Gerson has been at Bush's side ever since.

While the two men share a similar faith and outlook on life, that's where the similarities end, Gerson says. "He is outgoing and likable and gregarious and athletic, and I'm none of those things," the speechwriter says, laughing at himself. "But we do clearly share a couple of things. One of them is, he believes, and so do I, that politics is about big ideas and great causes and not about small things. And that really attracts me. I think the second thing is when an idea like the emergency plan for AIDS relief or malaria comes up— which I really pushed hard for in the system—when it comes down to that level of decision making in the Oval Office where the president sits down and the pros and cons are given and the costs are laid out, he has consistently been the biggest ally for these kinds of ideas within the administration, and I really respect that. I think both of those things, to a certain extent, come from a shared faith that believes politics is a cause. I think that has been part of the reason we've worked well together."

In February 2005, Bush promoted Gerson to the position of assistant to the president for policy and strategic planning, in which he advises the president on foreign policy, human rights, Africa, domestic AIDS, bioethics, and other issues that interest him personally. While he still writes some of Bush's major speeches, Gerson is spending more time traveling—at home and abroad—learning about the issues from people in the trenches. His latest endeavors have given him an opportunity to put his faith into action in a new, tangible way.

"When you're a person of faith who enters public life, your goal is to seek the welfare of the society you serve," he says. "Christians can and should contribute something distinctive, which is a belief that our political and social and cultural arrangements should not be organized only for the benefit of the strong. Justice requires us to serve the least. The way we know that's important, to some extent, at least in my faith tradition, is by how Jesus chose to spend his time on earth. Not with the powerful, the religiously influential, the politically prominent, but with lepers and tax collectors and former prostitutes and the unwanted and outcast. So there has to be some kind of special emphasis on the forgotten. There are a variety of ways to get at that. I've been privileged to be a part of some efforts where the government is trying to do that, whether it's the AIDS initiative or malaria or the faith-based initiative, where we're talking about mentoring the children of prisoners, people who are normally forgotten in the debates. We're trying to give the forgotten a voice in an acrimonious political debate. Obviously we do that imperfectly, but it's something we've tried to do."

By all accounts, Gerson was an important force in persuading Bush to turn his attention to the AIDS pandemic in Africa. In his January 29, 2003, State of the Union speech—which Gerson wrote—Bush announced a bullish aid package that promised $15 billion over five years to fight AIDS in Africa and the Caribbean. "As our nation moves troops and builds alliances to make our world safer, we must also remember our calling, as a blessed country, is to make the world better," the president said in the speech. "This nation can lead the world in sparing innocent people from a plague of nature."

A few weeks before our visit at the White House, Gerson traveled to Namibia to see for himself how the first installments of funds from Bush's AIDS relief package were being put to use on the ground. He tells a story from that trip that obviously moves him deeply. "I met people who are alive today because the president was willing to care and act on important issues. I've never had that experience before in government," he says. "I've never been more convinced in my life that government can be a source of good. I met a little girl whose parents were both infected with HIV and who was born infected with HIV. And now both her parents and she are receiving antiretroviral drugs. She was near death a year, year and a half ago, she had lost a tremendous amount of weight, and now she is just a perfectly normal little girl. It's like a miracle. It *is* a miracle. I guess it's fairly common in southern Africa to use names of significance, and her mother had named this little girl 'The world has no good in it.' Imagine the despair in a mother who would name her child that. And now there is some good in the world for that child. That's a good thing. That's something government, at its best, can do for people."

Bush—and by extension, Gerson himself—has been accused of sometimes giving the impression that America has a kind of divine mandate to do what it does in the world the way it sees fit, that, more simply put, God is on *our* side.

"Let me make this personal: I don't believe that God is on the side of America. But I do believe God is on the side of justice. And insofar as America is serving that cause, it's serving a noble cause," Gerson says. "To quote Martin Luther King again, when he says, 'The arc of the moral universe is long, but it bends toward justice,' that's another way of saying the same thing. The God who created the world is not indifferent to the cause of justice. So it is an area where you do have to be careful, but there is an appropriate language to talk about a source of justice that stands above human justice."

It's the oft-repeated "axis of evil" line from Bush's 2002 State of the Union address—one Gerson admits was, at least in part, his—and the president's frequent references to the concept of evil in general that have raised the most hackles among their critics. The wordsmith stands by his choice of words.

"You have to look at these things in context. We were at a point where the

Pentagon was still smoldering, an entire square block in New York was in ruins, the technique used was to turn citizens into weapons, children on the airplanes as weapons themselves," Gerson, the father of two young boys, says emphatically. "In that environment, there was no other adequate moral vocabulary except to call evil by its name. The techniques of terrorism in the political realm define that term. So some of it is just accurate description. And some of it is to help people understand what they have just experienced. That's what we faced in that circumstance. So yeah, it's a . . . I think it's . . . I don't know how to put it. The president believes and I share the belief that human evil is real and that courage triumphs and that justice and hope are the direction of history. Those things are very real and very needed in times of tragedy. So, yeah, it would have been hard to call it anything else."

I ask Gerson if prayer plays a significant role in how and what he writes. His answer is at first measured. He talks about the pressures of the job, the extreme highs and lows of ego involved in being so close (and influential) to the president, and the traumas suffered by the nation during the first George W. Bush administration. The more he talks, the more personal his answer becomes.

"Prayer is a way to come face-to-face with the reality that our value is not based on our achievements. It's a way of encountering God's unconditional love that doesn't depend on our merit or achievements. So that's a source of stability and peace. Those are the kinds of personal aspects. But more and more I've just discovered that it's impossible to have a rich prayer life in endless petition. It's in solitude and silence and trying to focus on what matters and what counts," says Gerson, who with his wife, Dawn, a childhood friend he married in 1990 (he has to take off his wedding ring to double-check the date), joined the Episcopal Church in the late 1990s. "I grew up Orthodox Presbyterian, and then just over time I found that tradition to be liturgically lacking. It's funny how people who come from liturgical traditions often don't appreciate them. I do. The words really matter to me. It's the great liturgy written in English. And I like frequent communion, so it's where we've kind of come home."

When I ask him to describe himself spiritually, he says, "I'm a mere Christian." It's probably the kind of inside joke that only a couple of Wheaton grads might enjoy. It's an allusion to *Mere Christianity* by C. S. Lewis, the great Christian apologist whose papers are kept in a special collection at

Wheaton's library (along with the famous wardrobe from the author's *The Lion, the Witch and the Wardrobe*). In *Mere Christianity*, Lewis lays out the basic beliefs of Christianity and argues that the boundaries that divide Christendom into factions and denominations are superfluous. "At the center of each there is something, or a Someone, who against all divergences of belief, all differences of temperament, all memories of mutual persecution, speaks with the same voice," Lewis wrote.

Gerson, who has a photograph of himself shaking the hand of Pope John Paul II on the wall behind his desk, says he draws from different Christian traditions to enliven his own faith and is pleased that more evangelicals today are doing the same. "I met him twice," Gerson says of the late pope. "He is one of my great heroes. I think he had the appropriately Christian combination of forgiveness and fortitude in the face of two great evils: Nazism and Communism. He had an uncompromising commitment to the dignity of the individual."

A voracious reader with an impressive memory for exceptional quotations, Gerson says that, along with Lewis, G. K. Chesterton, and Gerard Manley Hopkins, the work of the late Henri Nouwen—a Roman Catholic priest who wrote more than forty books on spiritual life, including the best known, *The Return of the Prodigal Son: A Story of Homecoming*—has had an immense impact on his faith and his life.

"Nouwen just had a tremendous sense of giving you a glimpse of what it would be like to live every moment as if you were infinitely loved by the creator of the universe, and that your worth never depends on your achievements or failures," he says. "What would that mean psychologically, how would you be different, if you were able to live that way?"

AUGUST 2005

DR. HENRY LEE

Forensic Scientist

Science doesn't always have the answer.

✳

BIRTH DATE: *November 22, 1938*

RAISED: *Buddhist*

NOW: *"I'm a believer."*

ATTENDS: *Nowhere regularly but visits various churches, temples, synagogues, and mosques when invited*

WORDS TO LIVE BY: *"If you work hard, you will have a chance. But you have to have faith. You can't just give up."*

Somewhere in Taiwan, where he was raised, there are people carrying around Dr. Henry Lee key chains in the hope that these will protect them from evil spirits. That his name and face would be considered a good-luck charm is a bizarre notion for Dr. Lee, one of the world's foremost forensic scientists. He deals with physical evidence—blood, fingerprints, DNA, bone fragments, ballistics, fibers, and bug larvae—to try to solve crimes with hard, scientific facts. Some say Dr. Lee is the best in the world at what he does, solving cases others believe are unsolvable and uncovering evidence other people don't find. But he does what he does with science, not magic.

"A lot of people think I have supernatural powers," Dr. Lee says in his office at the Henry C. Lee Institute of Forensic Science at the University of New Haven in Connecticut, where he has been a professor since 1975. Though Dr. Lee has worked on more than six thousand cases around the world, he is perhaps best known for two: his testimony at the O. J. Simpson murder trial

and his work on the investigation of the suicide of President Bill Clinton's first White House attorney, Vincent Foster.

"I handle death very well. I see a lot of tragedies. So particularly in China people think I must be immune because 'the ghosts' never bother me," Lee explains. "People collect little trinkets of me—key chains and badges—and think I protect them. I even know people who deeply believe in God—Christians—who think I have the power to deal with possessed people. One thought their house was possessed, and they had a priest do an exorcism. It didn't work, so they came to me. I said, 'Why do you come to me? No way.' I try to explain to them that I don't have supernatural powers. I don't! And I don't believe in ghosts!"

A native of China who was raised in Taiwan and came to the United States in 1965, Lee is every inch a man of science. But he is also a man of faith, if of a fairly nonspecific variety. "I don't have one definitive sort of faith, but spiritually I do believe there's something up there," he says, glancing at the ceiling. "I believe every religion. Yes, they have different formats, different procedures. But the bottom line is that they all want people to be good, to help others, to forgive their enemies. They all believe there is some superperson up there. It doesn't matter if it's Allah or Buddha or Jesus or God. The bottom line is that many things in this world are unexplainable. Science doesn't always have the answer."

That's blasphemy in many scientific circles. But Lee is not afraid to say he believes in something beyond what he can see in the physical world. "I believe something, but I don't know what," he says, his Chinese accent still thick after forty years away from home. Still, he makes himself clearly understood, emphatically so. His speech is precise, like that of a man who has a lot to do. "A lot of scientists believe something in their heart of hearts, but they don't want to say so. But I'm a straight arrow. I'll say whatever I believe. Whatever I think, I have nothing to hide. It's me. If you don't have faith, if you've lost belief in the spiritual, it's probably the end of your life.

"I've been a scientist all my life, and I've been a good detective all my life," says Dr. Lee, who was a captain in the Taipei Police Department before emigrating to the United States, where he earned a degree in criminal science from New York City's John Jay College, as well as master's and doctoral degrees from New York University. He went on to be the state of Connecticut's chief criminalist from 1979 to 2000. "Scientists believe in solid, physical evidence. We believe in logic. Whereas as detectives, we believe in experience and instinct. They are completely different ways of thinking. As a scientist, many times I cannot explain phenomena. As a detective, sometimes I've wondered why somebody drove on Interstate 95 and BOOM! had an accident and was killed. One second before that car, the driver escaped, and one second after that car, the driver escaped. Why that moment, that time, that individual? I've seen a billionaire who was murdered. I've seen winos in ditches. In my life, I've seen so many strange things that they force you to believe there is something else."

Lee has witnessed the very worst of humanity. Mass graves in Bosnia, horrific murder scenes, the grim handiwork of serial killers, even cannibalism—one particularly gruesome case where a son ate his mother comes to mind. He says he deals with the horror by compartmentalizing his mind, something for which he has an almost Zen-like talent. (He is known for being able to run half a dozen meetings simultaneously in different conference rooms in the same building.) "Is human nature born with evil, or is human nature born with goodness and kindness?" he asks rhetorically. "They are two extreme theories. Which one is correct? It's been puzzling me all these years. Why does someone commit a crime, take another life? Why does somebody violate a woman or a boy? Are we born with that evil spirit? Does everybody have that? Or is it because of a person's environment or his upbringing? Is it genetics or because of alcohol or drugs? Or is it because of a lack of faith, a lack of religious beliefs? Even today, I still don't have an answer. I see people commit crimes, but I do believe in the part of the human being that is kind and good and willing to help. If we one day lose that belief, it will be the dark age of the world, of humankind. You have to have that belief."

While he often toils in the dimmest side of life, Lee also has seen some truly amazingly good things, phenomena he cannot explain with science or with faith. "A young boy was in a traffic accident and became a vegetable," he says. "He was hooked up to life support for a month. I was in town to give a keynote speech at a medical center, and his physician said, 'Dr. Lee, we've tried every possible way. The best neurosurgeon has looked at the diagnostics and says there are just no brain waves, that he cannot function.' And then he said he had recently read something about the supernatural power of kung fu. I said that yes, I practiced kung fu a long time ago, when I was a kid. I practiced it, and karate. When I entered the police college we had to graduate with a black belt. I don't believe this can help, I told him. But the boy's parents were begging me to see their son. Just to see him. So after I gave my talk, I went up to the sixth floor to the ward to see this young man on life support. The physician said, 'Hey, Dr. Lee has come to see you.' There was no reaction. I put my hand on the boy's head and said, 'Be strong. Your family needs you, society needs you.' And all of a sudden the physician jumped up and said he heard a gurgling sound in the boy's throat.

"Everybody got so excited and said it was the first sign they'd seen of a reaction from him. 'Can you do more kung fu?' they asked me. I was just saying hello! I continued to talk to him a little bit and said, 'When you recover, you can come visit me and I'll give you a tour of the lab.' Two months later I got a phone call saying that the boy had recovered. Believe it or not, the physician insisted on coming to see me so I could teach him. I said, 'There is nothing I can teach you!'" Lee says, looking incredulous. "It's just a coincidence."

He tells another story about a woman who was in a car accident, in a coma. He visited her. She recovered. "They insist it had something to do with me, but I don't think so. I don't think so. I think it's just a lot of coincidences."

On the morning of our conversation, a family from Florida has arrived unannounced and without an appointment. Their child was murdered, and the case is unsolved. "Can I really help them? Maybe, maybe not," Lee says. "Because of jurisdictional things, I cannot just walk into Florida or Texas and say, 'Hey, let me work on this case.' But people don't understand that. They think, Oh, just go to Dr. Lee and Dr. Lee will make everything happen. But I do pray for them. I hope there is some solution for the case, because it's just eating them, consuming them. They want some answers. It looks like society has abandoned them, that no one cares about them. If I don't care, they're going to feel even more disappointed. So of course I'll talk to them, comfort them, and tell them I will do everything I possibly can do."

That's a lesson he learned from his mother. Lee is the second youngest of thirteen children born to his mother, An-Fu Lee, and his father, who died when Lee was four years old. "People ask me who I respect most, and I say my mother. They ask me who I fear the most, and it's my mother. People would ask me to give a speech and I'd say, 'But it's impossible. I'm booked until 2008.' And then they'd call my mother, and she'd call me and say, 'Why won't you give this talk?' And I'd say, 'I'm busy.' And she'd say, 'You never work hard enough.' So okay, Mom. I'll do it."

Lee's mother, who was a devout Buddhist, died in New York City in 2004 at the age of 106. While he does not consider himself a Buddhist, when he is home in China he will go to the temple to place his mother's name on the altar, light incense, and bow to the Buddha statue. "My mother was a very, very sincere individual, and she deeply believed in God. She deeply believed in good deeds. That's why all thirteen of us, we do good things," he explains. "Here at the University of New Haven, we have a scholarship in my mother's name for poor students who want to major in forensic science or criminal justice. We help a lot of people here. It's important. When I came to this country, I had only fifty dollars in my pocket and I didn't speak English. That's why I tell everybody if you work hard, you will have a chance. But you have to have faith. You can't just give up. When I first came to New York City in 1965, I had to work three jobs. I worked in the NYU Medical Center as a technician. I waited on tables, taught kung fu, and I went to school. You think I work hard now! I would walk home in the middle of the night—I couldn't afford the nickel subway or bus fare. I could have easily lost faith and said forget it. It paid off. Because I prayed? No. Did I pray? Yes. I walked home in the middle of the night saying, 'O God, please give me the strength to finish the semester.'

"Did I pray to God that I would become one of the top forensic scientists in the world? No. Did I pray that I would become a millionaire? No. Because I know it doesn't matter how you pray, you're not going to just sit in your house and become a millionaire. I see people who go to temple and they want to become rich, they want to get promoted, they want to become famous, they want to have babies. I almost want to tell them, from my personal experience—I have two kids—praying doesn't work. I thank God. I thank Buddha. I'm blessed with these two beautiful kids. But is it God that gave me the two kids? No. Buddha? No. The reason I have them is because I loved my wife, we had relations, and I got kids."

That's a fact. Which is different from the truth, Lee explains. People confuse the two all the time, and the confusion causes all sorts of problems, he says. "I don't believe in truth. I separate the truth and the fact. Facts are what happened and how it happened. Truth is an opinion. One person thinks one thing is the truth, and another person thinks the same thing isn't the truth. If I find your fingerprint, I can say that it's your fingerprint. The suspect could say, 'Oh, three months ago I was there and I left the fingerprint then.' Is that the truth? How do I know? But the fact is, your fingerprint is there. Now you know the difference between truth and fact."

So is it true that Lee has some kind of supernatural powers to heal and protect and ferret out the truth? He doesn't think so. But his key-chain-carrying fans do. What's the truth? It's simply relative, he says.

"Do I have a mission? Yes, I have a mission: To be a good, faithful scientist. That's my mission, and I've done everything I could do to fulfill my mission," he says, sounding very official. "Every day I feel accomplished. Every day I take one more step."

AUGUST 2005

MELISSA ETHERIDGE

Rock Star

My faith has been rewarded.

BIRTH DATE: *May 29, 1961*
RAISED: *Methodist*
NOW: *Spiritually "unlimited"*
ATTENDS: *Playing music is her spiritual practice*
WORDS TO LIVE BY: *"I know that whatever darkness I have, I will have at least as much light."*

"Morning!" a beaming Melissa Etheridge calls out, balancing a piece of toast with jam on the tips of her fingers as she opens a gate in the white picket fence surrounding her backyard in Los Angeles.

Etheridge's young children, Bailey and Becket, are busy in a nearby play-room as their rock-star mom, dressed in a worn orange T-shirt, bell-bottom jeans, and sneakers, walks by, followed closely by a mostly blind dog named Angel.

"I've been looking forward to this," Etheridge says as we settle onto an overstuffed couch in her sunny, lived-in living room. "In interviews, mostly I'm asked about music and my personal life—the gay thing. Every now and then they will say, 'Are you a religious person?' And I'll say, 'No, I'm a spiritual person.' And that's about all I get to talk about, unless you're over my house late at night and I've cornered you," she says, with a belly laugh. "Then I'll talk about it."

It's a bright, beautiful late summer morning. Etheridge is in a wonderful mood, full of mirth and optimism as she reflects on her faith and her life. A month later, in early October 2004, she will be diagnosed with breast cancer, cancel the tour in support of her latest album, *Lucky*, undergo surgery, and begin chemotherapy treatments. But on this particular day, with the specter of illness still hiding, Etheridge is feeling pretty darned blessed, readily admitting that she's in the best place spiritually she's ever been in her life.

"My faith has been rewarded," she says. "I have been rewarded for speaking the truth. I have been rewarded for saying, 'Okay, I'm in this really lonely, awful, I'm-eating-too-much-sugar place, and it feels horrible where I am, but I believe.' And that's faith. My faith is that I am on this earth, and I am an energy that is moving forward and can make choices and I'm in control. I know that whatever darkness I have, I will have at least as much light because that's just the way it is. I believe that. I have faith in that. And I've been shown that."

As she sees it, whenever she's been presented with a challenge or hurdle—in her work, her life, her soul—and has chosen the high road, she's been rewarded spiritually and, sometimes, materially. "I was hugely rewarded and sold millions of records after I came out—*millions*," she says, referring to revealing publicly more than a decade ago that she is a lesbian. "People say, 'Was it hard?' Once again, I was completely rewarded—huge, big-time—taking the step in truthfulness and trust and faith, taking that step. Hugely rewarded. I know in my heart and my soul that I am on the right path and that I am not wrong or going to hell or any of those labels that certain religions want to put on me," she says. "No. I know the way I breathe in this life, I know what's right. And I'm declaring my truth."

Etheridge lives in the hills of Brentwood, California, with the woman she calls her wife, the actress Tammy Lynn Michaels. The couple tied the knot in a 2003 seaside ceremony in Malibu. Etheridge's two children are the fruits of her relationship with her former partner Julie Cypher—and a little help from the singer David Crosby, who donated his sperm for the in vitro fertilizations. Etheridge shares custody of her daughter, Bailey, born in early 1997, and son, Becket, born in late 1998, with Cypher, from whom she split in 2000.

"What's going on, buddy?" the singer says when Becket appears in the doorway. "Hi," the barefoot, doe-eyed boy in a tie-dyed T-shirt and jeans says, sheepishly. "I was wondering where you were." Etheridge explains that she's doing an interview. "All right, buddy? So you need to close the door and I'll be out soon," she says warmly. Becket looks at her, smiles, and swings on the door handle, not going anywhere. With a little cajoling, after a few moments he leaves.

"Crazy beautiful" is how Etheridge describes her children. "Everybody was like, Why did you pick David Crosby? thinking they would have beards. No. I have gorgeous children. Someday, when they're adults, you will see what gorgeous children I have."

Bailey and Becket have taught her as much spiritually as she has tried to teach them, she says, recounting a recent conversation with her daughter as they drove by a church. "I remember driving by and saying, 'Some people have to go to church to talk to God.' And Bailey says, 'Oh, I don't. I just close my eyes and I can talk to God right behind my eyes.' You just want to leave that alone. You want to let that remain in there. So I leave it alone."

What does Etheridge think God is like? "That question would mean that I think God is one thing, and I don't," she says. "I think God is all things. So, you're God. This table is God. My children, that flower. For heaven's sakes, that flower is God. The sound of that saw, that's God. See, I went from religion to then studying physics and string theory and those things. You study, you get into string theory and all that, quarks and the time continuum, and you really start realizing God.

"I see in this world that science is the next great religion. I think science can set us free from religions. I think right now we're in a crisis of holding on to religions, and science is going up and we're all getting more aware of our world and those stories that used to control us, they don't control us anymore."

Etheridge was born and reared a Methodist in Leavenworth, Kansas. "White bread. It was as 'religion lite' as you can get," she says of the church she attended throughout her childhood and adolescence. Neither of her parents was a regular churchgoer, but her father made sure she got to services each weekend. "I remember being in church as a little girl, and I would cry and they'd have to take me down to the nursery, but I didn't want to be left alone in the nursery with the others," she says. "I remember first of all that church was someplace I couldn't be myself and I couldn't be with my family. That was my first impression and feeling about it. Then my father started taking me alone because, for my mother, religion reminded her of her own mother, who was a little bit nuts. So my father would take me, but he didn't like having people ask, 'Where is your wife?' He would get that a lot. By then

I was eight or nine years old, and I was playing guitar and I was in the choir and I wanted to go because of the music. For me, it wasn't about the church part, it was about the choir and it was social. Eventually my father would just drop me off at church. It came to that."

Today it's easier to say what Etheridge is *not* spiritually than what she is. "I am not bound to religion or religious dogma or creed. I am not limited spiritually at all, and that's where I'm at right now, realizing that it's infinite, that it keeps on unfolding. And the older I get, the more spiritual I get. So, I'm spiritually excited," she says. While she doesn't call herself a Christian— she shuns all religious labels—Etheridge says when she was a teenager she seriously explored Christianity. "It never fit, but I studied it. I recently ran across an old Bible of mine that I had underlined and written in. I studied the Bible. Not as someone chained to it, but as someone saying, 'Look, this has so much influence on the world I want to know what it's about. I want to know what's going on.'"

Etheridge believes Jesus was a real man and a great prophet, like Muhammad or the Buddha. But she doesn't believe Jesus was the son of God, born of a virgin, sent to Earth to redeem it. "I know too much about history that it de-mystifies the Jesus Christ myth for me. But I do believe that a man existed who was speaking incredible truths about our souls," she says and then adds, laughing, "And now I'm goin' to hell."

After she learned how to play guitar in grade school and fell head over heels in love with music, Etheridge had her first gigs in churches around Leavenworth. She vividly recalls playing in a local Baptist church, where she was asked to "accept the Lord Jesus Christ" and be saved. "And I remember saying to myself, 'I'm going to go up front, I'm gonna see what this is.' And I remember not feeling any different and not having the . . ." She pauses, searching for the right word. "It wasn't . . . it seemed too controlling to say, 'Do this and this and this and you go to heaven.' It spoke nothing of the day-to-day. It spoke nothing to my life. It spoke nothing to my mother, who was distant and didn't talk to me, or my sister, who was a freak that was scream-ing and hollering," she says. "It didn't fit."

As a teenager, Etheridge was involved deeply with a youth group at the Fort Leavenworth chapel. She even wrote and directed a musical about Jesus. "It was my version of *Godspell*," she says nostalgically. "I was completely obsessed with *Godspell* and *Jesus Christ Superstar*, because it's powerful, artistic music and show tunes! All the people who were interested were like me, ya know? You find, when you are a gay teenager—even when you don't know it—that you find people like yourself, or any shade of that, and you gravitate together. It saved my adolescence."

When she was nineteen, something else happened at the Leavenworth chapel that haunts her—in a good way—to this day. She recalls, "They had asked me if I would be the music director of the chapel. And there was a chaplain there—I forget his name. He ran the whole thing and I worked for him. By that time I was a full-on lesbian, terribly closeted, as you are when you're nineteen and don't know what's going on, and I had a run-in with my mother. She was like, Get out of this house. I don't know the nature of your disease, but you cannot bring it in this house. So I go to the chaplain and I tell him: 'I am gay and I don't know what to do about it and I need to tell you because I'm working with the youth of the chapel.'

"And he said, 'You know, there are people here who would tell you that you're wrong. There are other chaplains here who would tell you that. But I'm not going to tell you that. I don't believe that God would create a love that is wrong,'" she recounts, her eyes beginning to brim with tears.

"It was the kind words of one religious chaplain that gave me space, and that kept me from being like a complete atheist. I think he even said that his brother was gay or something like that, and I was just, Ahhhhhh," she said, throwing her head back and arms up in relief. "It gave me such hope. There's been a lot of hope injected into my life from different places that has kept my path really pretty amazing. That was one of them."

As an adult, Etheridge finds hope, insight, and spiritual guidance from a diverse collection of sources. Music, of course. String theory. Family counseling. Past-life regression. A bit of Wicca. The occasional clairvoyant. And, apparently, a little of what the Rastafarians call "herb." "Has anyone talked to you about drugs?" she asks during a lull in the conversation. "Why are drugs illegal? Why is alcohol legal—which is the stupid drug. It's drowning your brain. It's turning off any receptors. But that's legal. And smoking's legal. And that just kills you. That addicts you to something and kills you. Those two things are legal. Why are prescription drugs legal? Why are they trying to synthetically make these things to stimulate or depress things in our brains? But the natural substances—marijuana—that are not addictive and open, hugely open spiritual journeys and paths . . . I think, okay, why did they make pot illegal?

"It's one of those things that really opens up your mind, and you start going, Wait a minute now. And I think, just as there are many avenues of spiritual awakening—of faith—and there are things of this earth, on this earth, that can for a moment take you to spiritual highs. And I think that's very dangerous to our society and the control that society needs."

Etheridge isn't advocating drug use—at least not the use of synthetic drugs—and she doesn't deny that there's a problem with addiction in today's society. But she does believe that mind-altering natural substances, such as marijuana, peyote, and opium, may be the missing ingredients in modern religious rituals. "These natural things, I think, used responsibly, can enhance a spiritual awakening and experience," she says. "That is missing from our religions of today, if you look at other cultures and such, with their rituals and the herbs that they would use. I think it's repressed in our society, which is not a good thing."

When asked whom she goes to for spiritual guidance in times of great sorrow or great joy, Etheridge says she often turns to the spirit realm. Her most intimate guidance often arrives unsolicited. "My father was looking in my eyes when he died," she begins to explain. "I knew for sure when I saw him die that there is spirit and there is body and they are two different things. So I have no fear of dying. When I saw him die, I saw him in his body, and he was struggling and in pain and breathing hard. I took his hand and I said, 'You know what? You go ahead and go. Everything is okay here. I'll take care of everyone.' I said, 'It's like fishing,' because we used to fish when I was a kid. And I said, 'Go on.' I saw his spirit leave him. It wasn't like in the movies. I didn't see a mist and his body go away. But I saw his spirit leave. His body was still breathing, his heart was still going, but his spirit was gone.

"It's funny, I dreamed about him last night," she says, smiling. "He'll come in dreams. And in the dreams we're always fishing. In the dreams we discuss a lot—and even in waking consciousness. It's not like a ghost, it's like a spirit, whatever that dimension is that's right next to ours, that's so close to us. He's there, and I'm grateful for that."

Sometimes Etheridge turns to paranormal professionals for help. "There's a psychic I like to go to," she says. "I don't believe anyone can tell the future. It's not as simple as that. I do believe there are people who do use more parts of their brains than we do, who are blessed or cursed or however you want to look at it with a little more understanding of life and time, of the way life energy and force are. And these people have the gift to explain it in ways that we can understand. So if there are large questions of where am I going, about my career, larger sorts of spiritual concepts, I will go to a psychic." For instance, after she split with Cypher, Etheridge's psychic had some good news. "When I was single, I went to my psychic a lot saying, 'What's going on?' And she's like, 'You know what? You're learning. You're doing things. Someone is going to come into your life. This bright, amazing sunshine.' Even went as far as to say, 'Blond hair. Blue eyes,'" Etheridge says. Her partner, Michaels, has blond hair, big blue eyes, and a million-watt smile.

Back in the early nineties, Etheridge believes, another psychic healed her physically and helped her discover what could be described as her true calling. The rocker had a cyst the size of a golf ball on the wrist of the arm with which she plays the guitar. "I went to doctors, and they drained it, and then it would come back. They said they could go in and scrape it off, but that's your tendon and there are chances. I was like, Mmm, don't mess with my hand," she recalls. "So I went to a psychic healer, this crazy man. He had pictures of aliens all over his house. Completely insane. He says, 'Well, that's just an energy block for your hands. Do you sleep like this?'" she remembers, making a fist. "And I'm like, yeah. 'Well, you need to open up your hands. You need to touch more things. This is your energy. This is it. These are your receptors where energy comes in and out.' And he says, 'When you're onstage there's all this energy coming to you. You, it's your job to put your hands out and receive it. These are like antennas.'

"From that day forward, when I'm onstage it's a serious thing. I do this," she says, extending her arms out to the sides and turning her palms forward as if she's about to give the air a giant bear hug. "You can't see it, but it's food for the soul. It is spirit. And it's 'Thank you, thank you.' And it's not only taking from them but giving to them."

"This psychic healer said I am and have always been a healer. And that's my job," she says. "It's not about singing and performing and the rich and famous. It's about healing." For her fans. And for herself.

SEPTEMBER 2004

KURT ELLING

Jazz Musician

What is happening is a sacred thing.

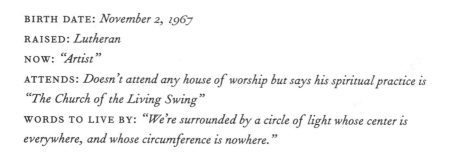

BIRTH DATE: *November 2, 1967*

RAISED: *Lutheran*

NOW: *"Artist"*

ATTENDS: *Doesn't attend any house of worship but says his spiritual practice is "The Church of the Living Swing"*

WORDS TO LIVE BY: *"We're surrounded by a circle of light whose center is everywhere, and whose circumference is nowhere."*

Grace comes in surprising packages. Sometimes grace, that hard-to-define-but-easy-to-recognize quality, arrives in a kind word from a friend, an extra week to pay a bill, a soft breeze on a sweltering day.

Two weeks after the terrorist attacks in September 2001, for me grace arrived, unannounced and unexpected, in the form of a jazzman.

It was the first Saturday night after life forever changed on 9/11. People waiting patiently to enter the Park West Theater in Chicago were unusually quiet as security guards checked and double-checked IDs, even for those who didn't intend to drink. A queer pall of uneasiness hung in the air.

Many of the smartly dressed folks waiting to hear the jazz vocalist Kurt Elling sing selections from his album *Flirting with Twilight* had had to force themselves out of the house that night, had to take a deep breath, say a few prayers, and put on something festive, even though that was the last thing they were feeling.

Inside, the nightclub glowed warmly with candlelight; a few concert-goers milled by the bar ordering cocktails while others found seats set up club-style in the intimate venue. But still, that nasty pall hovered.

Elling took the stage with his five-piece band and played the national anthem.

Everyone stood. Everyone sang. Some people cried.

Then grace entered the room.

"I came to sing for you tonight because someone wants us to suffer," Elling told the hushed crowd. "Someone wants us to fail—as a nation, a culture, as a people. We fold? They win. We stay home in fear or depression? They win. Culture must continue. Joy must come out. Life is stronger than death."

Then Elling, a Grammy-nominated jazz musician and all-around hip cat, quoted from the Hebrew Scriptures. The book of Job: "Though he slay me, yet will I trust him."

"We are not encircled by darkness. We're surrounded by a circle of light whose center is everywhere, and whose circumference is nowhere. We have beheld this glory; it is full of grace. If we were to ask such a God of grace, what do you think God would say?" Elling asked.

His band answered, playing the first few notes of "Not While I'm Around," a Stephen Sondheim tune from the musical *Sweeney Todd*.

Strange choice? Listen to the words:

"Nothing's gonna harm you, not while I'm around. No one's gonna harm you, no sir, not while I'm around. Demons are prowling everywhere nowadays. I'll send them howling, I don't care . . . I've got ways.

"No one's gonna hurt you, no one's gonna dare. Others can desert you, not to worry, whistle, I'll be there. Demons'll charm you with a smile, for a while. But in time, nothing can harm you, not while I'm around."

Yep. There you have it.

Grace.

There was hardly a dry eye in the house, and the pall blew away.

"It was a special honor and a challenge and a service, a moment of being a servant for whoever showed up," Elling told me a few days later, reflecting on that night. "People needed to be fed. I wanted to make sure they knew that they had access to this other way, that you listened to this music in this other way.

"I do have a belief that what is happening is a sacred thing."

Elling is a really interesting fellow. A Rockford, Illinois, native, he's the son of a music minister from the conservative Lutheran Church, Missouri Synod.

After college, where he studied history and religion, Elling enrolled in the University of Chicago's Divinity School. Were it not for a pesky German exam that he never passed, he says he'd have a divinity degree. Not that he ever intended to be a collared minister, or to use his jazz pulpit for anything more than singing. Elling, who refuses any religious label for himself apart from "artist," is definitely not the Michael W. Smith of the jazz world.

Still, his deep spirituality and religious background permeate his music. Just not in the way you could sum up on a bumper sticker.

That Saturday at the Park West, Elling was funny and profound, sexy and spiritual, following in the footsteps of other jazzmen like Duke Ellington. Elling wove songs about soul food and romantic love in between quotations from the German poets Rainer Maria Rilke and Friedrich Hölderlin, and from the Bible.

"I think music has this service to play. Most of the time it doesn't need to be explicit," he said. "People will accept whatever information that you lay on them in a way that they're ready for. I don't think that it's about spoon-feeding anybody what the deal is. Part of the beauty of it is the discovery of the individual. It's a beautiful thing because you're discovering art."

And, occasionally, grace.

SEPTEMBER 2001

251

ELIE WIESEL

Author, Holocaust Survivor, Nobel Peace Prize Winner

No faith is as pure as a wounded faith.

✳

BIRTH DATE: *September 30, 1928*

RAISED: *Jewish*

NOW: *Jewish*

ATTENDS: *A synagogue in New York City*

WORDS TO LIVE BY: *"God is to be feared, God is to be loved, and there should be a balance. Not too much of one, not too much of the other."*

W hat was he like?" a number of friends asked me after my first meeting with Professor Elie Wiesel at a Chicago synagogue a few weeks after the September 11, 2001, terrorist attacks.

"It was like sitting with God," I told them.

I'm not really sure what I meant, but I was certain of how it felt. I wasn't being flip. At that moment in time, after God's children once again had been so cruel to one another, I imagined God would be wearing the same mournful expression as the good professor. Woebegone and shrugging, with an inexplicable undercurrent of hope.

During that visit, Wiesel, a Holocaust survivor, author of more than forty books, and winner of the 1986 Nobel Peace Prize, had told me about how he was sitting in a cab in midtown Manhattan when the first plane hit the World Trade Center. He could see the smoke from the doomed towers rising in the taxi's rear window. His son worked in New York's financial district, and it would be more than an hour—an excruciating wait—before the man who had survived Nazi concentration camps that claimed the lives of his mother, father, and younger sister would receive word that his only child was alive and well.

"The question that kept working itself through my mind was 'What does it mean?'" Wiesel told me in 2001, the permanent furrow in his brow seeming to grow deeper as he talked. "What does it mean? Hours and hours, glued to the television. What does it mean? How could some man just do that? . . . Strangely, I had thought the twenty-first century was going to be a good century, better than the last that was so fraught with danger." During our brief visit that day in Chicago, we talked about violence, terror, goodness, and God. We both had more questions than answers.

In the spring of 2005, I had the chance to visit with Wiesel again, this time in his study on New York's Upper East Side. I wanted to know more about his spirituality, how he, of all people, had not lost faith in God or, for that matter, in humankind.

Why on earth does he still believe? I want to know. I *need* to know.

"Doubt is there all the time," he says, softly. "The questions are there, and all my questions are stronger than all my answers."

And yet you continue to wrestle with God?

"I continue because what is the alternative?" he says.

You could walk away.

"And do what, really? Could I not believe? If I were not who I am, of course I would not. But I am who I am," the professor says. "I cannot *not* believe. Not because of myself, but because of those who were before me. It is my love for and fidelity to my parents, my grandparents, and theirs, and simply to stop, to be last in the chain, is wrong. It would humiliate them. They weren't at fault. Why should I do it to them? I feel such a presence when I think about them and even when I don't think about them. I want to follow in their footsteps. I don't want to break the chain. And to choose what? Is it better to be agnostic or better to be an atheist? I don't know. I've never tried it. I accept having faith. I call it wounded faith, my faith is wounded. But I believe. A very great Hasidic master once said, 'No heart is as whole as a broken heart.' And I paraphrase it differently: No faith is as pure as a wounded faith because it is faith with an open eye. I know all the elements of the situation; I know all the reasons why I shouldn't have faith. I have better arguments against faith than for faith. Sure, it's a choice. And I choose faith."

When he was fifteen years old, on May 16, 1944, Wiesel and his family were forced from their home in Sighet, Transylvania, and deported to the concentration camps at Auschwitz-Birkenau, where his mother, Sarah, and younger sister, Zipporah, were murdered by the Nazis. Young Elie and his father, Shlomo, endured one camp after another until his father succumbed to dysentery, starvation, and exhaustion just two weeks before their final destination, Buchenwald, was liberated by American troops in April 1945.

In his 1958 book, *Night*, which recounts in stark detail his experiences of torture and depravity as a Jewish prisoner in Nazi concentration camps alongside his father, Wiesel described how witnessing such inhumanity led him to abandon faith. "Never shall I forget that smoke. Never shall I forget the small faces of the children whose bodies I saw transformed into smoke under a silent sky . . . Never shall I forget those moments that murdered my God and my soul and turned my dreams to ashes," he wrote.

His transformation—from a religious teenager who spent hours praying and studying Jewish texts to a disillusioned young adult with no use for the God he felt had abandoned him—did not happen in the concentration camps themselves. Quite the opposite, actually. "My father and I continued to pray at Auschwitz," he says. "Not begrudgingly. My father and I would get up early to pray, and not alone. There would be a hundred people with us at least. We stood in line in the barracks to pray because somebody bought a pair of phylacteries for ten portions of bread or something from a Pole who had managed to sneak them in. We still stood in a line to say prayers.

"If I could pray there, how can I say I cannot pray here?" Wiesel asks. "For a child, God is a loving God. Later on you realize that God can manifest himself not precisely in compassion but sometimes in punishment. There are two attitudes to have toward God. One of love for God and the other of fear of God. Both are powerful for the Jewish faith. God is to be feared, God is to be loved, and there should be a balance. Not too much of one, not too much of the other."

After his release from Buchenwald, Wiesel went to live in an orphanage in France. "I tried to be as religious as I was before," he says. "Later I had to ask myself, Why did I do that? In retrospect I understood why. I wanted to close the parentheses and say to the enemy, 'You will not succeed. You succeeded in taking my parents away, my grandparents, everything else, even my childhood. One thing you did not take is my faith. It is still here.' And *then* came the crisis."

When Wiesel was about twenty years old, he began studying secular philosophy, trying to find answers to his esoteric questions apart from faith. "I felt that I would not be honest with myself if I did not visit other possibilities," he says. "But there was never a question of whether God exists. I never doubted God's existence. I doubted his justice, his presence, his kindness, his compassion, his love, all the attributes I loved. And after a few years what saved me not only from total despair but also from insanity was my passion for study. The moment I came to France, I asked the orphanage for a copy of the Talmud, the same one I had to leave behind at Auschwitz, to continue exactly and open it exactly to the same page where I was interrupted," he says. "That passion sustains me to this day. I have a passion for study, not only for Jewish studies, which I do every day, but study in general. Plato or Euripides or Dostoyevsky. I love to study. That's why I'm a teacher and why I have never given the same course in thirty-five years." He has been the Andrew W. Mellon Professor in the Humanities at Boston University since 1976 and has also taught at the City University of New York and Yale University.

Wiesel says he continues to pray the ancient Jewish prayers he learned as a child. But I wonder if the quality of his prayer life is different from when he was young. "My prayers are the same, but I've turned them into arguments. I argue. I argue with God. I never stopped arguing," he says.

What about?

"Basically the same question," he says.

Which is?

"How can you allow these things to be done? But I don't have to go farther. In our tradition, the Jewish tradition, you can say that. The prophet Jeremiah goes much farther than I do. Jeremiah is the only one who predicted tragedy and survived tragedy to tell about it. He says, 'You, God, killed without pity.' I wouldn't go that far. But he says it. 'You killed without pity. You slaughtered without pity.' There is no other religion in the world that allows such attitude toward God, such language with God. In the Middle Ages people would have been burned at the stake for less, much less," Professor Wiesel says. He's referring to a passage in the second chapter of the biblical book of

Lamentations, which, according to tradition, was written by Jeremiah, in which the prophet says, "He has destroyed and had no pity, letting the enemy gloat over you and exalting the horn of your foes . . . You have slain on the day of your wrath, slaughtered without pity."

Does God cause bad things to happen to people? Or does God simply *allow* the bad things to happen?

"I love Jeremiah too much to dispute him, but at the same time, I cannot repeat it in my own name," Wiesel says. "I may quote him, but I cannot repeat it myself. I cannot go that far. I say maybe God is to be *pitied*. I had a teacher, a great teacher, who once asked me, 'Who is the most tragic character in the Bible?' I said Moses, because he was a solitary leader who had problems either with God or with the people. There was always somebody who didn't like him. Or maybe Abraham, who was asked by God to bring his son to be sacrificed. Or maybe it was Isaac, who realized all of a sudden what his father was going to do. My teacher said no, no, no. I said, 'Well, then, who is the most tragic character?' And he said, 'God.'"

What does the professor believe God was doing when he and millions of others were suffering at the hands of the Nazis?

"Look, God, by definition, is everywhere. That means he was there, too. So I have a choice to believe he was on the side of the perpetrators or on the side of the victims. I want to believe he was on the side of the victims. So therefore, the pathos of God, the sorrow of God, can move one to tears. Look what they have done, what the killers have done, not only to us, but to God," he says.

"I am a person who has problems believing, and yet, in spite of them or perhaps because of them, I do believe," Wiesel continues. "I think the right to doubt is one of the most important rights given to human beings. But I believe in God. In fact, I never stopped believing in God—that's why I had the problem, the crisis of faith. If I had stopped believing, then I would have been much more at peace. It would have been okay to be disappointed in human beings. What else could you expect from a human being who is the object of seduction and all kinds of ambitions, right? It is easier if God doesn't enter the equation. The moment you start to believe in God, then how can you accept the world? Do you then accept God's absence? Do you accept God's silence? God—why doesn't he try to make people better, make them lead better lives and be kinder to each other? Why doesn't he do it? A few times he gave up. But the floods were not a punishment for sins against God but for crimes against each other. What are they doing to themselves? God thought. So he brought the floods. And it didn't help. I cannot understand two aspects of human nature: indifference and nastiness. I cannot understand. At my age, I should be able to understand. But I cannot. I do not understand. Indifference and nastiness on every level, on petty levels and on high levels."

In the Jewish tradition, shaming someone publicly is the same as murdering them, Wiesel explains before revealing what he says is one of the great regrets of his life. "When I came here from France, I was very poor. I've said in my memoirs there were days when I had nothing to eat. My salary was $180 a month, including hotel, expenses, everything. There were days I had no money to buy bread, and I confess, I used to steal soap from the men's room at the United Nations. In order for sustenance, I joined the Jewish daily *Forward*, which was at the time a large Yiddish-language paper. And I remember once I wrote a review of a Yiddish novelist. And it wasn't very flattering because the book was silly. I regret it to this day. Why did I do that? Therefore, now, if I cannot praise a book, I do not review it." Nastiness. He cannot abide it.

Nor can he tolerate indifference. He recalls a trip to he made back to Auschwitz. Walking through the town that housed the concentration camp, "I saw four men on the street, one of them a priest. I said, 'Are you from here?' And the priest said yes. I said, 'Were you here during the war?' And he said, 'Of course.' I asked him, 'Where did you live?' And he said, 'That house, there.' I asked him, 'Where was the camp?' He said, 'There,' twenty feet away. I said, 'You could see it?' He said, 'Of course, through the window.' I asked him to describe a typical day, and he gave a full description about the music and the marching. I said, 'Could you sleep at night?' And he said, 'To be honest, in the beginning it was difficult. Then we got used to it.'"

My God. How chilling.

"Yes," Wiesel says with a tone of resignation, as if to say *And not much has changed*. "Look at Darfur or Rwanda," he says. "And suicide killings. The cult of death. They don't realize that when they're killing in God's name, they're turning God into a murderer."

Believing is hardest for Wiesel when he thinks of those who did not make it through the Holocaust. Like his father, mother, little sister. And so many millions more.

"Some people speak about miracles. I don't like them. If God made a miracle for me, God could have made a few more miracles for people worthier than I. It was just chance, luck. I was the wrong candidate for survival. I was always sick as a child, always. And how was I saved? I didn't do anything. I never took any initiative. I was a coward. I did not want to be beaten. Who knows? And why not others? A million and a half Jewish children were murdered. How many great sages would have come out of there? How many Nobel Prize winners? How many poets, how many scientists, how many doctors? I know now that since I don't find a meaning for my own survival, I must confer a meaning from it. That is why I teach, why I write. That is why I'm involved in all kinds of human rights activities. To justify my existence," he says. His legacy, he goes on, is his son, his grandchildren, and his writings.

"I hope my son and his children will live in a better world. Maybe to a small degree that will be because of the things that I've tried to do. Maybe strangers one day will be in a place and pick up a book because it is there on the table, and they'll read a sentence, and that idea or desire may help them get through one more event or one more sadness," he says.

Words are powerful and Wiesel understands that power.

When he was born, his given name was Eliezer. It is a biblical name, the name of Moses' son by his wife Zipporah. But the Hungarian government, which had control over the area where he lived, would not accept biblical (i.e., Jewish) names. So his name was changed to Elie. "Biblical names are so beautiful and meaningful. Eliezer means 'help of God,' and Elie means 'my God,'" Professor Wiesel says. "There is actually one thing I've tried to do; in all of my novels, the name of God is in the name of each of my main characters."

Elhanan in *The Forgotten*. "Whom God has graciously bestowed."

Gamaliel in *The Time of the Uprooted*. "Reward of God."

Elisha in *Dawn*. "My God is salvation."

Perhaps God *is* the main character?

"He must be," Professor Wiesel says, his pained stare lingering as he looks me straight in the eye, the silence between us indicating that we're not talking about his novels anymore. "If not He, who?"

NOVEMBER 2001, APRIL 2005

AFTERWORD

Dear B, Hef, Sandy, Studs, Senator Obama, Anne, Mancow, Billy, Dusty, Iyanla, Barry, David, Sandra, Hakeem, Mr. Robbins, John, Shanley, Reverend Al, Annie, Mr. Heaney, Jonathan, Mark, Jeff, Laura, Sherman, Harold, Russell, Mike, Dr. Lee, Melissa, Kurt, and Professor Wiesel—

Thank you.

Thank you for opening your hearts, homes, and lives to me.

Thank you for your candor, your vulnerability, your humor, your sincerity, your questions, and your answers.

Thank you for your struggles, your joys, your doubts, your inspiration, and your faith. In the divine, in others, in me.

Thank you for your hospitality, your charity, your challenges, and your gratitude.

Thank you for the gifts you've given me, for the insights, bits of wisdom, and glimpses of grace that I carry with me from the time we spent together.

Each one of you showered me with gems of insight into the world and the divine that I will continue to ponder for the rest of my life:

Ask yourself if what you're doing is kind.

Trying to prove you're a Christian is like trying to prove you're not a pedophile.

What would it be like if you lived every moment as if you knew you were infinitely loved by the creator of the universe?

The loss of faith occurs offstage.

Love. Why do we keep fucking it up?

Grace is the oxygen of religious life. Without it, religion will surely suffocate you.

There ought to be enough power to light this little ball up with peace.

Facts are what happened and how it happened. Truth is an opinion.

Forgive yourself. Love yourself. Forgive others. Love them.

Belief is like a muscle. The more you do it, the better you are at it.

No faith is as pure as a wounded faith.

Death has little meaning if you haven't lived.

Jesus met the woman at the well to save her, not to condemn her.

Emotions are like children on a bus that you are driving.

They're not icons. They're just things that I like.

Just keep smilin' and breathin', lady.

We can all make mistakes, even when we're absolutely certain.

There is a very good reason to help the poor: You may be poor yourself, you may be a stranger in a strange land.

When you're lost in the woods, stop running and just sit down.

The important thing to do is to go and be reconciled, to rejoin, to reapproach.

The door of repentance is always open.

Religion at its best comes with a big dose of doubt.

I'm no saint, but I know what's right and what's wrong.

It was the kind words from one chaplain that kept her from being a total atheist.

The essence of the spirit is love.

Culture must continue. Joy must come out. Life is stronger than death.

God made you for a reason. At the end of the day it has to do with how you serve others. But you can't serve others if you don't know who you are.

The Holy Spirit is when a flower smiles at you.

You will be forgiven, and you will be loved and you will be loved just as much as you were before you made the mistakes.

It can't hurt to have something that's keeping away bad vibes.

Teach me to love as well as those chimps just did.

Thank you for allowing me to share them with others.

Thank you for blessing us.

And may God continue to bless you abundantly.

PEACE,
CATHLEEN

None is worthy, but all are welcome.

—JUNE YOUNG

ACKNOWLEDGMENTS

One of the greatest joys of writing *The God Factor* was experiencing the out-pouring of blessings from friends and colleagues. I am eternally grateful for all of you and thank you for your presence in my life and for your influence on my work.

In particular, a special thank-you to my wondrous publisher, editor, and friend, Sarah Crichton, who took a chance on me when she decided to drop a dinner napkin with her name and number in my lap one red-winey night in Brooklyn. Thank you for your faith in me, for your guidance, patience, and collaboration. You are the most gracious of mentors. And for a thousand different reasons, thank you, Rose Lichter-Marck.

None of this would have been possible without the menschy matchmaking of Jen "The Bookmaker" Bluestein, who not only introduced me to Sarah but also let me hitch a ride on Bono's bus on World AIDS Day 2002, and, years later, invited me to finish writing my book by tiki-torch-light in her garden. I love you.

Everyone should have a Joanna Falk. She is my first reader and best friend, confessor and babysitter, playmate, coconspirator, and soul mate. I could not have done this without you. Your constant companionship and humor are priceless. *Lady, when you're with me I'm smiling . . .*

For the ridiculously hospitable denizens of 6F—Kathy, Chris, Nick, and Jake Reber—I am continually amazed and blessed by your generosity and kindness. Thank you for opening your home, hearts, and refrigerator to me, thank you for coming to my emotional rescue, for aligning my chakras and making me laugh. I adore you.

To my intrepid agent, Matthew Guma: you are a prince among men. This was so much more fun than Utah would have been. *Merci mille fois, cher.*

Michael Cooke: my guardian angel with the curry-stained wings and the funny accent. Thank you for your unwavering support from the very beginning. In the immortal words of your fellow Canadian Celine Dion, I'm everything I am because you, well, *hired* me. Ever faithful . . .

I am ever grateful for the incredible support this project received from my colleagues at the *Sun-Times* since its inception as a newspaper series. Thank you to the publisher, John Cruickshank, and my editors: John Barron, Don Hayner, Paul Saltzman, Dan Haar, Marcia Frellick, Nancy Moffett, and Phyllis Gilchrist. All of my fellow reporters and columnists have been fierce allies along this marvelous journey. Special thank-you to Annie Sweeney for her balance and wit; to Bill Zwecker for his cheerleading and friendship; and to Neil Steinberg for playing the devil's advocate. For taking such beautiful pictures, a huge thank-you to *Sun-Times* lensmen Brian Jackson, Tom Cruze, Rich Hein, and Bob Black, and a big kiss to Paul Natkin for making me look so good and for being a great traveling companion.

For their love, support, and prayers, enormous thanks to my marvelous tribe (blood and chosen): Maurice Possley, Helen and Muzzy Falsani, Captain Mark Falsani, Nell-Ayn and Jack Lynch, Jenifer Aloi, Frank Aloi, Mike and Britt Possley, Dan Possley, Tim Possley, Maura Possley, Casey Cora, Linda Midgett, Rick Kogan and Colleen Sims, Bill Zehme and Carrie Secrist, Bobby Richardson and Tatjana Vujosevic, Kelley and Steve Ryan, Melinda and Jason Pearson, Amanda Stulman, Jessica Moyer, Jean Sweeney, Roy Larson, Jenny and Eric Sheffer-Stevens, Stan Davis, Mike Pfleger, Dean

Balice, Joe Shanahan, Gustav Niebuh, Kathy Ferguson and Dennis Sherman and the Fairy Godmothers, Scott Mendeloff and Julie Stone, Lorna Propes and Ron Himel, Aileen Blackwell and Sheila Roche, Adam and Rachel "Hell Cat" Lisberg, and Jimma and June Young.

A very special thank-you to Lucy Matthew and the folks at DATA, to Paul McGuinness for his kindness and enthusiasm, to Candida Bottaci, and to Mr. Hewson, for inspiration (musical and otherwise) and for making me want to be better than I am.

One last thing: When I was a college freshman a thousand years ago, someone told me I should be a writer. For opening my eyes and giving me the irreplaceable gift of confidence, thank you, Linda Richardson.

ILLUSTRATION CREDITS

Sherman Alexie: © Rob Casey

Dusty Baker: Brian Jackson/*Chicago Sun-Times*

Sandra Bernhard: Richard Mitchell

Bono: By Andrew Macpherson, courtesy of U2 Limited

Sandra Cisneros: © by Ray Santisteban. By permission of Susan Bergholz Literary Services, New York. All rights reserved.

Billy Corgan: © Yelena Yemchuck

Kurt Elling: © Jeff Sciortino

Laura Esquivel: Courtesy of Laura Esquivel

Melissa Etheridge: Dan Winters/courtesy of Melissa Etheridge

Jonathan Safran Foer: Courtesy of Jonathan Safran Foer

Michael Gerson: Paul Morse

Seamus Heaney: © Keith Barnes

Hugh Hefner: Elayne Lodge/Playboy

Dr. Henry Lee: Courtesy of Dr. Henry C. Lee

Annie Lennox: Tom Cruze/*Chicago Sun-Times*

David Lynch: Richard Dumas

John Mahoney: Rich Hein/*Chicago Sun-Times*

Mark Morris: © Marc Royce

Mancow Muller: Courtesy of Mancow Muller

Senator Barack Obama: Bob Black/*Chicago Sun-Times*

Hakeem Olajuwon: © Keith Torrie/New York *Daily News*

Harold Ramis: Courtesy of Harold Ramis

Anne Rice: © Joyce Ravid

Tom Robbins: Courtesy of Tom Robbins

Jeffrey Sachs: www.arnoldadler.com

Barry Scheck: Courtesy of Barry Scheck and the Benjamin N. Cardozo School of Law

John Patrick Shanley: © Monique Carboni

The Reverend Al Sharpton: Courtesy of the Reverend Al Sharpton

Russell Simmons: © Corey Sipkin/New York *Daily News*

Studs Terkel: Rich Hein/*Chicago Sun-Times*

Iyanla Vanzant: Doug Turner Photography

Elie Wiesel: Brian Jackson/*Chicago Sun-Times*